The

D
Vill

THE VILLAGES OF BRITAIN SERIES

Other counties in this series include

Avon

Bedfordshire

Berkshire

Buckinghamshire

Cambridgeshire

Cheshire

Cleveland

Cornwall

Cumbria

Devon

Dorset

Essex

Gloucestershire

Hampshire

Herefordshire

Hertfordshire

Kent

Lancashire

Leicestershire
 & Rutland

Lincolnshire

Middlesex

Norfolk

Northamptonshire

Nottinghamshire

Oxfordshire

Powys Montgomeryshire

Shropshire

Somerset

Staffordshire

Suffolk

Surrey

East Sussex

West Sussex

Warwickshire

West Midlands

Wiltshire

Worcestershire

East Yorkshire

North Yorkshire

South & West Yorkshire

Most are published in conjunction with
County Federations of Women's Institutes

The Derbyshire Village Book

Compiled by the Derbyshire Federation
of Women's Institutes from notes and illustrations
sent by Institutes in the County

Published jointly by
Countryside Books, Newbury
and
the D.F.W.I., Derby

First Published 1991
© Derbyshire Federation of Women's Institutes 1991
Reprinted 1992

Countryside Books
3 Catherine Road
Newbury, Berkshire

ISBN 1 85306 133 6

Cover Photograph of Ashford-in-the-Water
taken by Bill Meadows

Produced through MRM Associates Ltd., Reading
Typeset by Acorn Bookwork, Salisbury
Printed in England by J. W. Arrowsmith Ltd., Bristol

Foreword

Derbyshire is a county of great contrasts, bordered by seven other counties. The most northerly countryside attracts many visitors with its high moorlands of peat, cotton grass, heather and tumbling streams which feed the reservoirs of the upper Derwent Valley. The long gritstone edges which flank the east and western borders enclose a massive limestone plateau studded with unusual rock formations, cliffs, caves and deep wooded gorges, carved over the centuries by the rivers flowing through the county. Continuing southward, the countryside changes to a more lowland pastoral scene.

The county is steeped in history, from ancient stone circles, to Roman settlements, to relics of past industry and the historic houses of Chatsworth, Hardwick, Haddon, Kedleston and Sudbury. To this day agriculture and industry play their part in the continual transformation of the countryside, but the most attractive feature of Derbyshire is its many small villages and their inhabitants.

The concept of this village book was a challenge eagerly accepted by Derbyshire's W.I. members. The enthusiasm and enjoyment given to researching the information for the village articles is very evident in the interesting stories, anecdotes and pictures within these pages. We hope that after reading this book you will feel encouraged to explore for yourself the many small villages and discover the beauty of the Derbyshire countryside.

Daphne P. Irvine
County Chairman

Acknowledgements

The Derbyshire Federation of Women's Institutes wish to thank all those members, their families and friends who have worked so diligently to research and provide the information for this book and who have provided the excellent drawings.

Also a special thank you to the co-ordinating ad hoc committee:
Mrs Shirley Aiton (Chairman)
Mrs Ruth Fennell
Mrs Jean Rawling
County Map drawn by Mrs Winifred P. Astle

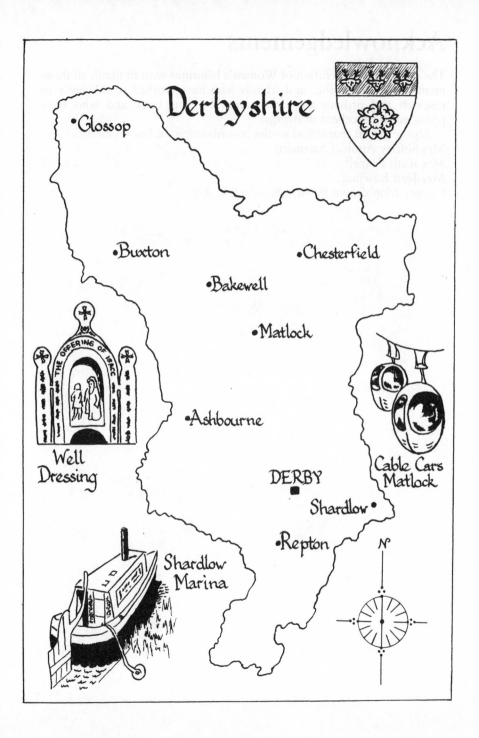

Hope Village

Abney & Abney Grange 🐚

Abney and Abney Grange are two hamlets surrounded by moorland, situated above the Hope Valley in the Peak District at approximately 1,100 ft. There was a settlement here in about 1500 BC. Abney was recorded in the Domesday Book in 1086, the name given as Habenai. The landowner was then William Peveril, the Conqueror's son.

William Newton was born at Cockey Farm, Abney. He was christened at Hope church on Christmas Day 1750. A carpenter by trade, he was also a poet and came to be known as 'Minstrel of the Peak'.

As well as agriculture, lead mining was predominant in the late 18th and early 19th centuries. Lead was brought from surrounding villages for smelting – the hills around providing plenty of draughts for this purpose. A census in 1821 showed that there were 23 houses and 143 inhabitants. In 1851 there were 20 houses and 87 inhabitants; apart from one joiner all these families were farmers and lead mining had therefore finished in Abney. Today there are 17 houses and 48 inhabitants, with only six families dependent on agriculture.

Unfortunately the Barn Dance (held in the old fashioned hay barn), cricket match and annual Wakes Week held at the end of August, are customs which have died away, though the Harvest Supper is still a very popular event.

There are ruined remains of old cottages, a cornmill and possibly a chapel in and around Abney. One cottage is reputed to have been a public house. In 1916 the then lord of the manor purchased a hut from 'Tin Town', which had been used to house workers building Derwent and Ladybower dams. The hut was given to the village for use as a church and village hall. After celebrating the Queen's Silver Jubilee the villagers decided that a new hall was needed. The old 'Tin Hut' that served the community so well for over 50 years was sadly falling into disrepair. With great enthusiasm and a lot of hard work sufficient money was raised, in three years, to build a new community hall. This was opened in 1981. It occupies the same site as the 'Tin Hut' and like its predecessor is used for church services.

In the late 1960s the Bowles family, who still owned Abney estate, sold the farms to the tenants. Change is now coming to the village as some of the older farmers retire and move away, commuters are buying up the properties. Gliding and hang gliding are popular activities in the area. Tourism has also arrived, by way of a caravan park, a stone camping barn, holiday cottages and bed and breakfast.

Allenton ✒

Allenton was once a quiet hamlet south of Derby, adjacent to the parish of Alvaston. It was originally known as Allentown after Isaac Allen – the gentleman who built the first houses in the area in 1878. It consisted of a few streets off the main Derby-Melbourne road and several houses on the main road.

A school was built at the corner of Allen Street and Poole Street in 1880 and it is still in use today as an infants school. On Sundays the school was used as a mission room by the church.

In 1885, an interesting discovery was made by workmen at the rear of the Crown inn. The men were sinking a well and at the depth of twelve ft found part of a large animal skeleton. It was a hippopotomus. Several other bones were found and identified as being the breast bone of an elephant and the femur of a rhinoceros. Later, digging in the same area in 1973, repairing major sewage pipes, workmen found the remains of a brown bear, hyena, ox or bison and hippopotomus. They had once roamed over Allenton and Alvaston in the most swampy ground.

By the late 1920s Allenton had groups of houses built on the main Derby-Melbourne road. Farming, however, was still a major activity in the area.

St Edmund's church was built in Sinfin Avenue at the edge of open country. White Mansfield stone was used in its construction. In 1989 the church celebrated 50 years of service.

At the south side of Allenton is the War Memorial Village, a cluster of over 30 houses in a pleasant setting with special features for the needs of the disabled occupants. It was the Derby Rotary Club who first brought up the idea for the village and the Town Council organised an appeal for subscriptions. On 27th June 1949 Princess Elizabeth and the Duke of Edinburgh visited the site and laid the foundation stone. Cemented into the foundation stone is a lead casket containing several medals and stars of the two wars, also a copy of the Derby Evening Telegraph of 27th September 1947 containing news of the launch of the appeal for funds. The first house was occupied in May 1950.

One of the best known landmarks in Allenton is the Spider Bridge – so named due to its shape. It is a series of bridges for pedestrians over a busy junction on the ring road. A good view of the surrounding area can be seen from the centre of the bridge.

Many people come to shop in Allenton with its free parking spaces and a variety of shops and stores. There is also a busy market on Fridays and Saturdays and an interesting flea market on Tuesday nights. Allenton has developed from a small group of houses into a busy part of the city of Derby.

Allestree 🌿

Allestree is situated two miles north of Derby on a ridge west of the river Derwent. Once a heavily wooded area, the name has come from Norman times and the thousand year old yew tree in the churchyard was known as Adelard's Tree. Who Adelard was we do not know, probably a headman or chief of the village. Allestree was mentioned in the Domesday Book and was given to Henry de Ferrers as a reward for his work in the Domesday survey.

The earliest inhabitants were farmers and evidence of strip framing can be seen quite clearly in areas around the present village. Not much farming goes on today, people mostly commute to the large city nearby for work.

The village has some fine old houses and just one building which is thatched, this being an old tithe barn, now a dwelling house. Allestree Hall is a fine 17th century house set in parkland. The house is soon to become a leisure centre and already has a golf course. The man-made lake in the park is shaped like a fish. One of the past owners of Allestree Hall used to drive through the village in his coach attended by two black footmen and a pair of large spotted dogs; this caused quite a stir among the inhabitants.

The church of St. Edmund, built of local gritstone, has celebrated 800 years of worship. In days gone by the church was really at the heart of things, the clergy used the chancel and the villagers the nave. The villagers held meetings and markets, stored implements and took shelter inside with their animals if necessary. There is a Norman doorway with fine carving and a Norman tower, but that is all that remains of the earlier church. The church was modernised in the 1950s.

Since 1833 there had been a school in Allestree supported by William Evans, a wealthy benefactor. When a new school was built in 1856, again he gave money to help pay for it. Today, the village has fine infants, junior and secondary schools taking children from a wide catchment area.

Allestree has grown considerably during the last two or three decades as new housing has been built on the edges of the village. This has made Allestree into a northern suburb of Derby, surrounded by parkland, and it is possible to walk by the river Derwent from Allestree right into Derby city centre.

Alport 🌿

Today the hamlet of Alport, where the river Lathkill cascades over limestone waterfalls and weirs to join the more sedate river Bradford, is much visited and admired by anglers, walkers and naturalists. But the present peace and serenity are in sharp contrast to the industrialisation and activity of former times.

Lead mining is said to have taken place in the district at the end of the 13th century. Alport was among the most bustling of the lead mining villages in the 17th, 18th, and 19th centuries. Water power was available and in the 17th and 18th centuries there were a number of water wheels. However in the 19th century the area was unrivalled in its use of water pressure engines developed by Richard Trevithick, and by 1848 six engines were at work for the Alport Mining Company.

The Hillcarr Sough, started in June 1766, became the longest sough in Derbyshire – four and a half miles from Alport to the river Derwent one and a half miles south of Great Rowsley. It was completed in 1787 at a cost of £32,000. Within two years the profits are said to have covered the expenditure due to the rich ore made accessible.

Cupola, the lead smelting works built about 1840, provided work which was anything but healthy. Fanny Needham born in 1847 and Alport's oldest inhabitant when the Youlgrave WI compiled an historical record in 1931, is quoted as saying 'the flues were cleaned out twice a year when the men had to have nose and mouth covered and to keep special clothes on shelves at the works. At dinner time all was spoon meat, broth or Irish stew or a posset in winter because they might not touch the food with their hands.'

The Portway, the ancient trackway from Nottingham to Castleton, passes through Alport over the ancient packhorse bridge, and through the ages there will have been a tremendous variety of travellers along this route.

Monks Hall (late 16th or early 17th century) is thought to have connections with the monastic granges.

There was a flourishing 18th century corn mill which is now a fish farm. The paper mill and the weaving shed have both disappeared.

There is an interesting Jacobean wall memorial to Roger Rooe of Alport in Youlgrave church. He died in 1613 and is shown kneeling facing his wife, with their eight children in line below. She is wearing a tall hat.

Ambergate ✺

Cradled in the arms of the hills between the rivers Derwent and Amber, lying snugly amongst the trees, is Ambergate, gateway to the Derbyshire Peak District.

Surrounded by beautiful deciduous woodland, once part of the ancient Duffield Frith, high in the Shining Cliff Wood is a cave bat house said to be of Roman origin. Close by is the now dead yew tree once inhabited by Betty Kenny along with her 13 children! Modern day accommodation is provided by a very well used Youth Hostel. Lower down this wood is a reservoir built to provide water for the near derelict but impressive Oak Hurst, family home of Thewlis Johnson, founder of the Ambergate Wire Works, now Richard Johnson and Nephew.

The parish church of St Anne was gifted by the aforementioned Thewlis Johnson, the foundation stone being laid by Mrs Johnson in July 1891. The site was donated by Albert Hurst of Alderwasley Hall, the stone for the church was hewn in the nearby Ridgeway quarry, woodwork prepared in Glossops, the local village woodyard, and much of the building work was carried out by willing local workers. These generous benefactors were friends of the more famous Richard Arkwright and George Stephenson to name but a few.

Thanks to the latter, Ambergate also had one of the very few triangular railway stations in the British Isles, standing 100 ft above the road. Sadly two arms of this unique station were destroyed by the demolition of two bridges in 1986. George Stephenson was also responsible for the cliff railway leading from the Crich mineral quarries feeding the Ambergate lime kilns. Few other places can boast four means of transport running parallel, ie canal, railway, road (A6) and river.

Every village worth its salt has at least one local hostelry; Ambergate has two, the White House and the Hurt Arms. The former club room of the Hurt Arms was used for religious services prior to the building of the church and was also the original venue of the annual flower show, this event being later transferred to the Wire Works show ground.

Ambergate has not been without its characters; the late 'Postman Jack', a one armed gentleman, whose daily task was to deliver letters and parcels on his bicycle, an overall journey of approximately five miles; Mrs Jackson, who sold her sweets from a pram at the entrance of Ambergate Wood; and last but not least, 'Dinky Day' the shopkeeper with his wooden shop near to the church. He had a most entertaining monkey, who on one memorable occasion escaped, climbed onto the church roof and tolled the bell!

The successful cricket club, one member of which is currently playing for the England Ladies Test Team, had its centenary in 1985. Football also has a long history in the village. Ambergate has also given its name to a race horse and an unusual daffodil!

Ashford-in-the-Water 🐚

It would be an interesting exercise to try to discover how many artists, over the years, have trodden the well worn path to Ashford's picturesque and ancient Sheep Wash Bridge in their efforts to immortalise it. Until recently, the sheep were washed there prior to shearing. The lambs would be penned within the stone-walled pen on one side of the river whilst their mothers were thrown in at the other side. They would naturally swim across to their offspring, thus ensuring a good soaking. Originally a medieval packhorse bridge it now attracts hundreds of visitors each year.

The people of Ashford still pay homage to the abundance of water by 'dressing' the six wells every year, in the old Peak District fashion of layering petals, leaves and other natural objects into a bed of clay to form an impressive picture. This custom had fallen into disuse in Ashford until about 40 years ago, when, thanks to a lady called Ida Thorpe, the custom was revived. The very high standard set by her is maintained to this day, as the hordes of visitors pouring into Ashford around Trinity Sunday bear witness. In 1990 over 12,000 people passed through the church during well-dressing week.

The village church of the Holy Trinity houses the relics of another ancient custom, the funeral garlands suspended from the roof. They were made from white paper, cut to form rosettes and were fixed to a wooden frame. They would be carried before the coffin of a young girl in the funeral procession. This practice was accorded only to virgins. The garland would then be hung in the church. There are four garlands still hanging there, the oldest believed to have been made in 1747.

Being a rural community, Ashford would have been capable of being self-sufficient, but not everyone was connected with agricultural work. The housewife of the past could well find herself with a part-time job in the home. She may have had a knitting frame in an upstairs room on which stockings were manufactured. In 1829 there were between 70 and 80 stocking frames. Today, one cottage remains with its typical row of small windows beneath the eves where the knitter could take advantage of the natural light. Or she may have been involved in creating small items from marble, again, in the home. The well known Ashford marble, not strictly speaking a true marble but an impure limestone, was first quarried in 1748 by Henry Watson. When polished, the black marble provided a perfect background for mosaic and inlaid patterns. Amongst other things it was used for vases, clocks and jewellery. A wonderful example of an inlaid table top is in Ashford church.

Work was also available in the candle factory. The house on the site today bears the name 'The Candle House' and is situated in Greaves Lane. According to the dictionary 'greaves' is the name given to dregs of melted tallow.

Leadmining was recorded in the Domesday Book as one of the main industries of the area and Ashford remained the centre of leadmining until the late 19th century.

One of the characters of note in Ashford's history was a lady called Molly Bray, known unfortunately as the Ashford Dwarf. She was born in the 1720s and although she lived to be 85 she grew no taller than three ft. She was not noted for her cleanliness. She liked to visit other people's houses, but when she'd left they would discreetly sweep where she had been sitting.

Ashover 🌿

Essovre ... the name, which first appeared in the Domesday Book, is derived from the village standing beyond the edge of the ash forest. Today it is known as Ashover and has been called 'the valley of silence and wild flowers'. The parish is now the second largest in England, far removed from its humble beginnings when in the Domesday Book the record told of a village with 14 smallholders, a church, a priest and an inn.

Changes there have been many. No longer do villagers make the shoes, baskets, lace and nails of the years gone by. Nor do the old Rattle cottagers – so called because their machines rattled so much – still earn their living from making stockings.

Visitors are no longer able to take advantage of the Ashover Light Railway, which transported many things between the Butts quarry and Clay Cross but alas, has only a few overgrown tracks left today. Yet what a landmark it was in its time, with scores of visitors stopping off for a welcome cup of tea at the Rainbow Cafe.

Many local people were employed by the lead mines and folk-lore tells us that one famous character was Dorothy Matly, a lady with the dubious reputation of being a 'curser, a liar, and a thief', Hardly surprising then, when a young miner lost twopence it was she who came under suspicion. This she hotly denied, with a dramatic protestation that if she had taken the money the ground would open and swallow her up. The ground did open and the miner retrieved his money.

History also tells of the Milnes brothers who in 1806 had a violent dispute about the lead vein that ran from Butts quarry to Kelstedge, a nearby hamlet. Their quarrel was never made up and they lived the rest of their lives in separate parts of the house. Butt's Grange, which they owned, was reputed to have been the place where arrows for the battle of Agincourt were made. And a tree standing nearby is called The Gospel Tree because, according to local tradition, John Wesley preached under it.

Standing opposite the Crispin inn is the fine church of All Saints, dating back to 1350. Inside are the alabaster tomb of the Babington family, the rood screen and one of the few lead fonts left in the country, where babies are still christened today.

How today's children would have loved the old Wakes weekend, held each year in July. Now no fairground visits the Rectory fields but still many older people follow the tradition of celebrating that weekend in July by eating the first new potatoes and fresh peas from the garden and gathering bilberries from the moors to make a delicious pie. Long gone too is the weekly Thursday market and hiring fair when the men used to offer their services to the farmers, but in recent years villagers have enjoyed a revival in the form of May day celebrations where colourful stalls, maypole dancing and Morris men have vied for attention. And the agricultural show, known as the 'friendly' show, attracts hundreds of visitors from far and wide.

Aston-upon-Trent 🌿

The village of Aston-upon-Trent, consisting of 1,793 acres, lies six miles south-east of Derby at the point where the river Trent divides the counties of Derbyshire and Leicestershire. Traces of Saxon pottery were found by the canal and there is Norman tooling on the fine Saxon church. A mound in a nearby field is thought to be an ancient burial ground.

A market cross stood near the stocks on the village green and it was here, in the early 19th century, that charities were distributed to the poor. Other charities included gifts of land, education in the cottage school for one boy and one girl, and for four almshouses to be built. The almshouses fell into disrepair many years ago but when a builder bought the land some 20 years ago it was agreed that he should build a charity bungalow near the site, so that charity lives on. There was also a lock-up in the village at one time. A village pump, though no longer in use, still stands in the centre of the village and the local magazine takes its name from this feature.

Documents of the late 19th century show tradesmen of every kind in the village; lace and stocking makers, wheelwrights, boot makers, maltsters, bakers, builders, butchers, farmers, rat catchers, constables, innkeepers, tailors, dressmakers, coal merchants, a schoolmaster and a blacksmith whose descendants still reside here.

Aston Lodge, a beautiful residence of the Bowden family, lace manufacturers, situated across from the church, had friendly rivalry with the occupiers of the Hall to see who could give the best parties. One of Bowden's daughters, for her marriage, had red carpet laid from the Lodge to the altar steps, some 400 ft. The house was eventually taken down and shipped to America, the stables were converted into flats and the grounds into sports and playing fields, part of which has recently been named Greatorex Walk to honour a village councillor for his many years in office.

The Hall was purchased by Col W. Winterbottom in 1889 and village life continued the same way. Men not working on the vast estate were employed in the gypsum mine, which in 1931 sold out to Derby Brick Company and the men transferred from gypsum working to brick making. On the death of Col Winterbottom in 1928 the Hall and estate were auctioned. Nottingham Corporation purchased the Hall for a psychiatric hospital.

Jubilees and coronations have been celebrated and for some years after the war the Harrington Hunt held point to point races in a top field. These same fields have recently been threatened, along with a conservation area with trees, by the planned route of the new Stoke link road. Many old buildings and customs – Wakes, beating the bounds, Rogation walk, have gone but we still retain our village atmosphere with a village quiz, Christmas walk, yearly carnival and pantomime.

Bakewell 🦡

Up to about the 10th century the river Wye at Bakewell was crossed by using either the Lum Ford, the Bakewell Ford or the Beeley Ford. These river crossings were at the sites of Holme Bridge, the town bridge at the end of Bridge Street, and the iron bridge near Granby Croft.

The present Holme Bridge dates from 1664 and has five segmental and two semi-circular arches. Its narrowness and comparatively low parapets identify it as constructed for packhorses whose panniers would overhang the sides. The cutwaters at river level are carried up to form refuges. Packhorses usually travelled in 'trains' of up to 40, and the most common early loads for long distance transport were salt, malt, wool (from sheep areas) or cheese (from cattle areas). The route which Holme Bridge served probably diverged from or crossed the ancient Portway some-where near Lady Manners School and passed to the west of the parish church before descending The Rock to the bridge, whereafter it climbed Holme Bank and followed the present footpath over Crackendale to cross the later turnpike at Rowdale and continue north through Rowland to Wardlow, Calver or Eyam.

Bakewell Bridge, with five pointed arches, is much older, 13th century, and although it was widened in the 19th century it was probably cart width originally. It lay on the route from the south-west (Leek, Harting-ton) via Conksbury, Edensor and East Moor to Chesterfield. Perhaps because of its proximity to the main town bridge the similar route using Beeley Ford did not carry a comparable amount of traffic and a masonry bridge was not justified, but the route can still be identified as descending The Butts from the south-west and climbing out of the valley again past the Outrake.

The first Bakewell pudding was the result of a misunderstanding between the mistress of the Rutlands Arms inn, Mrs Greaves, and her cook. Mrs Greaves was the first wife of William Greaves, who kept the inn sometime during the coaching days of the 19th century.

On a day when important visitors were expected at the inn for dinner, Mrs Greaves instructed her cook how she wished the pastry made for a strawberry tart; the egg mixture was to be mixed into the pastry and the strawberry jam spread on the top.

Mrs Greaves was called away to receive visitors and the cook either forgot or misunderstood the instruction and poured the egg mixture over the jam instead of mixing it in the pastry and what should have been a tart was now a pudding, went to the oven and thence to the table.

Dinner over, the guests sent for Mrs Greaves and complimented her upon her delicious pudding. Mrs Greaves thought it odd that her tart should be called a pudding and she questioned the cook who confessed what she had done.

This account was told by a Bakewell lady whose grandmother had the story from Mrs Greaves herself and handed it down in her family Mrs Greaves' very words to her cook were 'Continue to make them in that way', and so they have been made for nearly 100 years.

Bamford ✤

Bamford village is only a small part of the whole area of the parish, which includes many miles of high moorland. To the north it is bounded by the gritstone edges of Derwent and Bamford, and on the west by the peak of Win Hill. It lies within the Peak District National Park and attracts visitors who come to walk, fish, cycle, or simply to enjoy the magnificent scenery.

Approaching Bamford on the A57 from Sheffield the name 'Cut-throat Bridge' may strike terror into the heart of the traveller. This name was given by the local inhabitants who, in the 16th century, found a man lying there with many wounds to his face and neck. He was carried to a house nearby and then on to Bamford Hall where he died two days later. On these isolated moorland roads robbers and footpads were a constant threat to the lone traveller. In those days this road led down to the village of Ashopton, the river Derwent, and then into Bamford. Now it runs alongside Ladybower Reservoir, whose 504 acre expanse is fringed by steep woodlands and fields. The water mirrors the changes of sky and seasonal colours.

Starting in 1901 the first of three reservoirs was constructed in the upper Derwent valley seven miles north of Bamford, and this was followed by two more, the lowest of which, Ladybower, involved the inundation of the villages of Derwent and Ashopton. On the shore of Ladybower stands a gaunt, empty house, its vacant windows staring over the reservoir. Ginnett House was the home of Miss A. Cotterill until her death in 1990 at the age of 99 years. The house was built by her grandfather in 1880 as the family home, looking down onto Ashopton and its surrounding farmlands until they were submerged by the rising water. Miss Cotterill refused to move out, and so stayed on as a tenant of the water authority for the next 50 years. 'They didn't expect I would live so long, but I'm tough,' said Miss Cotterill. The house has no electricity supply; the stable and yard lie beneath the water which now laps at the front garden steps.

Like many farming communities Bamford had its own corn mill, and it was this mill, and the river which powered it, that caused the growth of the village during the Industrial Revolution. In about 1780 the mill was sold and converted to a cotton mill. The fine building which we see today was built in about 1820 by the Moore family, who rapidly became landowners and benefactors in the area. They were responsible for building houses for their workers, and a school. They also employed the Victorian architect William Butterfield to design a church and parsonage. By the end of the century the village boasted three churches, two schools and a green.

When the mill was sold in 1965 and converted to the manufacture of electrical furnaces, the last link with the cotton industry went. The railway opened up the Hope valley to commerce and industry, and people from Manchester and Sheffield saw opportunities to develop business in the area, and also of living in the country.

Over the years traditional country pastimes became established, including Bamford Sheepdog Trials which are held each year on Spring Bank Holiday Monday, attracting entries from far and wide. Spare a thought for the sheep! Roused from their slumbers in Chatsworth Park at 5.30 am, thus missing breakfast, then bundled into a lorry and eventually turned out in small groups to be chivvied by a man and a dog, it is not surprising they sometimes become rebellious. 'They are hungry, or they haven't been dogged', complained the Secretary one year, when various sheep invaded the beer tent, entered the President's enclosure and even chased a sheepdog! Good entertainment for the spectators, but frustrating for the competitors.

Barlow 🌿

Barlow is a village lying about four miles north-west of Chesterfield. Its recorded history dates back to William the Conquerer who gave it to one of his barons named Ascuit Musard of Honfleur. It was his grandson who adopted the name Jordan de Barley. In 1586 Peter Barley, the last of the family, died and from then the name changed from Barley to Barlow.

The parish is mostly agricultural; an area of small family farms growing cereals and root crops, and producing beef, milk, sheep, poultry and eggs. In many cases the ancient field names are still in use and the lay-out of the land has scarcely altered over the centuries.

At one time, iron and lead smelting were carried on, hence the name of Bolehill in one part, as also was the mining of coal, but almost every trace of these activities has vanished, and now Chesterfield, and to a lesser degree Sheffield, provide most of the employment.

The old houses are built of local stone weathered through the years, as is the church of St Laurence, which is 900 years old. It stands on rising ground in a well-kept, grassy churchyard and has an aura of restful timelessness about it. Not far from it is the Methodist chapel.

The one official ancient monument is the pinfold or pound, where stray animals were penned until their owners claimed them.

The great annual event is Well-Dressing Week, when three wells are beautifully decorated. They are done in the form of triptych pictures which are very colourfully composed of whole flower-heads (as against the more usual petals) and other natural materials such as bark and grasses. On the third Wednesday in August an early evening service is held in the flower-filled church and this is followed by a procession through the village to each well, where another brief blessing takes place. There is a tradition that this dates back as far at 1615 when, in spite of a serious drought, the wells managed to supply some water; but its origin is most probably a pagan rite of propitiation to a water god or goddess.

For those who enjoy walking, there are many footpaths through fields and woodlands. The sporting facilities are riding, fishing and football at the field. There are four small inns and two shops, one of which also does duty as a post office, as well as a cafe with an antiques section.

Barrow Hill 🌿

Barrow Hill is situated about four miles north-east of Chesterfield and one mile west of Staveley. It was built in the 1850s by the great coal and iron master, Richard Barrow.

Already a wealthy man, he came here during the Industrial Revolution to take over the Staveley ironworks from his brother. He built the village to attract workmen to the area to work in his blast furnaces and coal mines. Houses were built in threes with large gardens, an idea used to keep disease away, and became known locally as 'The Blocks'. The houses still stand today but have been designed for two families instead of three. Large villas overlooking the works were built for his managers to live in. A workman's dining hall complete with library was also opened. This hall is known today as the Memorial Club.

Richard Barrow died in 1865 and is buried in Staveley churchyard. By this time, the works had been formed into the Staveley Coal and Iron Company and a man named Charles Markham became the managing director. His wife Rosa was the daughter of Sir Joseph Paxton, the famous architect. His son, Charles Paxton Markham, succeeded him and was one of the greatest coal and iron masters of all time.

Plans to build a new church were made in 1889. A man by the name of Raymond Unwin, working as an engineer at Staveley works, was asked to draw up a design. He asked his cousin, and later brother-in-law, Barry Parker to help him. In a special service in November 1895 the church was opened and dedicated to St Andrew by the bishop of Southwell. In 1928 Barrow Hill became a parish and so the church became a parish church and one which people should be proud of, because the two men, Unwin and Parker, became world famous architects and this was the first building they designed together.

The Chesterfield Canal built by James Brindley and opened in 1777 is also close by. The owners of Staveley works used it to take coal and other goods to the river Trent at West Stockwith. The Chesterfield Canal

Society are busy restoring this historic waterway and hold their meetings in the local public house.

The railway played a very important part in Barrow Hill. There were extensive sidings at one time. Also, still in existence today is a unique turntable where steam trains used to be turned around. Railway enthusiasts are at present fighting to preserve this 'Roundhouse'. Today hardly anything remains of the coal and iron works and a giant chemical and pharmaceutical plant owned by the French company, Rhone-Poulenc, stands in its place.

Barrow Hill has always appeared to be shrouded in industry. However, if you go out of the back door of the village you step right into the heart of the former Staveley medieval park. The 17th century mansion called 'The Hagge', built by Sir Peter Frecheville, lord of the manor of Staveley, stands in the middle and the outlying farms mark its boundary.

Barrow-on-Trent

Barrow-on-Trent is an attractive rural village which lies between the river Trent and the Trent and Mersey Canal six miles south-west of Derby.

Although today the village is mainly residential with only two farms and a large market garden, there are still several old houses, cottages, the church, chapel and school, all of which contribute to the history of the village and the families who lived here.

The manor house and grounds together with the fishing rights in the Trent were given to the Methodist Ministers Retirement Fund by the last owners Mr and Mrs Hoult and in 1949 Manor Court was built. This comprises of five two-storey blocks of semi-detached flats facing south towards the river and were for retiring ministers who had to leave their manses and had no homes in which to live. Today the flats are sold as they become empty.

A very interesting feature of the village is a row of cottages owned by the parish and built by parish levy in the late 1700s. They were first let for a rental of 30 shillings per annum and thanks are due to successive parish councils for maintaining them in good condition.

There is a lovely old farmhouse facing the river called 'The Walnuts' and the family of George Turner the 19th century artist lived there. Many of his landscapes were painted in and around the village.

The church, St Wilfrid's, is mentioned in the Domesday Book but this was probably a wooden building as there are no signs of Saxon or Norman work in the present church which dates from the mid 12th century. From that time to 1540 the patron was the Grand Prior of the Order of St John of Jerusalem. There are devoted parishioners who add to the beauty of the church and grounds with loving care and floral arrangements. To walk into church on Christmas Eve and Easter morning especially is to hold one's breath with sheer delight and wonder at its loveliness.

The chapel has a fascinating history. The building had to be erected on arches to raise it to the level of the road three or four ft above and now called Chapel Lane. It is said that not all the villagers wanted a chapel and a young man living at Barrow Hall shot at the inscribed stone set in front of the chapel. The marks of the shot can still be seen today.

There is a Youth Club which meets in the village hall, a recently acquired field bought by the South Derbyshire District Council for community use, and an improved bus service which makes life easier. Community spirit within the village is good, problems, as in the past are faced together, whether it be repairs to the church and chapel or the ever expanding problem of gravel extraction.

Baslow 🌿

Down the centuries the village has been closely linked with the Duke of Devonshire's glorious Chatsworth house and parkland, being only two miles from the centre of the village. Visitors and villagers alike can enjoy this delightful short walk across the park with its wonderful variety of trees, so lovely in every season of the year, and the deer herd, always a good reason to pause and admire them and the surrounding hills.

The church, St Anne's, stands picturesquely at the side of the river Derwent, Derbyshire's longest and most important river, which in years gone by provided water power for the cornmill at nearby Calver.

There has been a church school in Baslow since the 18th century, although the school building is not on its original site. Today the village school is alive and well and in addition to its everyday use by local children is much in demand for local societies' activities.

Baslow has seen great changes over the years, yet still retains some old-fashioned village events such as the annual carnival with its procession of decorated floats and band playing and well dressings. There is the church fete with its stalls and teas in the vicarage garden and a lively barn dance in the evening.

During the 1880s the Baslow Hydro, known in full as the Baslow Hydropathic Establishment, was built. This proved immensely popular with the more well-to-do businessmen and their families who travelled from the cities, mainly Sheffield and Manchester, to 'take the cure' of Baslow's water, believed to be of benefit to those with aches and pains in joints and muscles. The Hydro continued until the 1920s but is no longer in existence, and the buildings were demolished.

The great bleak and desolate moorlands lie to the north and east of the village, their wild freedoms in sharp contrast to the evergreen quieter beauty of Chatsworth. An excerpt from one of the early brochures of the Baslow Hydro is as true today as when it was first written. 'If you look at a map of England you will see that Baslow occupies a central position. This is significant, for here, in the heart of England, is to be found the very essence of our country. River and pasture and parkland, green turf and noble trees, wild moors and woods, where in spring bluebells tumble in cascades down the hillsides; grey crags and green dales that hold the secret of beauty in their hollows, innumerable footpaths for the pedestrian, and the newer and stately Ducal Palace with its store of priceless treasures.'

Beeley 🐾

Beeley nestles in the valley between the moors and the river Derwent at the southern end of Chatsworth Park. The village is situated in the Peak District National Park and has been designated a conservation area.

The architecture of the church, dedicated to St Anne, supports its 12th century history. Tradition and superstition demand that bride and groom must not approach by the west gate and must pay coinage to leave by the roped narrow east gate – the wider one being reserved for funerals. In 1785 one lady died on her way to be married!

Burntwood Quarries, formerly the property of Henry Deeley and now closed, produced a fine quality, weather-resistant gritstone, much of which was used in the construction of Manchester, as well as locally to make grindstones.

The road system was altered early in the 19th century. The original packhorse route to Chatsworth left the village via Pig Lane, where the pigsties can still be seen, and it was replaced by the 'New Road' to the west of the village, making Beeley one of the first villages in the land to receive the benefits of a bypass.

The Duke's Barn was built in 1791 and housed the carthorses and drays which provided transport for both farm and estate. Today it houses a school for the deaf. For many years the old horses, their usefulness at an end, could be seen being quietly led down by the church and across the road into the Horse Pasture, where they were shot and buried. The sad little mounds can still be seen down by the river.

Beeley Old Hall, still a ruggedly beautiful old house and situated at the north-eastern end of the village, was the manor house until 1559, when it was replaced by 'The Greaves', subsequently renamed 'Hill Top' by the Savile family in 1667.

Sadly, Beeley no longer has either post office or shops – the post office and village store recently stopped trading. Many villagers still remember the home-made butter, 'beastings' for egg custards and home-pressed tongues made by Florrie Ollivant, who carried on the butchery business of her uncle, Anthony Holmes, from her shop along Brookside.

An interesting experience is to visit Hob Hurst's House, the Bronze Age tumulus up on Beeley Moor, especially at dusk. This ancient tomb is said to hold supernatural powers and if you listen carefully you may hear the voices of the original inhabitants.

One of the essential qualifications for being considered to be a 'Beeleyite' is to fall into Beeley Brooks – some achieve this at a very early age, others have been known to only be successful at a much more mature age!

Beighton ✍

Until the mid 1960s Beighton was a compact, friendly mining village surrounded by fields, woodland and lanes through which local people could walk to neighbouring villages – probably to Hackenthorpe which was part of Beighton parish with very close connections socially.

The history of the village began in Roman times – it is mentioned in the Domesday survey of 1086 and records show that mining was being carried out in the area way back in 1347. Mining began to flourish during the mid 19th century culminating in three collieries in the area, Birley, Beighton and Brookhouse. These together with farming provided most of the employment for the villagers. All three are now closed.

Railways also began to feature – three railway lines ran through Beighton. The viaduct carrying the track over the Manchester, Sheffield and Lincolnshire Railway was built in 1848 but heavy rain falling for several days resulted in the collapse of the bridge. Rebuilding commenced immediately and six months later, in April 1849, the viaduct was considered complete. It still stands and continues to carry trains from Sheffield to Worksop, Retford and beyond.

Beighton was notorious for its floods, which appeared after fairly moderate falls of rain, making travel between Beighton and Swallownest virtually impossible unless one used a boat – which many miners did to get to their work at Beighton Pit.

There were three nonconformist churches in Beighton, the Wesleyan chapel, the United Free church and the Primitive Methodist church, all very noble 19th century buildings. Two of these churches have been demolished leaving only the Primitive Methodist Church, which celebrated its centenary in 1990. The village church of St Mary was built in the 12th century. One of the features of Beighton churchyard and part of village lore is the gravestone showing the resting place of the Queen of the Gipsies, visited by almost everyone in Beighton in their childhood with a certain amount of awe.

During the Second World War Beighton had its share of tragedy. On 11th February 1942 a troop train carrying 400 naval and military personnel was involved in a crash at Beighton station. Fourteen soldiers and sailors were killed and 35 injured – the local doctors did sterling work that night. A few bombs and land mines were dropped during the blitz on Sheffield causing most of the windows in the High Street to be shattered but fortunately there were no human casualties.

By the 1950s massive housing developments had begun and most of old Hackenthorpe disappeared to make way for Sheffield Corporation's housing plans, creeping gradually towards Beighton like the lava of an erupting volcano. On 1st April 1967 the City of Sheffield took over Beighton – a truly appropriate date!

All the old familiar buildings began to disappear. The carnival parades around the village to the sound of Sothall jazz band, Beighton Feast which took place at the 'Rec' in High Street during the first week in August – the smell of the fair, mushy peas and candy floss, all remain forever in our memories. It is sad that the current generation of children are not able to see all the old buildings and take the walks one could take, letting imagination run riot when creating adventure playgrounds in the fields and by the fishing brooks along Skelton Lane, in the woods on the way to Hackenthorpe and around Bedgreave.

Beighton is now well known for its very modern shopping centre – Crystal Peaks – and for the Rother Valley Country Park, both very popular but without the atmosphere of the old village, which is now surrounded by closely packed red brick homes.

Belper

The pleasant old market town of Belper, combining urban and rural characteristics with a happy sense of proportion, may well be regarded as the southern approach to the Peak District. As Belper is situated in the pleasant valley of the river Derwent, the scenery around the town is of more than usual interest with railway, road, river and canal all running parallel.

Many changes took place in Belper which were brought about by the Industrial Revolution, but before this time, in spite of its smallness, Belper was already famous as a centre of a community of 'nailers' or nail-makers. The nailers were a rough lot of people even in the 18th century. Making of the nails was done in a nail shop, of which one still stands to this day in Joseph Street in the area known as 'The Clusters'.

One of the buildings that dominate the Derwent valley on the main Derby to Matlock road is what is known as 'The Belper Mill', founded by Richard Arkwright and Jedediah Strutt in 1776. The workers employed in the cotton mill in the beginning were mostly children, because with their nimble fingers they could tie threads together which had broken on the machines, and also could crawl behind them to keep them clean. Any misbehaviour such as tying bad knots, making waste yarn, stealing thread or riding on each other's backs, throwing tea, or using bad language was severely dealt with. Most of the mill workers were housed in Long Row which stands to this day just as it did when it was built in 1792–93.

St John's chapel is the oldest building in Belper, dating from 1250. Although not elevated to the status of parish church it became superfluous, as the 19th century St Peter's parish church is close by. Renovation has taken place recently and it is now used by many organisations as a meeting place.

Belper has always been a prosperous town. In the 1900s out-workers were employed to embroider men's socks up the sides, called 'chevining'. This process was usually done by the light of a paraffin lamp or candlelight by mothers at home at night whilst the children were tucked up in bed. The hosiery industry made a great impact on the community, employing many in the early days making lisle, then pure silk stockings and then later nylon tights.

The population has expanded from around 500 people and Belper was originally known as Beaurepaire. It has now grown to a population of about 18,000, with sprawling estates moving out in every direction. There is no mistaking Belper for a utopia, but taken together with its surrounding scenery, industrial history, and spirit of local enterprise, it is a place to remember with interest and to see again with pleasure.

Biggin

Even though it is well over 1,000 ft above sea level, the quiet limestone village of Biggin can only be entered by gentle descent from all sides, as it spreads unevenly over a shallow saucer.

Lying mid-way between Ashbourne and Buxton, just off the A515, Biggin was first mentioned in 1223. Then called Newbiggin, it consisted of a grange with several small farms, owned by Garendon Abbey and farmed by monks of the Cistercian order. It flourished for a number of years, but all that is left of that time is a small part of the original buildings at Biggin Grange.

The church, dedicated to St Thomas, was consecrated in 1848 and built of limestone acquired from a nearby field on The Liffs road. On the Sunday nearest to the 12th September the annual Wakes was kept, with special church services, and on the Monday, led by a band and carrying a banner, the Loyal Order of Ancient Shepherds would parade the village, ending at the Waterloo inn for the traditional roast beef and plum pudding. The school would close at mid-day, but 'Wakes' are no more in Biggin. Another custom lost is the locking-out of the teachers. On Shrove Tuesday, the older boys would arrive at school early and tie the doors. When the teachers arrived, the children would chant: 'Pancake Day is a jolly day, If you don't give us a holiday, We'll all run away'. The teachers would then pretend to be angry, but when the doors were opened, prayers said and register taken, the school would close for the day.

The Newhaven House Hotel was the last public house in England to have a perpetual licence. King George IV was so impressed by the warmth and hospitality of the then landlord, when he stayed there on his journey north, that he granted the licence, which applied until a few years ago when it closed for repair.

The Newhaven Fair was held on the 20th October and was not only a pleasure and market fair but also a hiring-fair. If you wished to employ or be employed, you would attend and strike a bargain for a year's work. In 1900, as an eleven year old, one villager's father was taken as a farm servant for 25 shillings per year, with one half-day off each month.

Visitors to Biggin, many of whom are walkers from the nearby Tissington Trail, often call at 'Pollies Cafe & General Store', owned and run by Mrs Webster (Pollie), now in her eighties, who is a native of Biggin. The little shop is a far cry from a city supermarket, but here you will find large jars of her homemade jams and pickles, free range eggs, fresh grown vegetables, complete with soil from her garden, alongside cakes and canned foods. If you are hungry, she will make you a mixed grill or a plate of fresh sandwiches and a lovely pot of tea, all while chatting to you about a wide range of subjects. Maybe she will tell you of the day when Biggin had a smithy, a wheelwrights and a bone-mill, or how the steep hill on the Grange Lane came to be called 'Dampy's Pinch'. If you are interested in ghost stories, she will tell you of the Victorian gentleman who walks down Main Street, in the moonlight, only to vanish into thin air near Biggin Hall gates.

Blackwell ✦

The parish of Blackwell consists of four hamlets – Blackwell, Newton, Westhouses and Hilcote. The total population is about 4,500.

There is one parish church situated at Old Blackwell, being the earliest settlement. This is St Werburgh's. Another building was erected at Westhouses by local churchgoers and was consecrated by the Bishop of Southwell on 26th September 1898 as St Saviour's.

There is evidence of farm settlements which are very old at Scander-lands and Hill Top farm. Apart from the agricultural work the only mention of other work in medieval times was coal pits. Most of that work was carried on in the Newton area but, as Newton was in the manor of Blackwell, all records refer to what is termed 'Blacwelle Pittes'.

In the mid 1800s rows of houses were built at Blackwell Colliery and Primrose Hill. An office block with six official's houses was also built near the colliery. The mining was by deep mine, with sunken shafts and cages to transport the men down and coal in tubs back. The lighting below was firstly by candles until the invention of the Davy lamp. Holes for explosives to blow the coal down were made by a long iron spiked rod called a 'ringer' and the cordite was rammed in and plugged with clay after putting in the fuse. It was terribly dangerous work in those days. An explosion occurred in the Low Main seam on the 11th November 1895 when seven men were killed.

The first evidence of a school was in 1835 on a site near the church lychgate. It was given by the lord of the manor who donated £20 to educate twelve children each year. Included in the houses built was a store, hotel and two shops. The store was opened by the Ripley Co-operative Society. One shop became a butcher's, the other a post office and stationer's.

A great degree of interest and amazement was caused during the First World War when a former resident of Blackwell Colliery, one Percy Toplis who had been called to the Forces, appeared in Captain's uniform. The story was that the colliery manager's interest in the Services occasioned a parade of the Territorials to be inspected by him. After he had left, the truth was learned, as is now known and has been the subject of television and films, he is reputed to have been involved in a mutiny of the services and was later shot whilst being pursued by the police.

In about 1920 by-product works were built adjacent to the colliery where coke, tar and other chemicals were processed. The fumes from these works were horrendous. They destroyed hedgerows, grass and crops for hundreds of yards from the site. They were closed and demolished about 1960.

A very old custom of the church was what was termed the 'Clipping'. This term means 'embracing'. The ritual was that the vicar and church members paraded round the outskirts of the parish, joined by any resident who was so inclined. The object was to mark out the bounds of the church and attempt to bring in the flock. This was done on the Sunday nearest the 21st June in accord with the birth of St Werburgh. It was somewhat akin to the ancient custom of 'beating the bounds'.

Bolehill

Bolehill lies on the slope of Barrel Edge to the north-east of the town of Wirksworth. Although part of Wirksworth parish, it maintains its own identity through a number of active village organisations and the Methodist chapel. It derives its name from the 'bole', or smelting hearth, which was situated on the hillside above the village.

In the 17th century the village consisted of a few miners' cottages situated close to the Bage Mine, with only tracks and a packhorse way connecting it to nearby towns and villages. The opening of the Nottingham to Newhaven turnpike in the following century improved communications although the route through the village was changed within a few years of the opening, probably due to land slippage. This is still a problem today, with Stoney Hill/Kernal Hill being closed to vehicles since 1969 despite several attempts to repair it.

By the middle of the 19th century the village was a thriving community with a wide variety of shops and tradespeople. The majority of the inhabitants were employed in the Bage Mine and other mines in the area.

When lead mining was at its peak the miners' holiday was a great event. It began on 12th or 13th May and lasted for a week. Country dancing took place on the green, the dancers making their way up the village and back again. There was a gingerbread stall, donkeys to ride and a greasy pole to climb – with a prize at the top, a leg of mutton.

The decline in the lead industry forced the people of the village to seek employment in the quarries, the mills and on the railways, and the growth of employment brought newcomers into the area. Today, although a few people work in the local quarries, most people travel further afield following a variety of occupations.

The Bage Mine was explored in 1980 by the Wirksworth Mines Research Group. They found the shaft very wet, but beautiful, showing yellows, blues and greens in its lower reaches. The group covered 9,000 ft of level passages and descended to a depth of 376 ft. One of the members, John Jones of Kegworth, found two rare specimens of Cromfordite, a very rare mineral formed from translucent green crystals. Its name derives from the place where it was first discovered 160 years ago.

The only buildings of any size are the chapel, the Men's Institute, the one remaining pub and the WI hall. The latter, which is used as a village hall, was erected on its present site in 1924 after use as a First World War army hut.

The High Peak Trail (the disused Cromford/High Peak mineral railway), which is officially designated a public leisure facility, skirts Bolehill's northern boundary. Today many people are attracted to this area to walk the Trail and visit neighbouring Black Rocks and the many other tourist attractions in the White Peak.

Bolsover

'Honour and principle did not seem to be known in the place, and we soon found that drunkenness and unchastity were no crimes, except in the clergy' – so wrote Mrs Hamilton Gray, the vicar's wife in 1829, referring to Bolsover. Let's hope this is no longer a fair description as Bolsover's famous 17th century castle, built by the Cavendishes, with its superbly restored murals and Derbyshire stone and marble fireplaces, is visited by thousands of people each year.

Bolsover's fame is not only linked to the castle. Across the main road is a public house called the Hudson Bay. Canada is a long way from Bolsover you may think, but this pub was originally built as a house for his mother by Peter Fidler, a local lad who worked for the Hudson Bay Company in the 18th century as a surveyor. A thriving Peter Fidler Society still exists in Canada.

Standing in front of the Hudson Bay, and looking down into the valley, can be seen the evidence of a hundred years of coal-mining. Not all of it is pit heads, dirt and coal heaps, as it includes a magnificent model village for the miners. Craftsman-built, solid family houses surround a vast attractive green giving light and spaciousness to the occupants.

Behind Sherwood Lodge is evidence of prehistoric habitation in Bolsover. Here are the remains of an Iron Age entrenchment which would have encircled the settlement, protecting its people from attack. This leads to an open space known today at Kitchin Croft, named after John Kitchin, a clay pipe maker of 1739. Pieces of clay pipe are still found and are known as fairy pipes, legend being that they were used by fairies under the earth.

This area must have been a hive of industry in the 17th and 18th centuries as blacksmith and potter also practised their crafts here. A more unusual industry was that of making iron shoe buckles. To test their strength, a loaded cart was wheeled over them!

Bolsover boasts many old public houses, of which the White Swan doubled as the moot court from the Middle Ages until the early 19th century. Bolsover received its market charter from Henry III in 1225, and the original grid pattern of streets is still discernible. On High Street today, if you look carefully, clues to Bolsover's long association with agriculture can be seen. One or two typical 17th century farmhouses are still standing, plus a barn now used by the Catholic church. Other such buildings can be spotted, disguised behind picture windows and modern doors.

The church of St Laurence, with its Saxon tower, is situated at the end of High Street. The churchyard boasts a gravestone not to be missed, the clockmaker's grave under the east window. Inside can be seen the Cavendish chapel, housing the tomb of Charles Cavendish (son of the indomitable Bess of Hardwick) and his wife. At the foot of the steps to the chapel and in direct contrast to the sumptuousness of the Cavendish memorial, is a rough stone in memory of Huntingdon Smithson and his son, John, who were the architects of Bolsover Castle.

Bonsall ༀ

Set in a limestone cleft, in the shadow of Masson Hill, the village was rich in limestone, lead, lapis-calaminaris and toadstone, so mining together with comb and lace making provided employment for the local inhabitants. In 1844 a flourishing home framework knitters' industry was in operation and to this day several buildings from this era can still be found – an excellent example in The Dale has its date 1737 engraved over the door; a later one built at Bonsall Cross had a stone chimney and was still working until after the First World War. In later years employment was found in lead smelting at the furnaces of Mr Alfred Allsop in Via Gellia, where there was also a colour works, Mill Close Mine, Hollins Viyella, Masson and Lea Mills and the various stone quarries. Many remains of lead mining can be seen around the village in abandoned mine-shafts, hillocks and stone cairns.

The 14th century stone church dedicated to St James stands in a prominent position overlooking the village. It has a fine tower surrounded by stone crowns and gargoyles and surmounted by a magnificent spire. The church still owns several acres of glebe land and benefits from the rents.

The village cross dominates the centre of the village and dates from 1628. To the right stands the King's Head inn, dated 1677, a popular calling place for both locals and visitors. A ghostly apparition has been seen several times by licensees. Over the centuries many inns and drinking houses have existed but now three serve the village, the others being the Pig of Lead and the Barley Mow.

The records of 1857 show the village boasted a large number of farmers, blacksmiths, butchers, joiners and miners. Several of the larger farms are still being worked today – mostly arable and dairy farming. A shallow brook ran through the village and every cottage in its path had a marble slab 'bridge' hence the stories of 'Marble-Arches'. The brook is still there today and can be seen as it breaks into open ground.

A free school was founded in 1717 out of the rents left by William and Elizabeth Cragg and with further bequests from Elizabeth Turner, for the education of 25 boys – 20 to be from Bonsall and five from Snitterton and Wensley villages. The boys' endowed school closed over 30 years ago and is used as the village hall. Bonsall primary school is situated near St James' church.

A well known village character was the late Mrs 'Dolly' Massey, who for a considerable number of years placed a life-sized Guy Fawkes on a seat outside her home, so lifelike that slightly inebriated customers leaving the King's Head have been seen to stop and converse – not even noticing his 'wife' hanging from a nearby telegraph pole! This tradition is still carried on by her daughter Mrs Eva Spencer. Dolly was also noted for her highly amusing and controversial entries in the carnivals.

Borrowash 🌿

Borrowash, which is part of Ockbrook parish, is situated between Derby and Nottingham, and although just five miles from Derby there are beautiful country walks to be taken – the Elvaston Country Park to the south and Ockbrook and Stanton-by-Dale to the north. The parish is now split by the A52 Borrowash bypass, which gives easy access to the M1 motorway for both its villages.

Borrowash was just a hamlet until the coming of the railway in 1839, when it became a village with its own railway station. Whilst under construction evidence was found of an ancient burial ground.

Sadly the village lost its station halt under Dr Beeching's axe, followed in a year or two by its canal. This ran alongside the railway but between 1961 – 1964 was closed and filled – all protests to no avail! It is difficult to imagine now, a busy canal with barges transporting goods, especially coal, between Derby and Nottingham and passing through the lock. Most people these days cannot remember the double row of cottages just over the railway line in front of Borrowash Mill called 'Teapot Alley'. They were so called, it is said, because the 'lady' of the village used to live in one of the cottages and used to 'entertain' bargees. When she was 'available' she put a large teapot in her window, which could be seen from the canal – and removed it when she was 'entertaining'.

In the past the village was very well served for shops and industry. At the junction of Derby Road and Victoria Avenue there was a wet fish shop kept by 'Fishy' Elston. He delivered on his bicycle and used to ride straight through his shop doorway on return. If he was not quite sober he accomplished this with very great skill.

A beautiful thatched cottage, owned by a Mr Coleman, stood near the old coaching house at Shacklecross Turnpike and long ago this was used by lady travellers for a rest and to powder their wigs, before going on to Ashbourne.

Industries in the 1930s varied. From Towles Mill the women workers at 6 pm every evening could be seen walking home, some living as far away as Ockbrook – this after a hard day's work! This mill was taken over by General Industrial Cleaners, who employed many of Borrowash's mothers and daughters. Sadly this closed in December 1990. Faire Bros Tape Manufacturers' factory was closed and demolished in the mid 1980s and the site was developed for executive housing. Barron's rose growers and landscape gardeners was also closed in the early 1960s, becoming the Rose Garden housing estate.

Little industry is left in the village today; the Birkin Lace Company, an upholsterer and a fishing float maker. There are fewer shops than in the 1930s and just one supermarket to date.

Brackenfield ❦

Brackenfield was known as Brackenthwaite in medieval times. The green is the centrepiece of the village (the second largest green in Derbyshire after Killamarsh). The population within Brackenfield's parish boundaries of 1,550 acres, has fallen from 346 in 1891 to its present 200 inhabitants – the smallest of any parish within the district of north-west Derbyshire.

The village green used to have a stream and many wells, which have been filled in, but in 1986 the villagers decided to start a well dressing event, in order to raise funds for the church. Every year since, on Spring bank holiday weekend there is a celebration which centres on the old school (parish hall) on the north side of the green.

Brackenfield has a picturesque reservoir, which is overlooked by Ogston Hall. The reservoir was constructed 1955 – 1960 in the valley where several houses and Ogston mill once stood. The old Trinity chapel is now a ruin, hidden on the wooded hillside. Trinity chapel was featured on all the county maps from the 16th century onwards, and is built on the site of the original medieval chapel, mentioned in the Domesday survey (1086).

Two infamous characters associated with Brackenfield's past are William Pugh and Samuel Mather. Many local people believe that Samuel Mather was a local sheep thief, in the early 18th century, who was hanged for his crimes at the crossroads on Tansley common and then buried at a road junction beneath a date stone, which is to be found set in a wall in the part of the village now known as Mathersgrave. Another version is that he was buried there after committing suicide in an old barn, not far from Brackenfield green. He took his own life because of unhappiness caused by an illegitimate daughter that caused him great grief and worry. Who knows the truth behind the legend? The facts are blurred by the mists of time.

William Pugh committed the murder of Lizzie Boot, at Lindway farm, Brackenfield, on 9th May 1896. Lizzie Boot's grave is to be found in the graveyard at Brackenfield church (which was built in 1856 to replace Trinity chapel).

Bradley 🌿

Today Bradley lies off the main road but until the late 16th century it straddled the old Ashbourne to Derby road and was the route followed by Bonnie Prince Charles' army.

It has a small church, All Saints, whose wooden bell-tower was destroyed by lightning. Although a church has been on the site for over 700 years the present building only dates back to the 14th century. Older than the church is the stone cross in the churchyard beheaded by Cromwell's men.

Originally the Hall was at the west end of the church but was demolished in the mid 18th century and the current one developed from the former stables. A frequent visitor there was Dr Johnson when staying in Ashbourne, and also Thomas Bancroft the 'small poet' from Swarkestone.

Until the 1950s Bradley's population was agrarian but today it includes commuters and non-agricultural workers.

The two centres at Moorend and the Pinfold still exist but there has been much infilling between the latter and the Hall. At Moorend the road, formerly gated, passes through a house: the Hole in the Wall. The other gate confining the park was at the smithy. Bradley Wood was given to the people of Ashbourne for their recreation by Capt Fitzherbert Wright in 1935. Sadly Bradley lost its post office in 1988, but retains its village school and has a public house which is one of only two nationally to have two official names: 'The Jinglers' and the 'Fox and Hounds'.

Bradwell ❧

Like so much of the Peak District of Derbyshire, the village of Bradwell owes much of its prosperity and architecture to the firm economic foundation provided by the 18th and 19th century boom in the lead mining industry. Today, despite the changing pattern of life, Bradwell remains essentially a home for working men and women.

But it was not only the lead extraction and associated smelting operations on which the village, tucked beneath Bradwell Moor, depended in years gone by. The weaving of both silk and cotton was commonplace within its cottages and Bradwell later became known as a centre of milliners and hatters, with no less than seven hatters in business at one time.

Opticians were also busy in Bradwell and were involved not only in the production of spectacles but also in the manufacture of telescopes. One of the village's most famous inhabitants was Mr Samuel Fox, who invented the folding umbrella, and who also founded the Stocksbridge steelworks. Born the son of a shuttle maker in 1815, in a cottage in Water Lane, he became something of a local benefactor, donating £100 towards the building of the parish church. He also presented a site for the vicarage and bequeathed a trust fund to be distributed amongst the poor annually.

Hazelbadge Hall, parts of which date back to 1549, has strong links with the Vernon family from Haddon Hall, regarded throughout the

'Cob Castle', Bradwell

34

17th century as local tyrants. The Vernon family also provide the local ghost. The last of their line, Margaret Vernon, is reputed to have become deranged after witnessing the marriage of her lover to a rival at Hope church. At intervals she has been said to have been seen riding on horseback between Hazelbadge and Hope.

The Bagshaw Cavern is a large series of underground caves which have famous dripstone formations, including the Dog Tooth stalagmites which curl up out of the floors.

Throughout the Dark Ages, Bradwell was the site of many battles and the Saxon King Edwin was reputedly killed following one such battle when he was hanged from a tree. It was thought to be from this incident that the place called Eden Tree derived its name. This is situated near the New Bath Hotel. The village name is probably derived from 'Broadwall', possibly referring to 'Grey Ditch', a broad fortification to the north of the village used by settlers to resist attack from the Brough side.

Since becoming a conservation area trees have been planted and overhead wires have been removed, but the essential character of the village has not changed and the grouping of the village buildings still suggests a tightly knit community. In his fascinating book *Bradwell Ancient and Modern* published in 1912, local author Seth Evans captures the essence of the village – 'Its steep winding streets, if streets they can be called – and all sorts of queer little out of the way places running in and out in all directions, break-neck, skew-tilted, beginning everywhere, leading nowhere . . .' aptly describes the village.

Brailsford 🎕

The name Brailsford is derived from 'a burial ground by the ford'. In the Domesday Book the village is listed as having a priest, half a church, 24 villagers, three smallholders and a mill. The reference to the church describes its position between Brailsford and Ednaston, shared by the communities. The church is thus in the fields away from the traffic, a delightful setting.

The people are down-to-earth, with no time for pretension but with an innate sense of the fitness of things and an appreciation of a quirky streak. Thus a diligent farmer, much plagued by a lazy and feckless neighbour whose fences were always in disrepair, found a way of dealing with the problem. Cows which strayed were milked before being returned; horses did a morning's ploughing and the ram served a flock of sheep. The point was made, no words were needed – the fences were mended.

The village of Brailsford has traditionally been occupied by a farming community. Although a small amount of development has taken place, the village still retains its country atmosphere. Its post office, baker, village institute, medical centre and school have helped Brailsford to retain its community spirit.

On the borders of Hulland Ward and Mercaston, on a lane between Cross-O-The-Hands and Brailsford, is the tiny place of worship called Halter Devil Chapel. The chapel was built in 1723 on to the end of the farmhouse and buildings by Francis Brown, who reformed after years of drunkenness. One dark night he attempted to halter his horse and mistakenly caught a cow which he thought was the devil. Hence the name Halter Devil Chapel. The lane lies in a valley known, in the 18th century, as Hell's Green. In 1794 a teenage girl, Sarah Kirkland, stepped out of her life in Hell's Green to become the first female travelling preacher.

An old character John Yates, a bachelor, who lived at Brailsford North, was a breeder of the shire horse. In the early years of the 20th century his first stallion was called *Agrivator*, which was the sire of his finest horse which he called *Brailsford All We Want*. The descendants of John Yates still breed shire horses to this day.

Brassington

The name of the village is thought to derive from Old English, Brandsige Farm, the farm by the steep path. Certainly paths are steep, stone-walled lanes narrow. Many of the houses are huddled together while others have space around them. Only council-built homes have numbers. For the most part, the lanes are not signed and many houses have no nameplates; so visitors find us intriguing or frustrating according to whether they come for pleasure or on business, especially in inclement weather or on dark evenings. Houses and cottages in which generations of families have lived are often called by the name of occupants former or present, their names known to few but the owners. Try asking for Rose Cottage or the whereabouts of a private business! Well, the postmistress may know.

St James' church houses the 'oldest inhabitant'. Inside the wall of the Norman tower is a relief carving, probably Saxon, of a man with his hand on his heart. Of three chapels the largest is now the village hall, the smallest sold for a house. The Wesleyan Reform is a 'Smedley Chapel', its building in 1852 encouraged by the mill owner, Mr Smedley. Noted for providing waterproof clothing and canteen facilities for his workers, he toured the district with a marquee, holding Revivalist meetings.

There are two public houses now, Ye Olde Gate and the Miners Arms; others are private houses – the Thorn Tree, George and Dragon, Red Lion and the Tiger inn. The turnpike from Derby and London ended at Brassington where the solid limestone made travel possible on the lanes to Buxton and Manchester. The inns served travellers and thirsty miners.

The village has changed from a self-sufficient community with butcher, baker, Co-op, cobbler, dressmaker, grocers, undertaker etc to one of a post office and one grocer's shop. Villagers still work at farms, quarries and local businesses but more travel out to work or are self-employed.

The district does not lack ghosts; old and young claim to have seen them. An elderly water and mineral diviner is used to them. His first cottage was haunted, the lady seen by family and visitors unforewarned. One moonlit November evening he heard one on Ballidon Way but saw no-one go over the hump of the road although the sound did! Across the road the Sand Pit boggart was a traditional source of anxiety for nervous children in past generations.

The village is a lovely one in which to live. All the year round the views are breathtaking. The lead miners left an interesting hillside with humps and hollows where cowslips, harebells and orchids grow. Mushrooms appear alongside the paths. In the winter the snow makes a beautiful setting when skiers and tobogganists are colourful and full of fun.

Breadsall 🐚

Breadsall village was once a small hamlet with a few cottages surrounding the lofty Norman church. It is now a busy expanding village on the borders of Derby Borough, a considerable number of new properties being added year by year.

The church of All Saints, which has one of the finest spires in the county, is steeped in history. When it was restored in 1877 an alabaster sculpture, a Pieta depicting the Blessed Virgin Mary with the dead Christ on her knee, was found beneath the flooring of the west end of the church. In 1914 the church was burnt down, reputedly by suffragettes, being restored over the next two years.

The Old Hall, an ancient building of stone and timber, dates back to the 14th century, and was originally a manor house built for the lord of Breadsall when the manor was divided into the Overhall and the Netherhall. Over the years the building has been used as a farmhouse, hunting box, school, village shop, public house, joiner's shop and post office. It is now used for meetings of various organisations, parish meetings and for private social functions. The Old Hall and garden belong to the church.

Breadsall Priory, the 13th century home of the Austin friars, became the residence of Erasmus Darwin, the poet, physician and philosopher, in 1799 and he died there in 1802. The Priory is now a successful country hotel with a country-wide reputation for its famous golf course.

Wakes Week was a great festivity, beginning on the first Sunday after 1st November (All Saints Day). Much drinking and feasting took place, pigs being killed, the chief entertainment being provided by the Guisers who walked into any house to perform. The play was acted by five blackened-faced youths, depicting such characters as Bull Guy, King George, the Doorboy, the Doctor and Belsie Bubb. On 21st December, St

Thomas's Day, the poor women of the parish donned clean caps and aprons and went from house to house begging for food and money.

Farming was once the principal occupation, but most of the working farms have now disappeared, the area of agricultural land being drastically reduced. Today most people commute into Derby for their employment.

The changes over the past 60 years have been great, and there are few people remaining who can remember the village as it was before the Second World War – a quiet, rural, friendly community, almost traffic free. It is sincerely hoped that Breadsall will maintain its village status, and not, as has happened with other villages in the vicinity, become part of the Borough of Derby.

Breaston 🌿

One of the most southerly of the Derbyshire villages, lying close to the borders with both Nottinghamshire and Leicestershire, Breaston has expanded rapidly in recent years and now has a population of more than 5,000; a far cry from the days when Roman soldiers stood on the ridge above the flood plain of the river Trent and waited for the waters to recede. There is evidence that there was in fact a Roman outpost in what is now part of Breaston.

The Domesday survey of 1086 records a small collection of thatched cottages made of timber, wattle and daub. This manor was given by William the Conqueror to Richard de Busli, one of his loyal followers. As was common practice, the land, unfenced and unhedged as we know it now, was farmed in strips by families. Clear traces of these strips can be seen on Breaston Park even today.

At the time of Domesday there was no church in Breaston, the people having to walk across the fields to St Chad's at Wilne, or All Saints at Sawley, to worship. The beginnings of the parish church of St Michael appear in records around the year 1200. The priest would come from Sawley or Wilne to say mass in the new little church, but for many years all baptisms, weddings and funerals took place at Wilne. There was no burial ground at Breaston and until 1824 coffins were carried on shoulders across the fields to Wilne; large, coffin-shaped stones once seen along the route enabled the bearers to rest their heavy loads. The 'Coffin Walk' is still a public footpath over the fields from Breaston to Wilne. As with all churches, many changes have been made to St Michael's over the centuries, resulting in today's mellow, grey stone building; make sure that if you visit, you ask to see the 'Breaston Boy'; one legend has it that, during the building of the church, a little boy would come and sit, day after day, chin in hands, watching the men at work, and that the 'Breaston Boy' is the mason's humorous portrayal of him.

Breaston village green is now a busy car park, catering for the many shoppers who use the village shops. In the year 1290, the unfortunate William de Naylestone was fatally mowed down, not by an impatient late-night shopper but by a three-horse coal cart from the pits at Morley!

Breaston had its share of cottage industries and small factories, for example Henry Plackett's lace factory on Longmoor Lane, which towards the end of the 19th century provided employment for some 20 to 30 families, as well as strips of scrap lace for whips in the Easter whip and top season!

The bed of the now defunct Derby Canal can still be followed behind the houses on the north side of Longmoor Lane, and at the Navigation inn a large basin which enabled barges to be turned round is clearly visible. Horse-drawn barges were a common sight within living memory, bringing sacks of grain to Slater's flour mill on the canal bank.

Bretby 🌿

Bretby is one of the most southerly villages in the country, in fact the parish boundary abuts Staffordshire at several points. In the 1086 Domesday survey it was described as an agricultural settlement with dwellings around the green. This remains the core of the village but there is a secondary settlement called Stanhope Bretby adjacent to the Bretby golf course and the main Burton on Trent to Ashby de la Zouch road. This was the site of the Bretby Colliery, coal mining being part of the life of this area for about 100 years, but the only connection now is British Coal's Research Establishment at the Bretby Business Park which covers several acres on the main road.

In the 13th century a castle and a church were built at the foot of the Mount. This is a hill which affords a 40 mile view over the Trent valley and the site of beacon fires over the centuries. The castle was demolished in the reign of James I when permission was given for a mansion to be built in a newly enclosed park of 600 acres. The ornamental gardens created there by the 2nd Earl of Chesterfield were reputed to be second only to Versailles. They included lakes, fountains, orangery, teahouse and aviary. Sadly only the lakes remain today. The present Hall, a large mansion with circular castellated towers at each of the front corners, was purchased in 1926 by the Derbyshire County Council and since then has been an orthopaedic hospital.

The 5th Earl of Chesterfield in the early days of the 19th century rebuilt farmhouses and cottages which are still in the village today and some bear dates between 1805–1815. Home Farm was acclaimed as a model dairy farm for Derbyshire and the marble dairy was visited daily by the Countess of Chesterfield for her glass of Bretby milk, giving rise to the name Lady's Walk for the road from the Hall.

A legend associated with Bretby related to the Cedar of Lebanon which grew on the east side of the Hall. It was planted in 1676 and because its branches were supported by chains to protect it from snow damage, it was said if a branch fell it foretold the death of a member of the family. When the Countess's descendant, the Earl of Caernarvon, the famous Egyptologist who financed the discovery of Tutankhamun's tomb in 1922 died, scores of people came to see if a branch had fallen. The tree was eventually killed by the chains which had been meant to preserve it.

Today's village reflects changing needs and fashions. The charm of the properties, with their wide ranging architecture and individuality, from the early estate cottages to suburban houses, bungalows and modern farms, together with conversions of farm buildings, smithy, schools and stables fills the needs of a commuter population in a still primarily agricultural area, making for a happy blend.

Bullbridge ✍

The small village of Bullbridge lies on a hillside about a mile from Crich. The population today is 224.

Bullbridge has lost most of its old buildings and treasures to industry. A flour mill belonging to Beavers for grinding wheat and powered by a water wheel driven by the river Amber was lost to make way for a factory car park. Part of the Cromford Canal with its interesting water-life was also taken for the siting of a factory warehouse. About 20 yards of the canal remains at this point, making it like a village pond with seven ducks and a few moorhens. The swans left their nest when the building began. Another stretch was sold for a building plot for a bungalow and the rest was filled in but the owner did leave the old swing bridge in its position on the footpath.

The mainline railway from Derby to Leeds runs through Bullbridge. In March 1830 Butterley Company's ironworks made an iron aqueduct bridge for the purpose of taking the canal over the railway. In Bullbridge there used to be nine bridges, now there are seven. The aqueduct bridge and road bridge which stood side by side were removed in 1968 for a road improvement scheme on the A610.

The name Gas Lane was changed to Drovers Way but it has no connection with the driving of cattle. The gas works used to be situated at the end of the lane with three or four gasometers.

The ruins of the old lime kilns which William Jessop and Benjamin Outram built in 1793 still stand on Drovers Way. They engineered a track to carry limestone from Hilts Quarry at Crich to Bullbridge. At first the trucks were horsedrawn but later engines were used.

In 1947 the old Ripley Urban & District Council began to build a housing estate, 34 houses beside the Canal inn with the avenues in the shape of crescents. Ten years later the estate was extended and 28 more houses erected.

The main occupation of the villagers is at the dye works. Mr Malcolm

Stevenson began his business with a shed between the river Amber and the Cromford Canal drawing water from both to dye hose. The business expanded to dye and finish fully fashioned knitwear, hose, half-hose, yarn, tape and garments. Now approximately 1,000 people are employed at Stevensons Dyers Ltd.

Beside the hill is a stone building which still has iron bars at the windows; it is now the factory shop. During the First World War it was a German prisoner of war camp. It is known locally as the Malt House, probably because it was used at sometime for the drying and storing of malt. In 1962 supermarkets were springing up in the towns and most families owned a car, so Elliott's General Stores suffered. It was closed in February 1962. The villagers travel into town to do their weekly shopping. There are two sub-post offices within walking distance for those who are fit, to reach either of them a hill has to be climbed.

Most who live in Bullbridge know everyone else and if help is needed it is always available. This proved to be so when on 7th December 1990 arctic conditions brought down power lines, the roads were blocked and the water taps dried up. Candles were shared and so was food and heating. The electricity supply was restored six days later.

Burbage 🌿

Burbage stands about 1,100 ft above sea level on the A53, approximately one mile north-west of Buxton and on the borders of Staffordshire and Cheshire.

The name means a mountain stream or the valley of a stream and if you stand on the hills around the village, you realise how well it is named, as you see the little stream coming from Axe Edge and meandering through the fields in the valley below – although now the fields are nearly all covered with modern houses. Residents fear that Burbage is losing its identity as a village and becoming a suburb of Buxton.

In the 17th century, Burbage was an agricultural area and there are still a few cottages and small farms left from that period. One farm, The Beet, which is still worked and the house still lived in, was mentioned in a case taken to the Star Chamber in 1604.

Later came the era of quarrying, lime burning and lead and coal mining, but it is thought that stone was quarried here by the Romans, because there are remains of a Roman road and an ancient burial ground, Poole's Cavern, was found under Grinlow Tower (known locally as Solomon's Temple).

The first lime workers lived in little houses made in the hillocks of ashes left from the lime burning. Until a short time ago one of these ash houses was used as a garage and there are still the remains of another in Dog Hole, that was used as a shippon. There were some very old cottages and two public houses on the green at Dog Hole but only Dog Hole House still stands. It was once the country residence of a Macclesfield silk

41

merchant. Four of his dogs, Bob, Don, Nell and Bold, are buried in the garden there and the merchant erected a large stone monument to their memory.

The quarry workers showed great interest in the Methodist church and in 1858 built a chapel in Ladmanlow, but when the Duke of Devonshire gave the land for a church to be built in Burbage, the Methodists took their chapel down – stone by stone – and rebuilt it, almost across from the church.

In 1776, the first school was built at Shay Lodge and is still used as a house. In the 19th century a council school was built near the church. This was closed in 1960, when a junior school was built near a new private housing estate, which had really joined Burbage to Buxton. Gone was the green belt, where there had been a golf course, farmland, a village cricket and football ground and tennis courts. There is one good bakery, three general shops, a post office and one public house, where once there had been 33 varied shops and businesses and four public houses.

The village is very proud of the Burbage Silver Prize Band which was formed in 1861. In 1915 the bandsmen, complete with their instruments, joined the Forces as a complete unit, and on a May morning in that year, they were seen off to war with much cheering and flag waving by the villagers. The bandsmen today show great interest in the welfare of the youngsters of the village and encourage them to join and practise with them.

Burnaston

Burnaston is a small hamlet of about 200 people, situated one and a half miles from Etwall and six miles south of Derby.

Around the turn of the century Burnaston had eight large working farms, two big houses (the Old Hall and Burnaston house), 15 small cottages, one of which was the village shop, and a small church. Today, only four of the farms remain and there is no church, no hostelry and no shops.

The present village hall, given to the village by a local farmer, Mr Stone, was originally the church. Services were conducted twice a month on Sunday afternoon by the vicar from Etwall. A local resident played the organ in both parishes and a member of her family recalls the wonderful Harvest Festival services which were held at Burnaston, with produce afterwards being taken to the Children's Hospital in Derby. The village hall is very small and is mainly used today for parish meetings and the Burnaston Women's Institute.

The village green no longer exists but it was originally circled by four cottages; it was a regular meeting place for the young men of the village, who congregated in a little wooden hut where a Mrs Wootton allowed them to play cards by candlelight. The village green also used to have an old stone trough and a water pump which were in regular use right up to the early 1970s, before two houses were built and the village green disappeared.

Before the Second World War Burnaston was mostly a farming community and the majority of the population did not go out of the area to seek work. Even today the village is without footpaths or street lighting, making it still a small rural community.

Until shortly after the Second World War, the only shop was in a small cottage at the corner of Tinderbox Lane. It was run for many years by a little old lady who used to sit behind the counter, in candlelight, waiting for her customers. Legend has it that the name Tinderbox Lane was derived from locals picking up flint in the area to fill their tinderboxes.

Before the Second World War Derby Corporation purchased Burnaston House, together with nearly 400 acres of land, to use as a municipal airport until it closed in 1961. In 1990 the site was resold by Derby County Council to the Japanese car firm Toyota. After many centuries as a small rural village, Burnaston is fast becoming internationally famous. Burnaston House had to be demolished to make way for the massive Toyota complex but the facade was retained and is, appropriately, being rebuilt in Japan. The actual factory site is approximately one and a quarter miles from the village and as yet the character of the village remains intact; we all hope this will remain so in the future.

Buxton 🌿

Although in no way can Buxton now be classified as a village, it started off as one and owes its development to its natural springs with their constant temperature of 28°C and the curative powers of their nitrogen and carbon gases. Mention Buxton Water today and most people think of the bottled variety but it is because of the thermal springs and their healing properties that Buxton has its place as one of the oldest and most fashionable spas in the country.

During the Roman occupation of Britain, Buxton was an important station en route from Manchester to Lincoln, and it is probably due to the Romans that the baths developed, only to fall into neglect on the departure of the legions. Buxton's fame revived during the Middle Ages at which time the chapel of St Ann was a shrine visited by the sick. After being closed during the early Reformation, prosperity returned when around 1600 the Earl of Shrewsbury built the Hall to accommodate visitors. Four times between 1573 and 1582 Mary Queen of Scots, in the charge of the Earl of Shrewsbury and his wife, Bess of Hardwick, was taken to Buxton to find relief from chronic rheumatism and neuralgia. In 1596 Queen Elizabeth I ordered her travels so that for three weeks she was near enough to Buxton in order that her favourite, the Earl of Leicester could have its water brought to him daily.

The influence of the Devonshire family, who inherited the Buxton estates by descent from Bess of Hardwick, is everywhere in evidence, and it was the fifth Duke who was responsible for the Crescent, built in 1780 and rivalling the one in Bath. The Devonshire Royal Hospital too is magnificent, said to have the widest unsupported dome in the world. The Pavilion and Pavilion Gardens are well worth a visit and the recently restored Opera House has world wide renown.

Lover's Leap in Ashwood Dale is a huge natural cleft in the limestone rocks and was so named because two runaway lovers on a horse leapt the chasm to avoid pursuit. The geology of the area is particularly interesting and there are collections of the local Ashford Marble and the unique Blue John stone in the museum.

Derbyshire's well dressings are well-known, but few can have been as dramatic as the Buxton well dressing at the beginning of this century when a swan glided in a specially built pool.

Buxton now as always caters widely for visitors and the many tourists who come to enjoy the attractions of the place, ranging from the magnificent buildings and beautiful gardens, Poole's Cavern and the woodland walks, the theatres and the museum, the market and the shops all of which combine with the healing springs to create the unique charm of Buxton, the highest town in England.

Caldwell 🌿

This hamlet in the southern corner of the county existed before the Domesday survey of 1086 and today consists of a few houses and farms, the Hall, the church and a public house.

The church of St Giles is quite small. There are two Saxon lights in the nave and another in the chancel. They keep company with a beautiful reredos of translucent alabaster with traceried panels and carvings of vines and grapes, crowned by two angels. In the west window are two medallions of old glass from Nuremberg.

Caldwell Hall was built on grounds surrounded by a moat. The present structure dates back to 1678, but the north-west wing is more recent. The owner in the late 18th century was Henry Evans of Burton, whose father Edward was a Burton brewer. One of Henry's daughters married the son of William Worthington, thus bringing about one of the earliest mergers of Burton breweries!

Following the death of Eva Milligan in 1960 there was a six-day sale of the Hall's contents, but the Hall itself was bought by Mr H. S. Waterfield of Swadlincote for a housing development. This never materialised and eventually the Hall was taken over by Messrs Topliss and Beard of Swadlincote who ran it as a country club.

When the club closed down, the Hall remained empty until, in 1971, Derbyshire County Council gave permission for it to be used as a special school, which it still is today.

Calow 🌿

Calow village is perched on a hill overlooking the Crooked Spire of Chesterfield. It's history goes back many years with the name Kalehal being mentioned in the Domesday book.

St Peter's church stands on land donated by the Earl of Manvers, a great landowner of this area in times past. The church was first of a simple square structure but to mark the occasion of Queen Victoria's Jubilee, tower and bells were added. Later to mark King George's finest hour a clock was unveiled which is today a well loved and trustworthy timepiece. The United Reformed church, built in the 19th century, offers a welcome to those of non-conformist zeal. Calow boasts some large imposing stone houses, Cobden House and The Lawn is to name but two. The Lawn's lands stretched far and wide – but today rows of brick houses are built there and appropriately named Lawn Villas.

Blacksmith Lane was where horses were shod by a strong blacksmith, and All Pits road is another clue to Calow's past reminding us when men mined iron-ore in the village.

Do not think Calow is just history no, it is a village of activity. The community centre was built as part of the local school, and caters for the needs of the senior citizens, mothers with toddlers, dancers, slimmers, members of the ladies club and the Women's Institute.

Calver 🌿

Calver, Calvoure in the Domesday Book 1086, is now very much a commuter village in the Peak National Park.

Evidence of a very early Anglo-Saxon settlement was revealed when skeletons were found in limestone rock during exploration in 1860. Lime burning was, along with lead mining, the earliest form of industry in the village.

Calver Sough Mine, an early lead mine, is at the northern end of a scattered village. With the coming of turnpike roads, two toll bars were built, one now a private house on the Sheffield road. The other on the Stoney Middleton road was demolished some time before the Second World War. This area is now a very busy crossroads. A boot factory, for many years a source of employment to local people, manufactured the metal-capped boots used by the mining industry at home and abroad. It finished production a few years ago and is now home to several different units and a bowling green that gives much pleasure to the older generation. At the rear of the factory is a popular garden centre. Across the Sough is the Eyre Arms public house, built on the site of an earlier Eyre Arms. Nearby a local coach company operates both local and worldwide tours.

Located in the centre of Calver village is the old cross; its original date and use is not known; but it has long been the site for gospel preachers and parliamentary candidates to hold forth. Many local and world affairs have been 'put to rights' by the elders seen to gather there on summer evenings.

From the Derwentwater Arms public house the local cricket pitch can be seen. The village cricket club's claim to fame is that a team played at nearby Chatsworth and was watched by the then Princess Victoria (before she ascended to the throne) while she was staying at Chatsworth House.

The old cotton mill was first built in 1785–6. Floods washed it and the first bridge away in 1799 and fire destroyed the next attempt but in 1805 it was again rebuilt and went on to become a thriving cotton mill employing a large number of local people. A gas works was erected in 1846 and during this time a school was built nearby by the mill owners. As the village had no church the school was licensed for divine service in 1850, the vicar of Baslow taking the Sunday afternoon service.

Calver village still has many old houses standing and continues to be a lively and thriving community with close ties to the nearby villages of Curbar and Froggatt.

Carsington & Hopton ✤

Carsington and Hopton are two old mining villages which lie between the market towns of Wirksworth and Ashbourne. In the 7th century, one of the Northern saints, a monk named Betti, came down from Northumberland and set up a preaching cross, which now stands on the village green. It was previously in the Hall grounds and was brought up into the village several years ago.

The church of St Margaret is of 12th century origin but was rebuilt in 1648 and stands on the bottom slopes of Carsington Pastures. An entry in the register dated 29th September 1668 reads: 'Sarah Tissington died. Born without hands or arms. She learned to knit, dig in the garden and do other things with her feet.'

Carsington Pastures is about 365 acres of open grazing land which rises steeply above the village to a height of over 1,000 ft above sea level. On the summit there is a large stone landmark, marked on the Ordnance Survey as the King's Chair, but known locally as the Lady Chair. The ground is scarred with remains of lead mines, the main source of wealth for the village for several hundred years and worked first by the Romans, who also brought the pretty blue and yellow pansy, known as heartsease,

The Green at Carsington

with them. A Roman pig of lead was found on the Owslow farm some years ago. Several of the old cottages in the village would have been originally the coes which were built round a mine shaft and at least one of them still has the mine shaft below the kitchen floor. A thick seam of lead was exposed during grave digging operations by the sexton in the 1930s, but could not be worked as the lead mining laws did not allow the mining of lead in churchyards, orchards or gardens.

For many years no building of any kind took place, but during the last decade a bypass has been built and the new Carsington reservoir is in process of building for the Severn Trent Water Authority. This has brought alterations to the villages with new houses being built and barns belonging to the farms along the valley being turned into desirable residences. There are only two farms left now in Hopton and the last farm in Carsington village was sold in 1990.

The Gell family lived at Hopton Hall for several centuries until it was sold in 1989 and their influence can be seen throughout both villages. The Hall has been rebuilt and altered over the centuries but there is a part of the original Elizabethan hall still standing with the red brick addition of later years surrounding it. The main road originally ran beside the school and across the front of the Hall until the later road was built. That is the reason for the Miners Arms inn standing with its back to the main road, facing the little lane which was the old road. The Miners Arms is a large three-storey building of the 16th century, and was recently bought from the brewery by the landlord.

The Hall gardens are enclosed by a high red brick wall, which is hollow with a stove at one end. The hollow wall conducted heat from the fire round the wall, against which were grown various kinds of fruit trees. This warmth, together with its south-facing position, ensured an early crop of peaches and other fruits for the house. This was built by Sir Philip Gell, who founded the almshouses in Hopton in 1719. The road to Cromford known as the Via Gellia, or Gell's road, was also built at this time to convey the world famous Hopton Wood stone, which was being quarried on his land at Hopton, to the newly opened Cromford Canal, from where it was despatched worldwide.

Castle Gresley

Castle Gresley is a village situated in rural countryside on the A444 in South Derbyshire and has approximately 1,500 inhabitants. Its history originated with the Gresley family. A parcel of land was handed down to two sons, one parcel of land contained the church and so became Church Gresley, the other contained a wooden castle that was built on a well known local landmark, Castle Knob. The castle was built between 1086–1090 and nothing remains of it today; this plot of land became known as Castle Gresley.

Every village has its ghosts and Castle Gresley is no exception. When fog or mist hangs in the air a lady dressed in white is sometimes seen in a wooded area known as the Nursery. There is a reservoir in the Nursery supplied by a spring, and many years ago a lady was drowned there – hence the name White Lady Springs. The reservoir was owned by the brewery and supplied the brewery with water; later it became a fertilizer factory, then a pickle factory, a mill, a tape-factory and now it is Toons Carpets, and this is where a second apparition appears as an old lady who visits the upper rooms. The Coal Board bought the land and a pumping station was installed which pumped water to supply Gresley Colliery.

The village relied heavily on coal for work, but in the 1940s and 1950s it suffered greatly from subsidence. Houses were propped up, some were demolished, cracks appeared in the roads, while the spoil heap at the Gresley Colliery poured poisonous gases into the atmosphere. The other colliery in the village was Cadley Hill. Both these collieries have now closed, Gresley in 1967 and Cadley Hill in 1988. Miners had worked coal in the area for 160 years. The subsidence and the spoil heaps have now gone and in their place is pleasant countryside.

From the past there are some amusing names – Rabbit Pen Row situated in Mount Road, Cat and Dog Street (Station and Princess Streets), Monkey Street (Bridge Street) – hence the name of the inn 'Drum & Monkey'.

Today Castle Gresley is a thriving village and over the past few years it has extended quite a lot. Businesses include a post office, chemist, hairdresser, newsagents, two video shops, two general stores, a garage, five pubs, a lorry depot, two farms and a carpet warehouse. There are also three chapels, the High Cross Banks built in 1870, the Baptist built in 1882 and the Wesleyan built in 1905.

Castleton 🖎

Castleton lies at the head of the beautiful Hope valley, encircled by hills and overlooked by Mam Tor – the 'shivering mountain' – with the remains of a Celtic hill fort on its summit. The village derives its name from the castle built by William Peveril, bastard son of William the Conqueror. The ruins are still standing today on a hill-top above the market place, and in 1986 the villagers celebrated the 900th anniversary of the castle. The parish church of St Edmund was the garrison church for the castle.

The village is unique for several reasons. There is the locally-mined semi-precious stone known as Blue John, which is found nowhere else in the world and which in former times was used for making large ornaments still to be found in many stately homes today. Nowadays it is mainly used for small pieces of jewellery which are on sale in the local gift shops.

The Garland ceremony is also unique to Castleton. It takes place on 29th May every year and is a survival of the ancient 'Green Man' fertility rite. It was suppressed during the Commonwealth years but revived in 1660 to celebrate the restoration of King Charles II, and has continued ever since. The 'King', wearing a large, beehive-shaped garland of flowers covering his head and shoulders, rides on horseback through the village with his 'Consort', followed by the village band, and young girls in flower-bedecked white dresses dancing to the Garland tune. After the First World War, maypole dancing was introduced and at the conclusion of the ceremony the 'Queen' (the top-most posy of the garland) is placed by the King on the village war memorial.

One of the local 'characters' of past times was known as Daft Sammy, but he wasn't as daft as all that! He worked on the surface at one of the lead mines on the Buxton road, and when a carriage came along on its way to Castleton he would throw down his tools and run to meet it and tell the occupants about the local attractions, and he always received recompense. He found this so profitable that he abandoned lead-mining and appointed himself guide to the castle. There were very few people who could shake Sammy off when he announced 'Awm't guide'.

The Castle Hotel dates from the 17th century and is said to be haunted by the ghost of a young woman waiting for her wedding breakfast. She had been left at the altar and died of a broken heart. It is also said that the body of a woman was buried beneath the entrance of the same inn, to bring good luck to a new building in accordance with pagan belief. The Castle Hotel is one of six old hostelries in the village.

Farming, lead-mining and rope-making were important village occupations in days gone by – the Romans came here for the lead, and the rope-making gear can still be seen in the entrance to the Peak Cavern. In the village there is an old house called 'The Walk' which has a long passage running beneath it to allow full stretch for the ropes. The lead-mining and rope-making are long gone, but farming continues and today there are also two electronics companies.

Visitors have always come to Castleton, attracted by the beautiful hill scenery and grand walking country, and the four deep underground caverns with their fascinating geology. Queen Victoria and Lord Byron were two notables amongst the many visitors of the past. Nowadays the tourists come in their thousands and their vehicles bring severe traffic and parking problems for the narrow village streets. Hostelries, restaurants, cafes and souvenir shops abound to cater for their needs. Yet in spite of the modern commercialism so evident in Castleton today, there is a wonderful community spirit amongst the residents.

Chaddesden ❧

Chaddesden, formerly Cedesdene, was mentioned in the Domesday Book. It is situated roughly two and a half miles east of Derby and today is a community of busy people commuting to Derby and Nottingham.

Reginald Road Day Nursery, at the corner of Old Nottingham Road, is the boundary line. The marked post says 'Village of Chaddesden' on one side and 'Derby' on the other. From this point, looking over to Old Nottingham Road cemetery, if you are very tall, you may be able to see angels wings above the vault where the Queen of Gipsies is buried.

The focal point of the village is the ancient church of St Mary the Virgin. In the churchyard there is still a small mound where six alms-houses once stood. These were founded by Robert Wilmot, member of the Wilmot family who were prominent in Chaddesden over many years.

In the 1500s the Wilmot family bought land in Chaddesden. Here they built Chaddesden Hall, a huge yellow brick building surrounded by woodland. The family continued to reside at the Hall until the early 1900s. Sadly in the 1920s the Hall was demolished. Today 'Mosey Yard', as the grounds of the Hall were called, is a well used park. On lovely summer days children can be seen happily splashing in the paddling pool, constructed where the Wilmots had their fishpond. The name of Wilmot is not forgotten. The Wilmot Arms on nearby Morley Road carries the family arms and crest. A little further on, the Wilmot Garage stands where once was a little cottage which had its own bakehouse.

Today it is taken for granted that public transport is readily available to journey into nearby Derby. Villagers of olden days paid a penny to ride in horse and trap into town. Others were not even that lucky. This was when farming was the main occupation. Women were to be seen at cottage doors busily weaving on their looms. William Davison, the village blacksmith and William Hodgkin, the wheelwright and joiner, worked from their own buildings, one called Oxo Cottage, now a row of shops. The local sheep dip was on the old Nottingham Road at the junction of Meadow Lane. Many of the farms are gone but some still remain. Much farming land was sold for development and housing estates abound all around the village outskirts. It would be difficult to find all the boundaries if choirboys still 'beat the bounds' on Rogation Sunday.

Chapel-en-le-Frith ✤

Chapel-en-le-Frith is known as the 'Capital of the Peaks', and lies just off the A6 road between Buxton and Stockport.

After the Norman Conquest, and possibly before, the area was part of the Royal hunting forest of the High Peak, and was part of the parish of Hope, which meant almost a day's journey to attend a funeral or a marriage. The foresters and keepers petitioned for a chapel of ease, which was granted and the first church was built in 1225. It became known as the Chapel in the Forest. Later it was dedicated to the martyred Thomas a Becket, and for 700 years the successors of the foresters preserved the right to elect their vicar. In 1648 the church was the scene of a great military scandal. About 1,500 prisoners of the Scottish army, under the Duke of Hamilton, were crowded into the building and kept in close confinement from the 13th to the 30th September. Registers show that 44 died before release and at least ten more during the march into Cheshire.

Chapel-en-le-Frith's largest and most widely known employer is Ferodo Ltd, producers of friction materials for the motor industry. The company was formed in 1897 by a local gentleman, Mr Herbert Frood, who had observed the problems of local carters on the steep hills of the Peak District. He patented a brake block made from woven cloth impregnated with resin, the first of its kind in the world, and from this small beginning sprang the whole range of friction materials that we know today.

The local beacon of Eccles Pike is situated to the south-west and rises to a height of 1,250 ft above sea level. Many people find it an invigorating walk to the summit which, when reached, gives wonderful views of the surrounding countryside. Each Good Friday local churches form a procession of witness and a cross is carried to the top and placed there. It is thought that this is the point used by our forefathers to light beacons warning of imminent danger, or perhaps a celebration, and was in all probability used as a link with other beacons around the area.

The market place is still cobbled and a very busy market is held every Thursday, bringing in people from surrounding districts. A focal point for many visitors are the old stocks. No one knows the exact age or when they were placed in this position, but it is thought possible they may have been erected in the Cromwellian period when stocks were placed in many towns and villages around the country.

On the first Saturday in July each year Chapel-en-le-Frith comes alive for the local carnival. The streets are gaily decorated, local shopkeepers deck out their windows, and a colourful procession wends its way to the Memorial Park.

Situated on Crossings road, about half a mile from the market place, is a medicinal spring well known in the neighbourhood as 'Nanny's Well'. According to historians the well was under the protection of St Anne or St Ninian, whose name has been corrupted into 'Nanny'. The water which bubbled up was said to be of the purest, possessing valuable medicinal qualities.

Charlesworth

Charlesworth is a pretty village nestling on the side of the Pennines. It lies on the borders of three Shires, Lancashire, Yorkshire and Cheshire but is part of Derbyshire.

The Grey Mare and the George and Dragon are two good inns serving excellent fare. Long Lane runs from the centre of the village to the 'Top Chapel' (Charlesworth Congregational chapel). Here, a traveller found refuge on his way over the Coombs and Monks Road, during a violent storm. He vowed to build a 'house of prayer' in thankfulness for his deliverance. The actual date of the building of the first chapel is uncertain but there is a reference to this as far back as 1291.

Leaving the chapel behind and coming down the hill, there are two rows of small cottages where the occupants used to weave cotton, many of the cottages possessing third storey rooms where this cottage industry took place. The weavers would have gone down Long Lane over Best Hill Bridge to Manchester for their supplies. Best Hill Bridge is still a narrow bridge, built for packhorses and the pony and trap, rather than the modern double-decker bus.

The Catholic church stands in lovely surroundings on the edge of the river Etherow, the boundary between Broadbottom and Charlesworth. This church was built in the year 1895 for the many Irish immigrants who came over to this country after the potato famine, settling in Broadbottom and working in the mills in the area.

When Rev Goodwin Purcell arrived in 1846, he found no church, no vicarage and no school. All three were realized by his hard work and efforts. He walked to Lands End and raised £1,500 and also collected money from wealthy individuals and the parishioners, to reach his target of £2,700. In 1849, the church of St John was opened and he turned his attention to a school and vicarage. This he was pleased to see opened in April 1851. In five years he had achieved his ambition and by 1873, 1,000 churchgoers attended.

In the past, when travel was limited, amusements had to be close at hand and Charlesworth Gardens were a great attraction. Peacocks strutted and parrots squawked. There was a 'dancing hut' and afternoon teas were served. Visitors arrived in waggonettes. This has now gone but on the opposite side of the road is a recreation ground bequeathed to the village. Here the children can play in safety. The cricket ground, lying in the shadow of Cown Edge, is an idyllic setting on a summer afternoon; a place where community spirit flourishes and an asset to the village.

Charlesworth still remains a thriving village, with its small business concerns and many organisations attached to the churches, schools and Community Association keeping alive the 'village' atmosphere. The summer carnival and events such as the Garden Show demonstrate the interest which people still have in 'their village'.

Chellaston

Chellaston is in the southern, gentler, corner of Derbyshire, one of a group of villages founded 1,000 years ago by the Anglo-Saxon adventurers coming up the river Trent.

The area was mainly agricultural for hundreds of years but during medieval times Chellaston gained great distinction from the pure white alabaster quarried here. There are records to prove that the stone was shipped to the continent and fashioned into uniquely beautiful altar pieces and table tombs to adorn churches in France, Italy and Spain. Nearer home, there are examples of the Chellaston 'kervers' craft at Lowick in Northamptonshire, Ashbourne and Norbury and many other old village churches. The Gothic revival of Victorian times and the Industrial Revolution resulted in the Chellaston quarries being reopened with plaster and brickmaking industries growing alongside.

St Peter's church, standing proudly above the High Street, is of 13th century origin, added to over the years with sensitivity. It is now the only ancient building left complete in Chellaston. There are parts of a wattle and daub framed cottage in Chapel Lane and a cruck cottage adjacent to the Corner Pin, one of the three public houses.

The expansion of the village began in 1873 when the Midland Railway Company opened the line from Derby to Chellaston, so bringing an influx of workers from the factories and offices in Derby four miles away. Development continued over the years until finally in 1968 Chellaston became a ward of the Borough, soon to become City, of Derby. Sadly it is no longer recognised as a village but its independent character still remains.

The old board school, opened in 1878 for 130 children, now houses 300 infants. In addition, there are separate junior and senior schools, both bulging at the seams. From an agricultural community with twelve farms and many smallholdings, Chellaston is reduced to one working farm and a market garden; from quarrying, mining and brickmaking, we now have a modern tent-making firm.

Will Chellaston ever again breed such characters as Mr Gibbons, a famous tulip grower who, in the middle of the 19th century, introduced about 100 first-rate new varieties; or the landowner who built the large mound of earth to ensure his privacy from his sworn enemy (the mound removed to make way for the building of the junior school); or Sam Ault who fell off the top of the church tower whilst oiling the weather vanes and survived but with one leg shorter than the other; or Billy Forman the village baker who always put racing before baking? Memories of the former village will remain clear whilst the paintings by the artists Frank Gresley and his sons Cuthbert and Harold, who lived and died here, are cherished and sought after by so many people.

Chinley & Buxworth

Until the making of the Peak Forest Canal and Tramway at Buxworth in 1806, and the coming of the railway through Chinley in 1867, both villages were only isolated areas with a few scattered farmsteads except for Buxworth Hall and Whitehough Old Hall. There were small farms, quarrying of stone on Cracken Edge, and a little coal mining. Chinley was well wooded as there is record of hundreds of trees being felled and sold in 1843. Buxworth used to be called Buggesworth and until recently Bugsworth. The natives did not like that, so it was changed to Buxworth.

After 1806 Buxworth grew and rapidly achieved fame as an inland lime port, despatching 70 narrow boats each week loaded with coal, limestone and powdered lime, stone and slates.

The nucleus of Chinley – as it is today – began when Mr James Waterhouse of Plarr Farm (now Heatherlea) built 20 cottages and a shop in 1852 at Chinley End where Wesley was entertained. In 1862 he built and gave the first Methodist church in the centre of Chinley, always known as 'The Preaching Room'.

After the widening of the railway line the new large Chinley station was built in 1902, a junction for Manchester, Liverpool, London and Sheffield. This railway venture involved the building of two joining curved viaducts, a brilliant piece of building. The station had five waiting rooms with big fires, a refreshment room and a bookstall. At first, a confused Stationmaster (Ould Sammy Hart the locals called him) in top hat and frock coat, with a huge timetable in his hand, rushed up and down the six platforms, sending trains 'all over t'country', as the locals said, highly amused. Something like 100 trains a day passed through Chinley station with 180 on August Bank Holiday.

Until recently there were two large mills in the valley, employing hundreds of people in bleaching and dyeing and paper and printing at various times. The mill hooters, formerly, could be heard at 6.00 am each day telling the workers to get up, and at 6.30 am telling them they should be at work. The workers stopped for breakfast at 8.00 am at another hooter.

During these years and until his death in 1951 at 83 years of age, Mr

Joseph Waterhouse of Albany House (built by saving all his threepenny bits over many years) chronicled the happenings of the village church and all his family in verse. These he would read in his high-pitched squeaky voice. He had a very dry sense of humour and his verses were witty and humorous. Some he would write in broad Derbyshire, then later bring up to date in King's English. He was a notable preacher and sometimes flautist and organist.

Eventually the railway and the now tarmacadamed turnpike roads took the trade from Buxworth, the port and buildings went into decline and the canal silted up. Now Buxworth Basin is being rebuilt as it used to be and the canal is also being cleared.

A large piece of limestone can be seen high in the gable end of the old British school, carried and placed there for a wager by a workman who had to walk and carry it from Dove Holes four to five miles away at 5.00 am.

Chisworth 🐑

Chisworth, in the north-west of Derbyshire between Glossop and Marple, is a very old village dating from Saxon times. It is noted in the Domesday Book as Chiswurde.

The village is a series of hamlets situated on the 'old' road – Holehouse, Chisworth (now Higher Chisworth), Sandy Lane and Chew. The main part of the village is situated on the 'new' turnpike road (now Marple Road), constructed in about 1790, and is known as Fattinghey.

Holehouse is the first hamlet to be approached on entering the village from the Glossop direction. A cluster of cottages was built round a mill – Mouse Mill – which has long gone. A bridge was constructed over a ford here in 1881. A toll house, built in 1803, stands at the junction of New Mills Road and Marple Road. Holehouse Mill and Chisworth House were also built around the same time. The relics of a 'flagged footpath' crosses the fields towards High Chisworth, most of the cottages in that hamlet being constructed in the 17th century.

Towards Sandy Lane are the relics and spoil heap of Alma Pit, one of a number of drift mines in the area. The last one closed in 1985. The weighbridge building for the pit still stands – it was used as a Sunday school at one time.

Chew had its own wool carding mill, built in 1795 and demolished in the 1960s. Two 19th century houses were built over an older inn, the Queens Arms, which was the only licensed beer house in 1780.

To the north of Chew are the remains of an old bleach mill and its vats, which was known as Bone Mill. A large 19th century mill – Kinder Lee – stands but hasn't been in use for many years. Plans are afoot to convert it into dwellings.

Fattinghey, the main part of the village, straddles Marple Road. Most of the houses here were constructed in the 19th century. The old Co-op has been converted into a house but the Commercial inn, dating from 1841 and renamed the Hunters inn thrives. There was an old mine – Gannister – in the middle of this hamlet too and the Gannister Arms, now a cottage, was another local hostelry. The Methodist church and school, built in 1834, are nearby. The school closed several years ago and is now used as a youth centre.

Today Chisworth is a thriving village with an active village hall where a committee organises functions throughout the year. The cottages, originally built to house workers from the local mills and drift mines, are much sought after by young couples who travel to work in Manchester, Stockport, Ashton under Lyne and even Sheffield. Everyone reckons they have the best of both worlds – several towns within easy access and the picturesque Peak District on the doorstep!

Church Broughton

Church Broughton lies close to the south-west boundary of Derbyshire. Because two of the large farms in the village were part of the Duke of Devonshire's estate until early in the 20th century, there has never been a resident lord of the manor. Apart from the church, built by the monks of Tutbury in 1300, with its little steeple atop a tower, there is also a timbered house and plenty of cottages from the 17th and 18th centuries, one of which is now a well-stocked shop and post office. The name Broughton means the farm by the brook. However the brook was never large enough for a mill, so the village's prosperity depended on the four large farms surrounded by smaller farming enterprises and outlying farms.

In the 19th century, the village was one of the largest in the area, the population rising from 414 in 1801 to 661 in 1850. The chapel was built in 1828. There was a busy brickworks, a wheelwright, blacksmith, four shoemakers, three butchers, a bakery and other small shops. The inhabitants were so unruly that the Duke had one of the first police houses in the county built in 1855 (now called Peel House, in Church Road). A cell for men opened into the hall, while that for women was above, by the bedrooms. They were probably only used overnight for drunks, but that cannot have given the resident police family a peaceful life. The school, opposite the church, always attracted well-qualified schoolmasters.

In 1864 Richard Bott, owner of the Tutbury and Rolleston water mills, rented and extended the largest farm, the Etchells, and lived in style. In the same year William Auden, uncle of the poet, came as vicar. He was followed by another nephew Alfred, who organised the closure of the Royal Oak public house in 1917. Improved transport led to the closure of the other businesses and changes in agriculture reduced employment on the land. The village population therefore declined, but the lively and involved rural community life continued.

Village activity has changed dramatically since the main sewer was laid in 1965, as three of the central farms have been taken over for suburban-style commuter housing and two outlying farms are about to go the same way. The leisurely daily trek of cows going through the village to the meadows has been replaced by hurrying motor traffic. Dogs can no longer safely lie sunning in the middle of the road outside the shop, as they once did.

A new primary school, which accommodates the children from neighbouring villages, Boylestone and Sutton on the Hill, was built in 1973 and doubles as a village hall (just as the old school did and for similar activities). The Holly Bush is a very busy public house, and together with the village shop and tennis club, it forms the main daily focus of activity in the village.

Clifton

Clifton with Compton formed a township in the parish of Ashbourne. In the 1890s Compton was taken into Ashbourne, leaving Clifton in the Morleston and Litchurch Hundred.

It is a very scattered village and once straddled the A515 from Collycroft to Lodge Farm near to the Nestle factory, but in the early 1970s a bypass was built.

Lodge Farm, with its small lakes, at one time formed part of the Cokayne estate and may have been used as a hunting and fishing lodge.

On one of the approach roads into Clifton from Snelston is a mound known as Margery Bower. It is reported to be the site where Cromwell's Roundheads, after the battle of Naseby in 1645, set up their cannons to attack the retreating Royalists at Ashbourne. A cannon ball in St Oswald's church is supposed to be a relic of this affray.

At one time there were two crosses in the village, one near to the church and the Cock inn being used as a market cross where butter, eggs, etc were traded. The other was by the tollgate house on the A515 which was demolished to make way for the bypass.

On Watery Lane there stood a corn mill built by J. Brindley. On the site of the mill a stone plinth was erected as a goal for the Royal and Ancient Game of Football which is still played in and around Ashbourne on Shrove Tuesday and Ash Wednesday. Depending on which side of the Henmore Brook you were born dictates which team you support, 'Upards' or 'Downards'.

The Staffordshire border is nearby, the river Dove being the county boundary. Bonds Mill stands within the boundary beside the river where tape and webbing are the main products, employing quite a few people from the village.

In the 1880s much of Clifton and Sturston (where the other goal for the football game is situated) was owned by the Smith family, who made their fortune by cheese-mongering. They were great benefactors, donating money for playgrounds, a cricket pitch, Holy Trinity church and its windows. At various times they lived in the Hall, Clifton house, now divided into two properties, and Clifton Cottage.

The village is fortunate in having a well stocked shop and post office and the Cock inn, thought to be the oldest building in the village. Two housing estates have been built during the last 40–50 years. There are several farms, one being the Hollies which does brisk business during the early summer offering 'Pick Your Own' soft fruits.

Numerous cottages of individual character are scattered throughout the village and Clifton boasts a flourishing golf course, a cricket club and a conservation area being constructed by the school children.

Coal Aston

Coal Aston appeared in the Domesday Book as Estune, but by the 14th century the name had changed to Cold Aston, meaning 'cold settlement', due to its exposed situation. The development from this to Coal Aston probably happened because of the mining which took place in the 19th century.

At that time Coal Aston was both a mining and a farming village. Silkstone Farm was so named because of the mining of the Silkstone seam of coal. There were two chapels, one a Wesleyan Reform and the other a Primitive Methodist, known locally as the 'top' and 'bottom' chapels. There were five or six public houses and many farms which also brewed and sold their own beer. There was also a thriving charcoal burning industry in the various woods around the village. This, together with the mining, has now disappeared but several farms still survive. The woodlands, some of which have been bought by the National Woodland Trust, still provide pleasant walks, interesting wildlife and, in spring, beautiful displays of bluebells.

Although only a small village, Coal Aston has its share of connections with the past and old buildings. One of these is Aston End, a cruck frame building thought to be one of the oldest houses in Derbyshire, dating from around AD 980. It boasts a carved head of King Richard (1230) and a carved truss dated 1450. There are signs of other cruck buildings around the same area.

The village was on the original 1757 turnpike route from Chesterfield to Sheffield and one of the buildings on the main road was a posting inn. This is still in use as a private house, as are many of the interesting cottages, farm buildings and the old village school. The Sitwells built a pond on this same route, to water their horses on the way to market. Sadly, this has been filled in and is now a grassed area, but the Royal Oak public house which stands nearby is still referred to by local residents as 'The Pond'.

Although there used to be several wells, when Coal Aston Women's Institute revived the old custom of well dressing in 1985, they chose the site of the old pond for their well-blessing ceremony. This has proved to be a popular annual event since then.

The two chapels, which still thrive, both add variety to life in the village by keeping up their own traditions. One of these is the celebration of St John the Baptist, known in the village as Feast Sunday. In the past this event lasted two days, with a procession on Sunday and games on the field and supper on Monday, ending with the 'Bidding' when a chain of dancers made their way round the village. Now the feast is celebrated on Sunday only, by a procession of witness around the village.

Because of its proximity to Sheffield and Chesterfield, Coal Aston has, to some extent, become a residential commuter area and has, over the years, expanded with the building of modern houses and bungalows. Nevertheless, the centre still retains its village atmosphere and is home not only to lifelong residents but also several artists who produce a variety of craft work.

Combs ❦

The village isn't easy to find – no main roads pass through it. Look out for the turning, just before the Hanging Gate pub, on the Chapel-en-le-Frith to Whaley Bridge road. You'll see a small sign, 'Combs' and find a lane going to the left. Combs Reservoir is on the right, a lovely stretch of water, especially on a summer's evening with boats sailing and the hills reflected in its surface. It was made to supply water to the Peak Forest Canal.

Combs could be said to resemble an octopus, its tentacles being the many little lanes which wend their way out of the valley into the hills. The only pub in the village, the Beehive, once overlooked a village green, but this has disappeared under tarmac. All the lanes radiate from this spot like the spokes of a wheel. In summer the pub is festooned with hanging baskets of flowers and customers sit outside and enjoy the scene. There is no main street, just one shop cum post office and a tiny Victorian chapel, which also houses the infants school and is the venue for most social activities.

The population numbers approximately 500, with many of the villagers commuting to jobs in Manchester, Stockport and other nearby towns. However, farming is still an important part of Combs. The hillsides are dotted with sheep and in the lower-lying fields you'll find dairy cows. There's really no arable farming in the area, hay being the only field crop now. There is evidence of grain being grown in the past and the ridges and furrows of early ploughing can still be seen, especially when the ground is covered with snow.

At weekends a few hikers pass through but on weekdays you will find us a peaceful haven. There's little traffic and you'll experience that rare quality – silence. Like most villages in England, Combs has buildings dating from various times. The stone used for the farms and cottages is the local millstone-grit and the newer buildings are in keeping with this. There are a few hedges on the lower ground but stone walls take over as the fields reach the hills. These gritstone hills stand guard over the valley, their aspects changing from hour to hour as the sun moves round. There is Combs Moss, Ladder Hill, Eccles Pike and Castle Naze – this being the site of a Roman fort. It was ideal for this purpose with a sheer drop to the valley.

Superstitions abound hereabouts and gain much from being passed from generation to generation. The tale of 'Dickie's Skull' is notorious – Dickie was Ned Dixon of Tunstead Farm, just outside Combs. He went away to the Huguenot wars, leaving his cousins to mind the farm. When he eventually returned, wounded, they killed him and buried his remains in the orchard. From that time ill luck dogged their paths, cattle and pigs died and they had no luck until they dug up his skull and placed it in the house. Twice it was buried in the churchyard but he created such a storm that they brought him back to his niche, where he remained until a new owner dared to bury him in the garden.

The railway line from Buxton to Manchester cuts through the valley and was completed in 1863. Many Combs men worked on this project and it had several set-backs, such as collapsing embankments etc. Local people thought the enterprise cursed because it trespassed onto 'Dickie's land'.

One or two famous people are connected with Combs, amongst them Florence Nightingale, who visited her father under the shadow of Combs Moss at Pyegreave.

Coton-in-the-Elms ✑

Coton-in-the-Elms is described in the Domesday Book under the name Cotune. Fifty years ago every road into the village had elm trees but they all succumbed to Dutch Elm disease; the last to go were three trees in the main street.

The present church of St Mary was built in 1846 but not on the site of the previous church, which was behind the Shoulder of Mutton inn. It is said that when the original church fell into disrepair, the bells were taken to Lullington (the next village), so we can still hear the old Coton bells on a summer evening when the wind is in the right direction; the present church has one bell. There is also a Methodist chapel, built in 1922 to replace a smaller building in Chapel Street which has, ever since, been called the Band Room. Coton had a very good band run by Mr Coates, who was also the post-master. They practised and kept their instruments in the old chapel. Officially it is now called the parish room, as it is the nearest thing to a village hall that Coton has.

There are a number of interesting stories about the village. For instance, one man who got tired of his considerable family went to live in a lane near Swepstone in Leicestershire. He lived in a hessian and mud hut and seemed content; his descendants still live in the village. Also, about half a mile out of the village there is a crossroads called Lads Grave; it is said that a young lad was hanged there during the Civil War for deserting.

Coton has never been a wealthy village, chiefly miners, farm workers and farmers. Now the local pits have closed and farms have become mechanised. The present Coton has many comparatively new houses; the old Elizabethan buildings were demolished to make way for some of them. Most people go out of the village to work, and because of that there are few activities in which all the village can take part. Coton band has long gone, but the community sticks together in times of adversity or celebration.

Crich ✑

Approached from any direction it is apparent how appropriate is the pre-Roman name of Crich, meaning hill. Geologically it is an anticline, being a mass of limestone rising to 955 ft above sea level, pushed up through the surrounding millstone grit. Lead was mined here from Roman times and the limestone quarried for lime burning and road making. An 18th century painting of Crich shows lime kilns in the centre of the village in the field known as Kiln Crofts.

In the 19th century a local home industry was framework knitting. The machines were hired out by Ward Brettle and Ward and installed either in upper rooms of cottages or adjacent outbuildings. Many such stock-inger's shops can still be seen with their long row of small-paned windows for maximum light. Many of the workers were women and girls. Cotton was distributed and work collected in village warehouses, although there are stories of people walking daily to Heanor. The rattle of the frames was a familiar day-long sound. *White's Directory* of 1857 mentions about 100 frames and three framesmiths.

Crich was then a thriving township of 2,500 inhabitants with most trades represented – a saddler, milliner, scythestick maker, candle maker, shoemakers, six tailors, blacksmiths, wheelwrights, joiners, also two surgeons, a druggist, a solicitor and three academics, not to mention nine public houses. An agent for the Clay Cross Lime Co is listed, as by this time George Stephenson had built the narrow gauge mineral railway to carry stone from the Cliff Quarry to the lime kilns at Ambergate, thence to the North Midland Railway. George Stephenson often stayed at the Wheatsheaf inn near the church.

Crich had two fairs, in April and October. As late as 1910 cattle were sold in the road between the church gates and the cross, and sheep were penned by the side of the Jovial Dutchman. The name commemorates the Dutch navvies who dug the Cromford Canal in 1794.

The parish church of St Mary is the most important building, dating from 1135 with a Norman nave, columns and font. The chancel and tower were added in the 14th century and the clerestory and porch a little later. From that date the exterior remained the same as we see it now. It is built of local gritstone as are all the old houses.

Another fine building is the Baptist chapel on the Market Place. Of even greater interest is the Wesleyan chapel built in 1765 and the oldest still in use in the country. John Wesley came here to preach in 1766 when the chapel stood on the edge of common land skirted by packhorse tracks. Behind the chapel rises the gritstone edge of the Tors, used as the parish quarry. From a favourite local walk along the ridge, Hardwick Hall can be seen to the east and the Derwent valley from Matlock to Derby in the west.

An even more spectacular view is from Crich Stand, the fourth monument on the site since 1760. It was built in 1923 as a monument to the men of the Sherwood Foresters who died in the First World War. It stands out as a landmark for miles around and its lantern shines after dark. On the first Sunday in July a pilgrimage is made to the Stand by men of the Sherwood Foresters & Worcester Regiment with their mascot, standards and regimental band.

Quarrying continues at a greater rate now with modern machinery, until it seems only the Stand prevents the total disappearance of the hill. The stone now goes to maintain the motorways, conveyed by huge lorries which thunder through the village. The old worked-out area of the quarry is now the home of the National Tramway Society which preserves and restores these beautiful vehicles. It is a strange sight to look up from a nearby road and see trams gliding 200 ft above the trees. A sight just as odd is the facade of the once elegant Assembly Rooms of Derby, forming part of an unlikely street scene amongst the rugged scenery of Crich.

The village is more fortunate than most in that there are still enough shops to supply daily needs: three grocers, a butcher, chemist, wool shop, a greengrocer, a florist, a fish shop, a bakery and a post office, as well as a craftsman making furniture and a nationally known pottery. Although there are many people living here who commute to nearby towns, Crich still retains its own character and inspires great affection.

Cromford 🌿

Sir Richard Arkwright – the cradle of the Industrial Revolution – the birthplace of those 'satanic mills' – are all synonymous with Cromford, but there was habitation here long before Arkwright came, it being mentioned in the Domesday Book as an outlier of the manor of Wirksworth. The original hamlet nestled beside the 'crooked' ford crossing the river Derwent – hence its name Cruneford, to Crumford then Cromford. The older villagers pronounce it 'Crumford'.

Sadly the only remains of this hamlet, destroyed by the Arkwrights, are the ruins of the Bridge chapel, one of the few surviving in Derbyshire. It is still possible to see the crudely carved cross by the doorway and the niche in the wall, where a light was placed at night to guide travellers across the ford. Here prayers were offered for a safe crossing.

The bridge now spanning the river is unique, as the upstream side has rounded arches and the downstream side three pointed 15th century arches – some of the oldest bridge work in Derbyshire, part of the original packhorse and footbridge. An interesting stone on the bridge marks the spot where, in 1697, Benjamin Heywood of Bridge house, returning home on horseback after an evening's jollity in the local hostelry, failed to take the bend on the bridge, went over the parapet, and horse and rider landed, unharmed, in the river. The annual Raft Race on Boxing Day draws crowds to the finish at the bridge.

With the arrival of Richard Arkwright in 1771 and the building of his three cotton mills, the need for housing for his workers led to the building of the village on its present site, nestling at the foot of the surrounding hills. North Street is a fine example of workers' houses, considered models for their period.

Alison Uttley is another famous name connected with Cromford. Born at Castle Top Farm where she lived until her late teens, she wrote the famous Grey Rabbit and Sam Pig Stories. Her books, *The Farm on the Hill* and *The Country Child*, evoke life in the village in the late 1800s.

The village remained virtually unchanged until 1921 when the Arkwright estate was sold and one or two new houses were built. After the Second World War the village, like Topsy 'just growed'. A large council estate was built, and later extended, and private housing estates were developed, so that today the original village is almost enclosed by these additions.

As the village altered, so did the occupations of the inhabitants. Previously employed in the cotton mills, lead mines and quarries, now they work at the County Offices in Matlock and commute to Derby, Chesterfield and further afield. September is the highlight of the year with the arrival of the Wakes. A legacy of the Arkwright era, it takes place on the weekend nearest to 8th September, the church's patronal festival.

The Market Place is dominated by the Greyhound Hotel built by Arkwright. Here the Manchester stage coach stopped for stabling and

The Dam, Cromford

victuals. Impressive Rock House – Arkwright's home – gave him a view over his mills. Gracious Willersley Castle standing above the Derwent, started by Sir Richard but burned down before it was finished and not completed until after his death, is now the headquarters of the Methodist Holiday Guild. During the Second World War it served as a maternity hospital for mothers from the East End of London, and there are many who can proudly say they were born in a castle.

St Mary's church, Arkwright's private chapel, also completed after his death, was built on the site of the old lead smelting hills. Here the Arkwrights are buried and there is a chantry memorial tablet to the family in the church. St Mark's, the village church, was closed in 1957 and demolished several years later.

Rose End Meadows, acquired by the Derbyshire Wildlife Trust in 1987, is a wealth of flowers, some rare, and moths and butterflies, showing that it has remained virtually untouched for three centuries, thanks to its previous owners, the late Mr and Miss Ollerenshaw, who farmed it the old fashioned way. What a legacy!

Cubley 🌺

The village of Cubley nestles either side of the old Roman road of Long Lane which runs from Derby to the Potteries, although recent archaeological excavation as yet provides no evidence of a settlement here in Roman times.

About a quarter of a mile to the west of the village stands the Howard Arms where the Roman road is intersected by the Ashbourne to Sudbury road. Because of the mounting block which can still be seen at the roadside, this pub is locally known as the 'Stoop'.

On the green hillside encircling a valley where streams unite, lies a quiet spot with memories of the great days of the Montgomerys, whose four centuries here ended four centuries ago. Their manor house stood opposite the church, where some of them lie in quiet isolation with the rectory and an ancient yew. The church of St Andrew is mentioned in the Domesday Book and from Norman days come the round arches and pillars of the nave, the pillars and the capitols of the chancel arch and the great round font.

Montgomery was the great name of this place but there was a humbler one, Johnson, that will not be forgotten. Johnson left Cubley to become a Lichfield bookseller and father of Samuel Johnson, the celebrated writer and socialite, who put all our words into the first great dictionary.

Cubley today is little more than a hamlet and probably the greatest changes have occurred within the memory of some of the older inhabitants. At the turn of the century the village school, which was built in 1871, had at times nigh on a hundred pupils but closed its doors to the village children in 1960. During the first half of the 20th century the majority of the village farms and cottages were owned by the Clowes family of Norbury. Mary Clowes was the benefactor of the village hall built in 1934 which has been the centre of village life ever since.

In the early 1900s the village boasted many tradespeople, including a tailor, a wheelwright and a brickyard which employed many local men but eventually closed because the bricks were found to be porous. The village laundry in the Row was run by Alice Harrison and her sister Mrs Prime who did a wonderful job, with a lot of elbow grease, starch and flat irons and were held in high esteem by the local gentry, whom they served.

The Wesleyan chapel, which is now disused, was built in 1874. It was said to have been built to 'spite' a very pompous vicar of St Andrew's called Cave Humphrey, who had upset the local people by preaching a sermon referring to their 'heathen ways'. In those days the rectory employed a coachman, gardener, cook, nanny and several maids, right up to the outbreak of the Second World War. The last vicar to live here was Richard 'Dickie' Nicholls, a kindly man of ample proportion who took a keen interest in the youth of the village and provided a tennis court on his lawn for their use as a tennis club. When he left the village in the late 1950s, the rectory was sold into private ownership and a new one built near to the Howard Arms.

Curbar

Overlooking the main part of the village of Curbar there is a ridge of hills which stretch for a couple of miles. It is always interesting to see people trying to climb the steep rocks.

Commencing at the bottom of the hill the Bar Road climbs up through the village. When one reaches the top of the hill, one realises that it was a Roman road and there is a straight road across the moor just over a mile long. This road is used a great deal.

In years gone by the people had to fetch their water from the troughs in the village and the villagers were thankful when taps were installed in the houses and they were linked up with the Severn Trent Water Company. There is still one round trough in the village which supplies the water for animals.

Just over 30 years before the Plague in Eyam, Curbar suffered in a similar way. On the moors there are the gravestones of the Cundy family, who lived at Grislowfield Farm, Curbar. A man by the name of Sheldon is also buried up there. There are also a number of tombs just below the Wesleyan Reform chapel which are dated 1632. It would appear that Curbar suffered before Eyam.

Near the moor there is a small square house with a round roof; originally this was used to house prisoners who were being taken across country. During the last 70 years this little house has been occupied by two families.

Cliffe College is in Curbar. At the end of the 19th century it was used to train missionaries but eventually they were moved to London for training. It is now used for the training of those who wish to be useful in their own church or for those who wish to train as ministers or as special workers in the church. Extra buildings have been erected and are often used for conferences.

All Saint's parish church was commenced in 1867. The school and the church are in Curbar parish and serve both Calver and Froggatt. The Curbar Wesleyan Reform chapel was built in 1862 and the stone was quarried in a nearby field.

Part way up the Bar Road there is the pinfold, in which wandering cattle were housed until they were claimed by their owners.

Cutthorpe 🌾

Cutthorpe is a small, sleepy village approximately four miles north-west of Chesterfield with a village school, a butcher's shop and a small post office/grocery store, and three public houses. The main road straggles through the village for three miles, reaching the Grange at its highest point, with commanding views all around as far as the eye can see.

Yet Cutthorpe boasts proud ancestry – Thomas Linacre, Physician to Henry VIII and one of the founders of the Royal College of Physicians, lived in Cutthorpe Hall, and the surrounding woodlands named after him still show a profusion of daffodils in the springtime.

Legend has it that a secret passage runs beneath the Hall and the 16th century Old Hall a quarter of a mile away, and that highwaymen were alerted to passing travellers. Certainly French soldiers from the Napoleonic war were housed in the building now used as a dovecote.

Monks from Beauchief Abbey, Sheffield, walking to Holymoor stayed for refreshment and lodging in one of the old inns. Besom and basket-making took place in Abbey Farm – baskets were used to carry ore in the Sheffield steel industry, and the ground is riddled with old coal workings.

The old custom of well-dressing has been revived, and a local committee raise funds for charities – each year raising thousands of pounds. In the small village institute – which is used for communion services once a month – many activities take place.

There is also a Methodist chapel – over 150 years old – where a small band of regular worshippers meet, the Sunday school, and also a ladies' choir, whose members regularly entertain in different churches in nearby parishes.

Cutthorpe boasts a recreation ground, with a good local cricket team, and a Sunday football team.

Dale Abbey 🙢

Not the most accessible of places, Depedale, or Dale Abbey as it is now called, has close ties with its neighbouring village of Stanley, and what it lacks in size it makes up for in history. Here one can find the great east window of the ancient abbey, and a tiny church just 26 ft long by 25 ft wide said to have the largest chalice in use in England – being nine inches high and 15 inches round.

The church shares the same roof as a farmhouse which was rebuilt on the same site in 1883. The building was used as an infirmary for the abbey and later a pub known as the Blue Bell. They owe their origin to a Derby baker named Cornelius who, between 1130 and 1140, had a vision to go to Depedale and live a life of meditation and solitude.

On the south side of the valley Cornelius cut a hermitage, measuring six yards by three yards, in the sandstone cliff. Well-preserved, the cave has a doorway and two windows. He discovered water nearby – said to have healing qualities. There were also claims that it was a wishing well (the water had to be taken three times on Good Friday between noon and three o'clock, to make one wish come true).

The abbey was completed in the early 13th century and the magnificent window arch, 40 ft high and 16 ft wide, still stands as a reminder of this important and wealthy settlement – dissolved in 1538. While this arch stands farmers are said to be exempt from paying tithes. Abbey remains can be found around the village, including Abbey House, Manor House and part of the Gatehouse which was used as a lock-up when prisoners were transferred from Nottingham to Derby.

All Saints' church was a 'Peculiar', which meant that it did not come under the authority of the Bishop and prior to the 1754 Marriage Act couples could marry without banns being read. Erected in 1902 the Methodist chapel, initially built as a Wesleyan chapel on the same site, became redundant recently and is now the Gateway Christian Centre, useful for a day retreat, conference centre or refreshment stop.

The Carpenters Arms, where Mr John Herety holds the licence, has been in his family for almost 60 years. Constructed in two stages, the front part was added to the original and built and paid for by the Hollingworth family with Mr Jim Hollingworth using his carpentry skills. Haymaking was a jolly time, with as much beer drunk as hay gathered, the youngsters fetching the beer in one gallon stone jars from 'The Carpenters'. At the turn of the century it was not unknown for cock fighting to take place in the pub.

Though under restoration at present the Cat and Fiddle, thought to be Derbyshire's only surviving post mill, stands on the site of an earlier mill. It provided a landmark for miles around and was workable until 1987 when the 18th century mill lost its sails in a gale.

Two centuries ago Dale Abbey experienced its own industrial revolution and had a blast furnace, on the site of Basset Farm, which produced about 400 tons of pig iron yearly. Now, perhaps, the only clue it ever existed is Furnace Pond (a dried out ironstone mine) lying to the east of the village.

A flourishing silver band was run by Mr Stephen Smedley of Ash Tree Farm with over 90% of the members being named 'Smedley'. On Whit Monday the Dale Abbey Friendly Society marched behind the band carrying their huge ornate banner – the last march being held in 1934. After speeches a meal with 'lashings' of roast beef was served in the Club Room – built in 1845 and now converted to a bungalow. At Easter and Whitsuntide children from surrounding villages walked to Dale Abbey where a fair was held in the village street and the pub car park. The local 'helter-skelter', a steep hill behind the church, was known as 'grass hill' and was a favourite spot for picnics.

Meandering up Tattle Hill (thought to have derived its name from the words 'tittle tattle') we find another eye-catching treasure in the thatched barn (built as a cow shed to house four cows, it was last used during the Second World War and re-thatched about that time). A new strain of prize winning gooseberry, called 'Woodpecker', was cultivated by 'Essa' Lynham – engineer in charge of the steam pumping engine at the colliery – in his garden at Manor house.

Danesmoor ✺

St Barnabas' church, the only surviving place of worship in Danesmoor, stands in what was once the centre of the village. The Bethel chapel stood on land near the Park House Hotel, and across the road was the Methodist chapel, now used for sporting activities such as boxing. In the 1940s and early 1950s the close community of Danesmoor attended church regularly, and joined in with the many activities such as dancing and social evenings held in the church hall, which is still in regular use.

The church had a large choir and congregation in those days, compared with the very small number going today. Whitsuntide was a great occasion, when the church and the two chapels joined together in the Whitsuntide Witness ('Whit walk'). There were about 120 children and adults walking around the district, led by a brass band. The younger children sat on decorated drays whilst the older ones walked, but the honour was for the four girls chosen to hold the ropes of the banner representing each place of worship. All children wore new clothes and shoes, and what a struggle it was to keep the tar off new shoes as it melted underfoot. The walk ended at Clay Cross Hall, where each child received an iced bun. On the corner of the church grounds, on Guildford Lane, stands the war memorial erected in memory of those who lost their lives in the two World Wars.

Danesmoor was a mining community, and the majority of men worked at Parkhouse pit and others at Clay Cross Company, now called Biwater.

The work was hard and dangerous and at the pit there was an explosion in November 1882 in which 45 men and boys died. A statue called 'The Weeping Mary' was erected in Clay Cross cemetery in their memory. The pit no longer remains.

The houses were mainly owned by the Coal Board and consisted of the Blocks, six blocks of eight houses situated at the bottom end of Danesmoor, the Square in the middle, and houses on 'the hill'. These houses consisted of a walk-in pantry, some had sculleries, a living kitchen and a parlour, which was only used on special occasions such as Christmas, and what a performance to get the open fire going! Upstairs were two bedrooms. Toilets were across the yard, and also in the yard was a washhouse with coal-fired coppers or boilers for heating water for washing the clothes. The Blocks have now been demolished and in their place stands Worcester Engineering and Ashton Containers, two firms bringing many necessary jobs after the closure of the pit.

The village has two public houses, namely the Park House Hotel, also called Bottom pub, and the Greyhound inn, called Top pub by the locals. There were several small shops stocking almost every item it was possible to buy during the hard years of war and after. Some of them were the front rooms of houses opened to become shops. there was, and still is, a post office and grocery store, a butcher's shop and a fish shop. There was also a cobbler's hut where children had many an enjoyable time watching shoes and boots being repaired, and at the bottom of Danesmoor, the Co-operative store, now turned into a house.

The extended area called Old Danesmoor consisted of farms and farm land, and a few old but beautiful cottages scattered around. Very few remain, and in the whole area of Old Danesmoor now stand hundreds of local authority and private dwellings. The Old Danesmoor gone but a new generation come.

Darley Abbey

Travelling north along the A6 from the City of Derby for a little over half a mile, one observes a sign 'Darley Abbey Old Village'. Following the sign and leaving the busy A6 one quickly enters a true oasis of peace and tranquillity; a village of delightfully restored mill cottages built in rows or squares and with a particularly fine public park close by on the Derby side. Perhaps this latter feature has prevented the village being physically absorbed into the industrial city of Derby as have so many peripheral villages this century. Bounding the park to the south-east is the picturesque river Derwent.

To get a real picture of the early village we must look back to the 12th century when there existed an Augustinian abbey at Darley. Little or no evidence of the site of such a building remains though a restored building, now the Abbey pub, constructed of stone and ancient timbers, appears to have some connection with monastic buildings as during its renovation 12th century pottery was unearthed. Centuries later in the 1920s when mains water was being laid, a lead coffin was discovered half under the front room of a cottage in Hill Square! On the orders of the then owner, Mrs Ada Evans, the coffin was left in situ.

In connection with the development of Darley Abbey, one family name is still revered, the Evans family. Originating from the Youlgreave area, they brought industrial prosperity to Darley Abbey alongside the banks of the river Derwent. To this day there remains the mill and mill yard, approached from the village by a toll bridge, which in the 18th century housed brick works, paper mill, a red lead factory, corn mill and cotton mill. For some 150 years the Evans family were almost the sole employers of the village folk and indeed cared for employees and their families in every way – subsidised rent, coal, hot meals for the sick and old, houses painted regularly inside and out, shawls and blankets provided in cold weather (for a deposit returnable if returned to the Hall in a clean condition!). Health was taken care of too. There was a sick club and a convalescent home in Llandudno, and innoculation against small pox. Villagers were buried at the expense of the Evans and memorial tablets erected.

There was a price to be paid for the Evans' guardianship. Hard work and long hours were the norm – some 70 hours per week. Children were employed from the age of nine and if short in stature were provided with pattens so that they could reach the machines! A respectable standard of social behaviour was expected – no swearing, no being away from home after 10 pm, drunks were put in the village lock-up (now demolished) overnight and had to appear before the Evans on the morrow. This paternalism continued in some form until the death of Mrs Ada Evans in 1929. There ended an era and from that time properties became privately owned.

St Matthew's church, of Gothic style, built in 1819 by the first Walter Evans, stands proudly on the hill overlooking the village and is worth a visit. It has just been beautifully restored. St Matthew's C of E school, now used as architect's offices, provided accommodation for boys and girls.

In the time of Miss Elizabeth Evans the girls were inspected once a week and their ribbons and hair cut if ribbon were deemed too gaudy and hair too long.

The latter half of the 20th century has seen development in housing but a careful watch is kept in order to preserve the somewhat unique character of the village.

Darley Dale 🦜

The village of Darley Dale appears to be just a string of houses and industrial buildings along the A6 north of Matlock and almost stretching to Rowsley. It is a village that has no real centre, no village green, even the parish church is not situated at the heart of the village. However, if you leave the main road and begin to explore you will find that the settlement has much history to discover and buildings that are of great interest.

It is possible that the present name of Darley Dale may have been invented by the railway company who, around 1890, considered that 'Dale' would make their Darley station more attractive. The growth of Darley Dale was, to a large extent, influenced by the railway. Many older residents still consider that Darley is a railway village and reminisce about railwaymen and so on, although the railway line, the station and the sidings north of the village have long since disappeared. Peak Rail, a group of railway enthusiasts, are at the present time working on reopening the railway line from Matlock through Darley to Buxton, and have done a great deal of work renovating Darley station, so it seems that in the not too distant future steam trains will again run through Darley Dale.

Sir Joseph Whitworth of Manchester, remembered as a successful manufacturer of machine tools and armaments and the inventor of the Whitworth screw thread, became a generous benefactor to Darley Dale in the 19th century. It is after him that important areas of Darley Dale are named and it was his philanthropy and that of Lady Whitworth that founded the local Whitworth Hospital, the Whitworth Institute and the Whitworth Park. Although Darley Dale was greatly improved by Whitworth generosity he was very unpopular with the villagers. He built many miles of high boundary walls around Stancliffe Hall, where he lived, to protect his privacy, and on more than one occasion he was in dispute with local landowners.

It is said that in order that the local people should not see him on his way to the church in his carriage, none of the houses were built with windows and doors facing the road.

Sir Joseph Whitworth spent many years planning to build the Whitworth Institute in Darley Dale, but in fact it was erected in 1890 after his death, by Lady Whitworth. The Institute had been planned as the centre of a model village and intended as a school for all the people of Darley Dale – it contained a library, recreation room, a gymnasium, swimming bath and a museum. Large portraits of Sir Joseph and Lady Whitworth hang in the upstairs ballroom and the building contains a Victorian timber-framed roof, wrought iron staircase and wall panels of Hopton marble. Very much unaltered, today the Whitworth Institute serves as a community centre for the people of Darley Dale.

Many years ago Darley Dale was noted for the many acres of land used for nurseries, stretching up the hillside from the village to the moorland above. The soil was particularly suited to the cultivation of conifers and heathers, the species of heather *Erica Darleyensis* named after the area. Most of these nurseries have now disappeared except for the one at the edge of the village still managed by descendants of the Smith family who began the original nurseries at the end of the 19th century.

The parish church of St Helen stands between the edge of the village and the river Derwent. Past the church runs the old road known now as Church Lane but once called Ghost Lane, because in the 17th century a pedlar was murdered near the church gates and his ghost is supposed to haunt the lane. The Darley yew tree overshadows much of the church-yard, although it is much smaller than it used to be. Estimates of its age range from 600–4,000 years old. William Wray, a vicar of the parish in the 18th century, erected a sundial to encourage his congregation to be early for services as in his opinion they spent far too much time gossiping under the yew tree.

Denby

Denby is mentioned in the Domesday Book as Denebi, and means the village of the Danes. Rykneld Street, which is the old Roman road, runs on the western part of the parish for 2,440 yards, in a straight line from Bottle Brook to the northern boundary of Street Lane.

Denby is reputed to be the second largest parish in acreage in Der-byshire, consisting of 2,437 acres. In times past there were 28 farms and in 1831 Denby contained 240 houses, most of which were thatched, 243 families and 1,272 inhabitants. Of the families 50 were chiefly employed

Denby Free C of E School

73

in agriculture, 30 in trade and handicraft and the other 163 were directly employed in working the extensive collieries and ironstone pits. Most of the land and collieries were in the ownership of the Drury-Lowe family of Locko Park, Spondon, Derby. The family have been patrons of the church for well over 400 years.

Several charities are still in existence today. One dated 1893 provided for £500 to be invested, the dividends or income to be used for the purchase of Welsh flannel to be distributed to the aged poor residents of the village in the month of October. The second was for £5 19s 2d annually to be invested and the revenue to be used for the purchase of coarse Yorkshire cloth and flannel, to be distributed to the poor and needy of the village. Both charities are in the names of the vicar and church wardens. There is no mention of the parish church in the Domesday Book, the oldest piece of stone dates from the year AD 950. The tower contains a peal of six bells, the oldest dating from about 1371.

In 1334 Richard, Lord Grey of Codnor, obtained a charter for a market on Thursdays and a two-day fair (known as Denby Wakes) on the festival of the nativity of the Virgin Mary, to whom the parish church is dedicated. The market and the fair are no longer held, but the church celebrates on 8th September with a flower festival and concert.

A building of interest in Denby is Breach Cottage, the meeting house of Quakers from 1678 to 1834 and where the remains of 200 members of the Society are buried.

The village was once a very prosperous coal mining area, coal having been worked in the parish since the 13th century. Other rich minerals are clay and ironstone. In 1806 a turnpike was constructed from Denby to Alfreton and as it passed through Denby a bed of clay was uncovered. This was found to be the finest stoneware clay in Europe, hence in 1809 Denby Pottery began production of its now world famous stoneware. Iron ore was worked in the parish in very early times by outcropping of the ironstone layers.

Denby has two famous men; one was John Flamsteed, born at 'Crowtrees' Denby Village, who was the first Astronomer Royal. The second one was Benjamin Outram, an engineer who built the Outram railway line from Smithy Houses to Little Eaton for the purpose of carting coal by horse-drawn trucks to the canal wharf at Little Eaton.

Denby can also claim another first. In 1903 a wagon carrying several barrels of tar was jolting along the turnpike, when one of the barrels fell off and burst, covering a stretch of the road with wet tar. To cover up the spillage someone sprinkled the tar with slag debris from the nearby blast furnaces. It was later noticed by a road surveyor that this area of road was remarkably free from both dust and wear and thus started a product, tarmacadam, which was to revolutionise road making in this country.

Denby primary school was founded by Mrs Jane Massie in 1760, carrying out the wishes of her husband's will for 'the teaching of boys and girls in the parish to read and write'. The John Flamsteed School today is unique, a large comprehensive school in a village.

Dethick, Lea & Holloway 🪴

Dethick, Lea and Holloway are a trio of attractive villages nestling in the hills of the Derwent valley.

In the 13th century a manor house and a chapel were built for Geoffrey Dethick, who took his name from the place. In the 17th century the manor house was partially demolished, and the hamlet now has three farms and a church, St John the Baptist, still in use. However, it has its own claim to fame as the home of Anthony Babington. He played a crucial role in the plot to release Mary Queen of Scots from imprisonment in nearby Wingfield Manor, and was executed for his pains.

Lea has a different character; in fact a dual personality. Upper Lea, as it is sometimes called, was the home of local gentlemen of business and property. The 14th century Lea Hall was formerly the home of the lord of the manor, and close by are believed to be the remains of a monastery, complete with monk's pathway. Lea Green was, at the turn of the century, the home of John Marsden Smedley, a landowner of some consequence. The creation of the now famous rhododendron gardens is a tribute to his knowledge, skill and love of the flower. Year after year, visitors from all over the country arrive by car and coach, simply to admire and enjoy the gardens.

Lea Bridge, on the other hand, is a complete contrast. It was once the largest, and one of the last, lead smelters in the county. When the nearby canal cutting was opened in the 18th century by Peter Nightingale, lead could then be carried more quickly by barge, drawn by either two men or a horse, to the railway. At the same time, hats for soldiers and gentlemen were being turned out at Peter Nightingale's hat factory, so that altogether the village had a thriving industrial life. An interesting fate awaited the hat factory, however. It gave way to the production of mineral water taken from one of the many springs in this locality.

Lea Bridge's heyday may be over, but it still echoes to the sound of machinery. Lea Mills is famous for its fine woollen underwear and outerwear. Bearing the logo of a 'Jay' – the trademark of John Smedley & Co – the knit-wear is exported to several countries, and has a popular following here. The mill, built by Peter Nightingale in 1784, was a cotton mill, but in the early 19th century John Smedley leased the mill and began spinning fine wool; another success story for Lea Bridge and its workers, because he not only built houses for them to live in, but also established one of the first factory hospitals in some nearby buildings, now known as Post Office Cottages.

Lea Mills has, of course, its ghost. He is said to be one Aaron Wigley, who worked there until a great age and still walks the factory floor! The mill also had its own football and cricket team, skittle alley and a brass band.

Holloway is south-facing, overlooks the Derwent valley and boasts a distinguished former resident. Florence Nightingale lived part of her life in the family home at Lea Hurst, amid rolling parkland. Older folk can recall a choir singing on the lawns and refreshments being served by Mr Shore Nightingale. The family were actively concerned in the life of the village, and provided a site for the building of a Memorial Hall. The foundation stone of the Florence Nightingale Hall was laid by the then Prince of Wales in 1932, and in 1982 Princess Anne laid the foundation stone of a much-needed extension.

In the early 1900s Holloway had 28 shops. Now it has three. In the 1920s there was a Wakes Week of continuous entertainment. Now there is a carnival on one day in June. These are signs of great change in village life, but even today it is still a working village where some get their living in Matlock or Derby, and others on the farms or in the mill. The oldest parts of Holloway are surrounded with woods which, in spring, are covered with bluebells. Natural underground springs give a lushness to the landscape, whilst canal and river are home to little grebe, heron and, if one is lucky, kingfisher.

Doe Lea & Bramley Vale 🌿

Doe Lea Cottages was the official description in 1895 of the original small colliery hamlet that was situated partly in Ault Hucknall parish and partly in Heath. The name of that community had been taken from the river Doe Lea, a stream rising locally and joining the river Rother near Renishaw. When the Sheepbridge Coal and Iron Co Ltd started mining activities at Glapwell Colliery in 1882, the village at Doe Lea developed considerably. The Mansfield to Chesterfield railway ran through Bramley Vale, the tunnel being opened in 1890. Glapwell station, situated more or less in Bramley Vale, served this part of the Doe Lea valley from 1890 to 1930. Forty years after its closure it was a meeting place for the Full Revival Gospel Mission. During the Second World War the tunnel was a store for explosives and valuables. The station and tunnel have now been demolished and part of the track is used as the Rowthorne trail.

At Doe Lea the Primitive Methodist chapel was built in 1892. The Church of England authorities established St Andrew's Mission, which was used for worship and also, on Friday evenings from 6 pm until 7 pm, the Yorkshire Penny Bank was held there. The Jackson Memorial Hall was opened in 1933 in memory of Mrs W.M.B. Jackson of Glapwell Hall.

Local residents at the turn of the 20th century included Albert Evans, shopkeeper; Thomas Fisher, farm bailiff; Edward Glassbrook, grocer; George Bland, hairdresser; Lucy Perkes, schoolmistress; T.T. Smith, cashier; Elizabeth Farnsworth at Hagg's Farm and Robey Townrow in Bramley Vale. Local carriers were John Ashmore and John Brookes.

After 1923 colliery workers' modern housing was being built at Bramley Vale and a number of Doe Lea residents moved there. The plans of the hot water heating system for each of the houses (supplied by the

Sheepbridge company) were displayed at the British Empire Exhibition held at Wembley in 1924 and 1925. The first car in Doe Lea and Bramley Vale was owned by Mr F. Haywood who was under manager at the colliery; in 1917 the brass fittings of the French Darracq amazed all those who turned out to witness its arrival by rail.

People still talk about the fire on Pancake Day, 1931, when the school at Doe Lea burnt down. Shrove Tuesday was a half day holiday and it was presumed a lighted coal had fallen from the stove. One seven year old danced for joy thinking he would never have to go to school again! The present primary school for the neighbourhood is in Bramley Vale and backs on to a pleasant wood. Lent was the season for whip and top, battleboard and shuttlecock, new skipping ropes and bowls – name for the steel hoop used by the boys.

The Doe Lea Allotment Association held an annual show, and one year in the 1920s the prize was a bedroom suite!

Today at Doe Lea, near Junction 29 of the M1, there is still a small drift mine which is probably one of the oldest in the area, and one of the few mines which has never been nationalised. Glapwell Colliery ceased operations in 1974 and this rhyme was no longer used locally:

'O Lord above, my back is sore,
Lift up this tub, while I shove o'er'

The land has been reinstated, trees planted and sheep now graze beside the A617, east of the motorway.

Doveridge

Driving from Uttoxeter towards Derby on the busy A50 trunk road, you could be forgiven for thinking that Doveridge, most of which cannot be seen from the highway, isn't much of a village at all; more a disagreeable 30 miles per hour area to be negotiated as quickly as possible. However, if you leave this thoroughfare, you will find the village named after the older of two bridges which cross the river Dove, the natural county boundary between Derbyshire and Staffordshire.

Like many old villages, Doveridge is mentioned in the Domesday Book boasting, amongst other things, a parish church and a water mill. Approaching St Cuthbert's by the main path you enter a 'tunnel' of branches formed by an ancient yew tree, reputed to be some 1,200 years of age. According to legend, Robin Hood was betrothed to his lady under its boughs. In recent times these boughs have been propped up with timber and restrained by chains to prevent them blocking the way.

Dropping down from the church, a footpath passes the site of the old water mill which was demolished in the 1970s after being left in disrepair for many years, the last working parts being sold off in the 1950s. Villagers consider this a great shame because it was a unique part of the village's history and also a listed building.

Back on the main road is the village 'local', the Cavendish Arms, named after landed gentry of yesteryear. In the centre of the village is a working men's club, and other meeting places include the village post office, a general store, playing fields, an antiques shop and the village hall.

The village primary school is today housed in a modern building but in the 18th century the few lucky children who received education were taught in dame schools which were held in various houses throughout the village, notably 'The Gables' in Lower Street, a fine old house which has recently been carefully restored. In 1797 the first purpose-built village school was completed, paid for with money from bequests by two village ladies, Mary Burgh and Lucy Bakewell. This building is still standing and is used as a private dwelling. Less fortunate was Doveridge Hall, which fell into disrepair and was eventually demolished in 1938.

Heading from the centre of the village towards the church one arrives at a crossroads on which stands Doveridge Well. The village has several wells but this one is of most importance, being a handsome focal point. The well is now capped over and a garden surrounding it is maintained throughout the year by members of the Doveridge Women's Institute, who also supplied a seat which was installed there in 1951 to mark Festival of Britain Year.

Much new housing has been built in recent years, mostly on two pleasant estates, one of which was constructed on parkland once belonging to Doveridge Hall. Development has brought to the area many new people who today add much to the pattern of life in Doveridge.

The road bridge over the river is of modern construction and lies side by side with the original bridge, which is constructed of local stone and can be reached by a footpath. It is now closed to traffic and you can stand upon it and dream of the days when horses and carts were all that trundled over its six magnificent arches.

Draycott & Wilne

The Romans started it all. In order to get their Derbyshire lead from Derby to the river Trent at Trent Lock, they built a straight road between the two. A small community developed along it about six miles from Derby. It was mentioned in the Domesday Book in 1086 as Draicott or Dry Cote.

About a mile to the south by the river Derwent there was a settlement which we now call Wilne, the original name meaning 'a clearing in the willows' which sounds a wet and marshy place. A church was recorded there in AD 822 dedicated to St Chad, the bishop of Lichfield whose diocese covered the area. The Domesday Book also records a manor and a mill; the latter has survived in various forms through the ages, and at present it is the maker of fireworks and military pyrotechnics.

As may be expected, the folk at Wilne gradually moved to Dry Cote as this was higher and dryer, not subject to flooding. Eventually they merged. At present there are only two houses with the mill, the fine old church, and a modern lake has been added recently, encouraging wildlife. The church was gutted by fire in 1917, reopened in 1923 and is now the parish church of the combined parish of Draycott & Wilne.

In the 18th century a canal followed the line of the road from Derby, and in the 19th century a railway. About three miles beyond, there used to be the only station in the country where one could sit and watch two trains going in opposite directions, both going to London.

For centuries it was entirely a farming community, but as industry grew so did Draycott. Coal was mined in the more northern areas of the county, and transported in carts drawn by donkeys as far down as the river or the canal. Draycott folk are traditionally called 'Neddies'. The reason was that the market place was the changing point for the coal-cart donkeys. They surely needed a rest.

The landmark in Draycott is the large Victoria Mill, its clock-tower visible from miles around. This mill really brought industry to the village. Its size was the same as Noah's Ark; 300 cubits long, 50 cubits wide and 30 cubits high. When it was completed in 1907 (having been badly damaged by fire in 1902) it was the largest manufacturing mill in Europe. Until the advent of the railway, freight was carried by canal, which remained in use until the Second World War.

The village ghost is frequently seen in the Draycott lace mill. He is Mr Stocks the founder, who died a quarter of a century ago. The workers seem to take him as quite a normal visitor.

Dronfield 🐝

Dronfield is thought to mean the open land where there are drones (male bees). It is situated in the north-east of Derbyshire halfway between the city of Sheffield to the north and Chesterfield to the south. It is bordered on the west by open countryside which adjoins the Peak District National Park – a mere three miles away. Dronfield has grown rapidly in the last 20 years, and is now a mixture of modern housing and fine old buildings.

Many of the old buildings are in the High Street and Church Street area. One of the more unusual and interesting buildings, situated near the top of the High Street, is the Peel Monument. Built of gritstone in 1854, the Monument is a tribute to Sir Robert Peel, and celebrates the repeal of the Corn Laws in 1846. It is probably one of the most photographed and sketched features of Dronfield. The market cross and stocks were previously on this site.

In 1662 Dronfield was granted a market by Charles II, but in the 18th century, due to the nearness of Sheffield and Chesterfield, the market went into decline and ceased to exist. It was revived on a nearby site in 1980, and is thriving today.

Close to the Monument on High Street, is a house known as 'The Cottage', dating from the 16th century. It is believed to have been owned by Lord Byron (1788 – 1824), though there is no proof that he ever lived in it. Two tales in Dronfield concern funerals. It was said that the first person to meet a funeral would be the next to die. A woman living in Dronfield was in the habit of following funerals to see who was the first person to meet the corpse! Secondly, at funerals in Dronfield the coffin was laid on a table, which was put outside the house and covered with a white cloth. The neighbours laid flowers on the cloth and sang a hymn.

It is said that a smell of thyme may always be noticed near a footpath leading from Dronfield to Stubley. The supposed reason is that a young man murdered his sweetheart there when she was carrying a bunch of thyme. There is also a story that a headless woman appears where three roads meet between Coal Aston, Dronfield, and Bowshaw.

There was a recent examination by the Boundary Commission of proposals to merge Dronfield into Sheffield and hence South Yorkshire. Thanks to concerted representation by the local community this proposal was turned down, and Dronfield and its traditions is to remain part of Derbyshire.

Duckmanton 🌿

Duckmanton is a village in the north-east corner of Derbyshire. It is in fact almost two villages; the old agricultural village and the newer mining village. The mining village consists of Markham Colliery, British Coal central workshops and central store, and also the houses built for the miners employed at the colliery. In recent years these houses have been sold off and there is now no one common type of work. The other end of the village is still agricultural with some residential property.

There was mining in Duckmanton as long ago as 1350. In recent times there has been much open-cast mining and this has brought to light bell pits as evidence of the old methods of obtaining coal. This method of mining must have fallen into disuse when it was inadequate for the extraction of coal and the village reverted to an area of small farms.

Mining has always been a difficult, dirty and dangerous undertaking. There are still men who remember working in water and 'getting' the coal with pick and shovel. Each man had a 'stint' to work and was paid piece work. It was the custom to give the overman an orange as a Christmas present. In the orange was inserted a gold sovereign. This 'sweetener' it was hoped would ensure the miner being allocated an easy 'stint'. Even now with automation and computerisation it is a hard life but at least miners are now more adequately rewarded.

In 1750 the Adelphi Ironworks was founded in Duckmanton and here cannon balls for the Napoleonic wars were manufactured. In fact the gates were later called 'Waterloo Gates'. The iron for this manufacture was brought from Staveley by water along underground 'legging tunnels'. This name arose from the way the barges were propelled. Men lay on their backs and 'walked' with their feet on the roof of the tunnel.

There was a church in Duckmanton in the 13th century but by the time Sir Francis Leake of Sutton Scarsdale had bought the former monastic lands from Henry VIII on the Dissolution of the Monasteries, the building had fallen into disrepair. The rectory at St Mary's, Sutton Scarsdale, was also in a bad condition, so the two parishes were united. In 1840 the present church was built. It was originally used as a reading room for itinerant workers building the new railways. When this present building was begun, 16 skeletons were discovered, each measuring six ft from head to ankle, none having any feet. What happened to the missing feet?

The Arkwright family lived at Sutton Hall, so strictly speaking do not belong to Duckmanton, but they owned all the land at Duckmanton, buying the estate from the Leakes. Mr Richard Arkwright went to the auction of the estate in London dressed in very shabby clothes. The auctioneer, it is reported, was concerned as to whether this man could honour his bid. He was suitably surprised when a note for £100,000 was produced, together with the statement that only two notes of that denomination had been issued and Mr Arkwright also possessed the other one.

Duffield

Duffield is situated on the A6 five miles north of Derby. It is an interesting and appealing combination of old and new. As one enters the village, the hall on the left is an imposing building; once a stately home, then a girls school, it is now the headquarters of the Derbyshire Building Society. Change over the last 50 years has been tremendous: housing estates where farms used to nestle. Duffield in Appletree was mentioned in the Domesday Book of 1086, being one of the five Wapentakes or Hundreds listed under the County of Derby.

The railway runs through the village and Duffield station was once known as a 'Top Hat' station as several of the railway hierarchy lived here. A row of houses was built specially for railwaymen who were transferred to Derby from the North. Nowadays Duffield station is just a 'halt' and one can board a little train and take a very pleasant journey to Matlock.

Duffield endowed school has been in existence since the 1600s and there is now also the Meadows primary school and Ecclebourne school. There was formerly a girls school. The headmistress Miss Dorothy Benner was quite a character. Most children, although respecting her authority, were scared of her. The cane, a thickly pointed type, was always lying on the top of her desk which was on a platform. This dear lady, carrying a lot of weight, used to make the floor shake when she dropped off her stool to point to the blackboard. Another colourful character of the 1920s and 1930s was Mrs Laura Butler of Tamworth Street, who used to light the gas lamps in the village each evening in winter.

Duffield Cricket Club have played cricket on Eyes Meadow for over 100 years. There are football, rugby and hockey pitches as well. The Duffield Carnival, organized by the Community Association, is also held annually on Eyes Meadow.

People of all denominations are catered for. There is the 12th/14th century parish church of St Alkmund, Trinity Methodist church, the Baptist church, St Margaret Clitherow Roman Catholic church and the Emmanuel community church. Duffield is also fortunate to have a variety of shops, mostly on the A6 which runs through the centre of the village. Duffield has grown considerably during the past years and like so many villages, the character and appearance of the shops has altered as times have changed. The little bay-windowed cobbler's shop, which sold leather nails, etc to the people who mended their own shoes; and the draper's where one could buy pure wool at 4d per ounce are long gone. There are now several newly built and modernised shops including a new post office, a Co-op supermarket, two butchers' shops, two delicatessen shops, and a flower and greengrocery shop. There are also shops at Meadow Vale, Flaxholme and New Zealand Lane for the convenience of the people living on the outskirts of the village.

Earl Sterndale 🦢

Earl Sterndale, five miles south of Buxton, lies 1,100 ft above sea level in the Peak National Park. It is ringed by beautiful hills such as Parkhouse, Chrome and High Wheeldon. Chrome is recorded as being the highest hill in the county, and High Wheeldon was given to the National Trust as a memorial to the men of Derbyshire and Staffordshire regiments who gave their lives in two World Wars. In the hillside is a cave in which were found prehistoric remains and exhibits are now in the Buxton Museum.

The first recorded mention of Earl Sterndale is in 1244, when it was known as Stenredile. This may reflect the nature of the terrain in those days and for many centuries – a stony and sterile dale. Today, it is a pretty upland village.

Most of the cottages are built of stone, hand-got from small quarries in the village. The Duke of Devonshire once owned most of the land in the parish and, in the past, lead mining and quarrying provided employment as well as agriculture, although occupations now are diverse. The first chapelry was built in the reign of Edward IV, around 1400. This was a wooden structure and was reputedly burned down. The present church of St Michael was built in 1828 and it has a Saxon font. This font, a treasure of the church, was shattered when the church was virtually destroyed by incendiary bombs on the night of 9th January 1941, the only one in the Derbyshire Diocese to be damaged by enemy action. The font was repaired, the church rebuilt, and rededicated in July 1952. The Wakes, one of the feasts of the church, is now always the Sunday nearest to the 11th October. Tradition has it that the man who is most drunk on the Friday before the Wakes is elected Mayor for the year.

The church register begins in 1768, and there is mention in it of a workhouse and asylum, now the walled garden of a private house. The road adjacent, Griffen Lane, is named after the workhouse keeper. Children having previously been educated in the Quiet Woman inn and Sycamore Cottage, the present school was built in 1850 in the grounds of the church. The same year saw the building of the Wesleyan chapel.

The only inn still in existence is the Quiet Woman, which is reputed to be over 400 years old and was in the occupation of the Heathcote family for nearly 300 years. This unusual name, one of only three in the country, is said to derive from the too talkative wife of a landlord who was decapitated in consequence! It has the sign of a headless woman and the quotation 'Soft words turneth away wrath'.

Earl de Ferrers gave great tracts of land to the Basingwerk Monastery, and Abbots Grove, at the southern end of the village, was built about 1780 on the site of an earlier building in which the abbot stayed when visiting monastery properties. There are many Granges in the village where the monks lived and worked the land, such as Cronkstone, Glutton and Harley, etc. It is said that Bonnie Prince Charlie's men, looking for food, found cattle belonging to Cronkstone hidden up a narrow dale. They killed them and had a great feast – thus giving the name Glutton to the Grange in the dale.

During the 1850s, the buildings at Abbots Grove housed the local tannery and many interesting artefacts have been unearthed there. At the end of the century, one Thomas Bradley, resident there, deserted his wife for another woman. On his death, he bequeathed his wife one shilling. She was so infuriated that she nailed the shilling to the kitchen door and it was still there in 1974, disappearing shortly afterwards during renovations, leaving only the imprint which remains today.

Woodbine Cottage was once the home of Billy Budd, who fought in the Afghan War in 1880, and who marched from Kabul to Kandahar, a distance of 350 miles, wearing no boots but his feet wrapped in cloths. He is buried in the churchyard.

Eckington 🌿

Eckington, which is in north-east Derbyshire, is seven miles north of Chesterfield. The name Eckington is of Saxon origin, meaning the township of Ecca.

In medieval times it was a small but important settlement, which was later engulfed by development when coal deposits were extensively worked throughout the area. It is a long sprawling village, with typical picture postcard scenes of its manor houses and cottages built of the local Derbyshire stone. The main street through the village is just over a mile in length. There are eleven public houses, some dating back many years.

The main occupations were farming and mining, but since the closing of the local colliery, although some miners still work at nearby colleries, several light industries have become established and a lot of farming land has been lost to building development.

The parish church of St Peter and St Paul dates from the year 1100 and is of exceptional architectural interest, still retaining the original Norman doorway. In a field at the back of the church, near the river Moss stands the Priest's Well where the parish priest used to draw water for the needs of the church. Up to the 1930s gipsies used the field as a winter camp, drawing water from the well for all their needs. Close to the church is the rectory, a late Georgian house with Venetian windows.

Sir Reresby and Lady Sitwell live at Renishaw Hall, which is surrounded by parkland and a golf course on the outskirts of Eckington. The Hall has been the family home of the Sitwell family for nearly 400 years and has become famous through the writing of Edith, Osbert and Sacheverell Sitwell, father of the present owner. A novel feature at the hall is the vineyard begun in 1972.

A market is held each Friday on pedestrianised Market Street, adding life and colour to the centre of the village. The Civic Centre, also on Market Street, is widely used for many different functions and activities, and stands beside the swimming pool and library.

There are many pathways for people to enjoy to the surrounding villages and through the wooded valley of the river Moss, a tributary of the Rother. This area, now rich in wildlife, was once a centre of industry, relics of which can still be seen today.

Edale 🎗

The valley is deep, 1,250 ft in the middle so that the sun sets early and frosts are keen. The five small communities or booths that formed the old centres of life are strung out in a line along the south facing side, upslope from what was once the marshy, wooded, wolf and fugitive-concealing valley floor. Two newer groups of houses lie near the station and a mill on the river Noe and a small number of isolated farms and barns are dotted among the fields. Just a few private houses line the road.

If Edale has a centre, it is the middle booth, Grindsbrook, where trees conceal the church, school, post office, council bungalows and two old public houses. Nearly all are made of stone and the wide fields are contained within stone walls which stretch up the valley sides until the land becomes too steep to improve and fields give way to open sheep

Edale Church and the Old Chapel Inn

pasture or bracken and heather moor and eventually, on the northern rim, to crags of millstone grit which edge the Kinder Plateau.

The past scene is of a few families with many members, visited only by jaggers (packhorse men) who plied their trade, cheese and salt from Cheshire for woollen bales from Yorkshire, along a narrow track from Hayfield, past Edale Cross in the west, through the booths to cross the rushing brook at Grindsbrook by way of a lofty stone packhorse bridge and on out of the valley up Jaggers' Clough and Crookstone to Derwent. They could stop at the Nag's Head inn en route for refreshment. Edale was noted as a subsidiary settlement to Hope in the Domesday Book and until the first chapel of ease was built in 1633, worshippers had to climb the two bridle paths to Castleton, a journey of three miles and a climb of 600 ft. Edale did not become a parish until 1863. Even 50 years ago housewives depended on visiting tradesmen.

New blood arrived when the old corn mill was replaced or enlarged to make a cotton mill, a local man taking three Manchester men into partnership. An even greater influx came when the railway was built. The population rose from 335 in 1881 to 960 in 1891 and a shanty town grew up near Barber Booth where the one and a half mile long Cowburn tunnel was excavated in 1888. The mill stayed open until 1934 and many workers or their descendants still live here.

In the 19th century, much of the land was in the hands of important landowners such as the Champions and the Duke of Devonshire. The Champions were great benefactors but their moors were closed to the public, policed by gamekeepers and only open for shooting parties. By the 1940s the Duke's land had been sold to the Water Authority for the Derwent Dams project or to pay death duties. It was also planned to flood the Edale valley but its shifting shale and sandstone sides would have made a dam unsafe. The Champion family still farms here but on a much reduced scale. Today's landowner is the National Trust, which has amalgamated small farms and let the farmhouses.

Not many Edalians have actually walked the Pennine Way but they have shown lots of people where it is and they share the valley with thousands of walkers and campers who come to enjoy the freedom to walk. The three shops, two cafes and two pubs benefit from the trade as do those who provide hotel, bed and breakfast and cottage accommodation. It is thought a privilege to live in a place so many want to visit.

Edensor & Pilsley

Edensor and Pilsley, and the hamlets of Calton Lees and Dunsa, all lie on the Chatsworth estate. Almost all the inhabitants work for it, and Chatsworth House, the home of the Duke of Devonshire, is the pivot.

The Saxon village of Ednesoure, now Edensor, which thanks to the idiosyncrasies of the local pronunciation is called Enzor, is a small model village surrounded by a wall. There are some older houses, but most were built from individual designs around 1840, when the 6th Duke removed the village from along the river to its present position; so you find a Norman house and a Swiss and Tudor cottage among others. These are tied houses but their occupants and their widows and widowers may keep them for life. No new houses have been built but the stables have been converted into eleven flats for pensioners.

St Peter's church dominates the village, and was built on the site of the old church in 1870. A patronal festival is held on 29th June and the people from Pilsley, Calton Lees and Dunsa (naturally pronounced Dunza) join in a weekend of celebrations. Many Americans come to see the grave of Kathleen Kennedy in the ducal burial ground. She was killed in an aircrash after her husband, Lord Hartington, the present Duke's brother, was killed in the Second World War. President Kennedy came to see his sister's grave in 1963 in a visit shrouded in great secrecy for security reasons. The only casualties of the day were the churchwarden's hens, which were swept up with the presidential helicopter and never seen again!

Sir Joseph Paxton is also buried in the churchyard. He had long associations with Chatsworth and, among many other achievements, designed the Crystal Palace.

The school which stood on the green was demolished in 1950. The last schoolmaster was the redoubtable Mr Wragg, a martinet who taught his pupils to write in beautiful copperplate, instantly recognisable in the handwriting of some of the older generation.

To preserve the 'model village' appearance, no vegetable gardens or pig sties were in evidence, allotments were provided up the village and washing had to be hung in the drying ground, again out of sight. Now everyone takes a great pride in their gardens, which are a delight to see, and what they do with their washing is their own affair!

One of the houses in the village used to be an ale house, but that ceased to be in 1870 and since then there has been no pub but there is a shop and a post office and a cafe.

Pilsley stands on a hill looking over to the moors and limestone edges. It has a school, a post office and a pub. The old bakery is still there but not in use – hence Bun Alley alongside. Duck Row is further up the village. The school is the heart of the village, enlarged to take in more children when Beeley school closed.

The smithy, now no longer needed, was a hive of industry in its heyday. Horses, from ponies to the great shires, would wait to be shod and a big stone trough stood outside in which the cart wheels were soaked. The fine range of buildings of the old shire horse stud farm now houses the farm shop. Four workshops are in the rear buildings and an upholstery business thrives in some great old barns on the other side of the village. Well dressings are combined with a Pilsley Carnival and many visitors come to join in the junketings on the green, when money is raised for charities. The old chapel has been turned into a village room and twelve new houses have been built in recent years.

The hamlet of Calton Lees has a farm and a small group of houses, but there is activity there with the sawmills and forestry yard. The garden centre is run by tenants of the estate and attracts hundreds of gardeners and non-gardeners alike, so great is the variety of things they sell. The large free car park is occupied all the year round.

Dunsa is a small collection of houses, dominated by an Italianate Paxton house, now the home of the Comptroller. The farm buildings have been updated, and a shed for 1,000 lambing ewes built.

With most people involved in work for the Chatsworth estate, these villages form a close-knit community drawn together in loyalty to 'The House'.

Edlaston & Wyaston

Although Edlaston and Wyaston have a long history of separate townships they must be regarded as a single village. The church is in Edlaston and only a few hundred yards away is the village public house, the Shire Horse. The address of this is Wyaston, as is that of the community beyond.

It is on record that the ancient church of St James was repaired in 1682 and the ecclesiastical parish is united with Brailsford, Shirley and Osmaston. Inside the church are several notices of charities dating from 1694 of monies left to the parishes of Edlaston and Wyaston with Yeldersley and Painters Lane. The chapel was closed and is now a house. There are two wells which over the years have been the scene of well dressings, but this is no longer continued.

The village school was closed on the 21st July 1961 and is now domestic property. Nearly all recent development has been in the form of renovation of old property with the exception of a scattering of new houses as infill. The village hall originally consisted of two wooden huts, used for almost 30 years until funds were raised to build the present hall which was officially opened by Sir Ian Walker-Okeover in March 1980.

Wyaston Show is an annual event, which started as a small gymkhana in 1957. The Wyaston Show and Gymkhana Committee was formed in 1958, when the first show was held incorporating cattle together with arts and crafts. The show is now held on the Polo Ground at Osmaston on the first Saturday in June.

Egginton

Egginton is a small South Derbyshire village of 590 residents, just off the A38 (the old Rykneld Way) between Burton-on-Trent and Derby.

In late Stone Age times it was a swamp settlement on the higher ground bounded by the present streets Fishpond Lane, Duck Street and Main Street. The fishpond is to be found to the west of Fishpond Lane by the track to the Hilton Brook called Watery Lane, and ducks still waddle by the roadsides! Until recently flooding was a frequent problem, but happily there is now a flood-bank to keep the waters of the nearby river Dove at bay. Even so the Town End Bridge was washed away by the swollen Egginton brook in 1977, and essential supplies reached the village on a farm tractor.

In the 17th century the village and its lands were owned by the Every family. The old Tudor Hall was burnt down in 1736 and a new Hall built in 1780. At the same time the surrounding Tudor cottages were removed to create open parkland round the Hall, so all the estate houses date from the late 18th century. During demolition of a cottage in the early 1800s a beautiful Cavalier sword was found in the thatch, no doubt hidden by a fugitive from the battle of Egginton Heath in 1644.

The row of cottages opposite the Park wall in Fishpond Lane is now only two dwellings, though previously it housed eight families. Strangely, all the 'front' doors were at the rear until recently. It is said that a certain Squire Osbaldeston of Atherston began to hunt coverts which belonged to the Egginton Hunt. When Sir Henry Every remonstrated with him, he challenged Sir Henry to a duel, but as duelling had been made illegal a generation before, and under persuasion from his Hunt Committee, Sir Henry refused. Fearing that the villagers might think him a coward and gossip about him as he drove past in his carriage, he had the front doors of the cottages blocked.

Private development has occurred mainly since 1938, following the sale of the estate. Sadly the Hall was demolished in 1954 and only ruins of the stables can now be seen.

Egginton is now largely a commuter village, though some of its families stretch back over many generations. It offers peace and tranquillity to its inhabitants, and a range of clubs and societies for all ages. There is no pub within the village, but the Every Arms, an ancient coaching inn, is half a mile away on the A38.

In Duck Street, still in good condition, stands the pound, once used to house stray cattle found wandering in the village. During the First World War it held a machine gun, which was melted down to make armaments in the Second World War.

The present church of St Wilfrid, built on the site of an earlier Norman church, dates from the 13th century, and contains some original stained glass, many memorials to the Every and Moseley families, and water colours of the interior before the major alterations of 1892. Of particular interest is a map showing parish field names, some of which are perpetuated in house names.

The festival of St Wilfrid's Day is still celebrated in October each year with children's games and a variety concert put on by village organisations, and the village supports Etwall by 'dressing' one of their wells in May. Sadly, the Osier Feast has lapsed, though osier beds are still to be seen from Watery Lane, and older inhabitants can remember 'stripping the willow'.

The school is unique, in that it is rented to the education authority for use during school hours, but reverts to being the village hall at other times. It was bought by the village as a memorial to the fallen of the First World War. The School House serves a triple purpose, housing the caretaker, post office and the village shop, where a warm welcome is typical of this very friendly village.

Elton 🌿

Elton is a friendly village with a happy knack of integrating its newcomers, of whom many choose to stay. A former lead-mining village, it is situated in the South Peak, on the spring line between the limestone and the gritstone. Houses and field boundaries are built from both rocks and remains of some of the old pumps and wells can be seen, notably in Well Street. There are many disused leadmines in the surrounding fields. Most are now capped although occasionally a cow has to be rescued from a hitherto undiscovered shaft.

Most of the 18th century miners' cottages have been enlarged and modernised and more recent houses have mostly been built during the 20th century. The oldest dated building is Elton Hall, now the Youth Hostel, which bears a stone dated 1668. Along Main Street are a number of former shops, workshops, smithy and slaughterhouse now all used as garages for storage. Only one shop remains, a post office cum general store which used to be a public house, the Nelson Arms. In former times there were as many as four ale houses. The one remaining is still an unpretentious village pub.

All Saint's church, which stands in the centre of the village, was rebuilt in 1812, the former building having collapsed as a result of extensive mineworkings below. The font is a replica of the original 12th century one which former parishioners, unaware of its worth, allowed to go to Youlgreave church. Later, when its historical value was realised, they tried to retrieve it but without success. Residents are justly proud of their church and churchyard which are well-kept and a credit to the village.

Sixty years ago the main occupations were quarrying, farming and lead-mining, the men in the latter case walking over three miles to the Millclose Mine at Darley Dale. Others travelled daily to the brickworks at Friden. Girls went into domestic service, worked on the farm or cycled to the mills on Via Gellia. Today professional and skilled industrial workers travel to work in nearby towns while farmers (fewer than in the 1930s) and self-employed builders, carpenters and other craftsmen work from premises within the village.

Elton was the last village in Derbyshire, and perhaps in England, to retain its rural fire party. The County Fire Service provided a firebox kept near the centre of the village, containing a standpipe, hosereels, a stirrup pump and a hand-operated siren which was to be used to call out the volunteers. Occasional training sessions were held but 'real' fires were few and far between and fortunately not serious. However, on one occasion the party was able to contain a potentially serious barn fire until the arrival of a fire engine from Matlock, some six or seven miles away. The party stood down for the last time in 1987, partly because the County Fire Service was concerned about the increasing risk to volunteers presented by burning chemicals.

Although the population is only about 400, there is plenty going on in Elton. There is a primary school, church and chapel. The village has its cricket and football teams and a ski club which sets up its tow on a steep hillside known as The Bonks. A residential qualification applies to membership of the Elton Cricket Club: to play you have to live in the village or to have been born here. Elton folk have worked hard over the years to provide facilities for their community. They celebrated the Silver Jubilee by raising money for a recreation ground in 1977 and five years later bought and converted a redundant chapel for use as a village hall.

Elvaston

Not strictly a village, Elvaston is a large rural parish east of Derby and uneasily sharing a boundary with the city. The parish encompasses the hamlets of Elvaston, Thulston and Ambaston (originally Ealvoldstune, Torulfestune and Eanbaldstune), ancient settlements named after their respective chiefs. This area has been populated for at least 3,000 years and farming was so well established by 1086 that there was 'land for 17 ploughs', calculated as about 500 acres, a quarter of the present parish area. Also, Elvaston had one of the two smiths working in Derbyshire at that time.

In the time of Henry VIII the local manor with its lands came to the Stanhopes, who lived in what is today the Castle in Elvaston Country Park. When the estate was sold 30 years ago, the local authority bought the Castle, its surrounding parkland and the Home Farm. In 1969 this was opened as a 'Country Park', one of the first in the country, now identified by English Heritage as a 'Park of Special Interest, Grade 2'. At the top of the avenue from the A6 there is a fine pair of iron gates, painted in blue and gold and known locally as the 'Golden Gates', which are reputed to have been taken from Madrid by Napoleon and acquired by the Earl of Harrington, possibly as 'spoils of war'.

Cricket has been played by Elvaston Cricket Club (earlier known as the Earl of Harrington's XI) for over 140 years on a pitch in the castle grounds.

The parish church, dedicated to St Bartholomew, is close to the castle and some distance from the nearest hamlet of Elvaston. The present building dates back to the 12th century, with additions and alterations in the 14th century, and contains some fine monuments and carved screens.

Two interesting buildings in Elvaston are the village hall, formerly the village school (dated 1852), where numerous parish organisations and societies meet, and the three-storey house known as the 'Clockhouse', built as a 'Refuge for the Aged Poor' in 1862 and after a period as a private residence now a retirement home. Thurlastone Grange, an attractive Georgian Grade II listed building in Thulston, is also of interest, having had a varied history as a private residence, the vicarage for nearly 100 years, home to the army, a boys' preparatory school and back into private ownership.

The remaining public house is the Harrington Arms in Thulston, where for many years a 'Guisers' or 'Mummers' play was performed at Christmas time. An even older tradition (c1600s) was that of brewing ales jointly with the neighbouring parish of Ockbrook. Residents were then obliged to buy the ale from the other parish for the 'support and repair of the church'. Present day residents are still supportive of charities, in particular the Fun Run around the park which annually raises several hundred pounds.

A charitable trust exists in the parish, combining three charities left in the 17th and 19th centuries, for the provision of a small pension to retired long-time residents of 'good character'. Small sums for tools for apprentices (nowadays interpreted as books for students) are also allowed for.

Agriculture (mostly arable, beef and sheep rearing) is still the most important industry, although only a fraction of the residents work on the land. Most now commute to employment outside the parish. Calico weaving and stocking framing were recorded in a 19th century census and in the 1700s alabaster was mined at Bellington. Today sand and gravel are extracted in the same area and to the dismay of parishioners this seems likely eventually to affect most of the parish.

Although most residents are new to the area, there are still some families who can trace their presence here for hundred of years. Indeed, some are recorded as being liable for Hearth Tax in the mid 1600s.

Etwall ﷽

A photograph taken from St Helen's churchtower a hundred years ago shows little change from the view today – the curving road with its large old houses, the top pub, the rectory, the almshouses and beyond that the open country. In spite of its proximity to Derby and now largely a commuter village, the post-war housing developments which led to a threefold increase in population between 1951 and 1981 have not been allowed to encroach on to the countryside to the north and east of the village.

Originally named after the Saxon king Eata, whose well or spring lies below St Helen's church, Etwall still has the remains of up to 70 wells. Mentioned in the Domesday Book as Etewelle, it would be interesting to know for what reason the village came to be called Etwall; late into the 19th century there was a thriving brick industry and many WI members live in properties built with local bricks stamped firmly 'Etwell'.

The almshouses, rebuilt 300 years ago round an open courtyard close by St Helen's church, are perhaps the most outstanding feature of the village. Recently they were transformed internally to provide ten attractive and much sought after homes for retired 'locals', married or single. Quite a change from the days when a fence was erected and a Warden appointed to lock the men in at night and throw any women out! Up until the 1960s, almsmen and women wore special hats or bonnets and a dark blue cloak with a silver clasp. They were always buried in their cloaks.

The final transformation to the almshouses was the addition of the famous, now refurbished, Robert Bakewell gates which had for some years languished in a school cellar. What now proudly welcome visitors to the almshouses, had for over 200 years and flanked by two lodges, guarded the entrance to Etwall Hall.

The site of the Hall with its lake and grounds became the site of the John Port school. Dilapidated after war-time occupation by the forces, its home-farm land sterile, it appealed to Jack Longland, Director of Education, as a suitable place for setting up two new schools, a grammar and a secondary modern in the centre of the village. Later these became the focus of the present John Port comprehensive school which now has over 1,700 students travelling from a wide radius. The name of the Port family, who bought land and married into local gentry, has been associated with Etwall since the 15th century.

There are great contrasts between the life of the village today and that of a century ago, when Etwall supported a small population mainly serving the surrounding farms and rural industries. The coming of the railway in 1879 allowed us to send fresh food out daily, as far afield as London. There was a cheese factory whose piggeries took the by-products and a privately owned gas, light and coke company sited near the railway sidings. There was a builder, blacksmith, wheelwright, saddler, tailor, draper, bootmaker and a coffin maker. Basket makers used the local grown willows. All in all, Etwall was quite a self-contained community.

Now relatively few residents are directly connected with farming, though luckily there is still a hard core. No longer are the shops sufficient for all needs and now the biggest industry is education.

Eyam 🦔

Eyam, situated in the Peak District, five miles north of Bakewell, derives its name from the Anglo-Saxon 'Ey' meaning water and 'Ham', a settlement. It is pronounced 'Eam' as in 'steam'. The geological structure of the hills to the north of the village, permeable millstone grit sandstone above Eyam shales, is impervious to water and ensures that rain water issues out from the shale as a series of springs down the one mile length of the village street.

In 1588, twelve sets of stone troughs were built at convenient places along the village street and the spring water was conducted to the troughs by pipes; thus Eyam became one of the first villages in the country to have a public water system. This trough system continued to provide the village water supply until the 1920s, when piped water came to the village.

Eyam is famous as the Plague Village. A widow, Mary Cooper, and her two sons lived near the church in what is now called Plague Cottage. Lodging with them was a tailor named George Viccars. Tradition states that cloth he had ordered from London, where plague was raging, arrived damp and was spread out to dry. This released plague-infected fleas. Within days Viccars fell ill and died of a strange fever. He was buried on 7th September 1665. Fifteen days later fear spread when young Edward Cooper died, quickly followed by several neighbours. The death rate rose in October and some families fled.

William Mompesson, the rector, supported by Thomas Stanley, a former incumbent, fearing the infection would spread widely, asked the villagers to quarantine themselves from the outside world. They arranged for food and medical supplies to be left at agreed points on the village boundary, eg Mompesson's Well and the Boundary Stone. The church was closed and services were held in Cucklet Delf, a valley nearby, where the Plague Commemoration Service is still held annually. There were no funerals and families buried their own dead near their homes, as at Riley, where Mrs Hancock buried her husband and six children in eight days.

The plague ended in October 1666. In 14 months it had claimed 259 lives out of a population believed to have been about 350. Many of the houses and cottages existing in the village in 1665, whilst retaining their privacy, are identified by information plaques.

The church of St Lawrence, with its interesting sundial, Celtic cross and tombstones outside and its Saxon and Norman fonts, nave roof, murals, Plague Register, together with the Rev William Mompesson's chair and the Jacobean pulpit inside, is well worth a visit.

Over the centuries the villagers have been employed in the silk and cotton industries, boot and shoe manufacturing, lead mining, limestone quarrying and agriculture. Silk weaving looms, aided by child labour, brought some prosperity to Eyam in the 19th century. An Eyam weaver, Ralph Wain, discovered the process of producing patterns on both sides of the material. But, being unable to read or write, he was 'persuaded' to sell his idea to a Macclesfield firm. His workplace at Townhead still stands and over the years has been a boot and shoe factory, a printing works and is now a furniture factory.

Lead mining reached peak production in the 18th century, when exhaustion of major veins, increasing extraction costs and the reduction in demand caused a decline. Recession was offset by an increasing demand for previous waste products, fluorspar and barytes, which are still mined and processed locally. The processing plant was located in the centre of the village until 1965 when the plant was enlarged on transfer to its present site on Stoney Middleton Moor.

Eyam is not obsessed with its unhappy past, nor is it a dormitory village, it is an active vibrant community where all ages take part in a variety of interests and activities. All organisations and individual villagers co-operate during late August and early September to prepare for the Plague Commemoration Service, Well Dressing, the Carnival and Sheep Roast and the Annual Village Show.

Fairfield 🌿

Although Fairfield is now part of the town of Buxton its origins stem from a medieval hamlet within the Forest of Peak. The earliest recorded history of Fairfield is in the 13th century when application was made for the establishment of a church in the village 'in order that the difficult and dangerous journey to the mother church at Hope [a distance of eleven miles on foot over wild and bleak terrain] might be avoided'. The application was granted and a church has stood on the site since that time. The present St Peter's Church dates from 1839 and is the focal point of the original parish. Various extensions have been added and in the early 1920s a stained glass window was dedicated as a memorial to the 72 parishioners who died in the First World War. Incorporated into the design, for the first time in a window erected in England, was an aeroplane.

Methodism has strong roots in Fairfield and John Wesley is known to have preached here. The church of the 1800s was demolished several years ago and a new church, together with Wesley House, sheltered accommodation for the elderly, was built on the site.

The village still retains several old houses and cottages dating from the 1600s. Fairfield can also lay claim to a very large 'village green' in the form of The Common, an open area of over 100 acres. It is the last remnant of some 800 acres left to the parish in perpetuity from the 1772 Enclosures Act. For the past 100 years it has been home to the Buxton and High Peak Golf Club and until the mid 1920s provided pasture for cattle and sheep.

Around the mid 1700s a racecourse existed on the western side of The Common, with a fine grandstand designed by the architect Carr of York. Here each summer until 1839 the Sport of Kings held sway with side-shows for boxing and cockfighting, gambling booths with thimbleriggers and the usual assembly of light-fingered gentry. It attracted large vociferous crowds from the neighbouring counties. Nothing now remains of the racecourse or grandstand and the only sound to rend the air on summer evenings are shouts of 'fore' from the golfers but the area is still referred to by locals as 'standside'.

One of the area's finest assets is the Fairfield Silver Prize Band. It began life as a drum and fife band and became a brass band around 1870. A strong family tradition is carried on by the Kitchen family; three generations being current members. Charlie plays the cornet, and his father was a member of the original drum and fife band – between them the family can notch up over 390 years' playing service.

Fairfield, though now grown and spread over a much wider area, strives to retain its individual identity. The Carnival has been revived in recent years and is now a successful event each summer. Fairfield Endowed School, though moved to a new site, still keeps its title and links with the church. There is a thriving community centre and local groups of scouts, guides, cubs and brownies flourish.

Fenny Bentley

Life in Fenny Bentley has for a long time revolved around the school, the church and the pub. The old school closed 20 years ago, and is now leased to a scout group who use it as an outdoor activity centre; the new FitzHerbert School was opened in 1970. There are still many people in the area who remember going across the fields to school, even back to the days when school uniform consisted of knickerbockers and hobnailed boots for the boys, and white pinafores for the girls.

The beautifully proportioned church of St Edmund has a dominant position in the village. The annual summer fete that the church and school run jointly is still eagerly looked forward to by everyone in the village.

The Coach and Horses dates from the 16th century, and as the name implies, it was formerly a coaching inn. There was also another pub nearby, the Wheatsheaf, which is now a private house. Fenny Bentley must have had some very thirsty inhabitants to be able to support two pubs in such a small village.

Perhaps the most imposing building along the main road is Cherry Orchard Farm. This dates from the 15th century, and at one time had twin towers and battlements. It was the seat of the Beresford family. Sir Thomas Beresford fought at Agincourt, and is buried in the church. His wife, Lady Agnes, had 21 children, and everyone with the surname of Beresford is said to be descended from them. In fact there is an annual convention in the village, when Beresfords come from all over the country, and indeed from abroad, to reunite.

Before the Second World War, most people in the area were employed in agriculture. Sadly, Cherry Orchard Farm is the only working farm left in the village itself today. However around the turn of the century, Woodeaves Mill was working nearby. It produced cotton velvet, and provided employment for many village people.

Until recent years, the village was mainly built along the main road. The Bentley brook follows the main road, and in the days before the widespread knowledge of public health, it was a convenient form of sanitation for those living in cottages facing the road! Several of those cottages have since been demolished.

The road itself was widened at the bottom of Tissington Hill, as vehicles were inclined to go out of control and cannon into the houses on the bend. Residents in the village can remember when the road was only ten ft wide, and herds of cattle would be driven along it to Ashbourne Market.

Nowadays, even though the A515 splits the village in two, Fenny Bentley is still a close-knit community, and the school, the church and the pub still hold their own.

Findern 🦚

Findern is a village in the south of Derbyshire, spreading over a small hill rising out of the Trent valley. Because of its location, Findern is almost a dormitory village – situated halfway between the city of Derby and the town of Burton-on-Trent, both with many industries and shopping facilities.

Findern is one of the few villages in South Derbyshire with a traditional village green. The form of this has changed over the years. Early in the 19th century there was a duckpond there, then pathways criss-crossed the grass. Now it is surrounded by posts and chains, given by the Women's Institute to mark the movement's Golden Jubilee and the restoration of the green in 1966–67. The post office, shops and cottages edge the green, and it is overlooked by the parish church of All Saints.

Before the times of fast and easy travel, Findern was a self-sufficient village. Around the green was the post office, bakery, forge, wheelwright's shop, ale house, two farms and cottages. Below the green was Lower Green (known as Bumpton). More cottages clustered together near the well, and with the village lock-up and cattle pound. Here, in 1862, a Mrs Clark gave £10 for the land near the well to be purchased so that a Methodist chapel could be built. Also in the village were a butcher, stonemason, saddler and miller. In the cottages was carried out the village industry of velvet weaving – in 1846 there were as many as 22 velvet and silk looms in the village.

In Main Street is the village pump which was used until the 1930s when the water mains were installed. Now the pump is 'dressed', like many Derbyshire wells by the WI for the village fete in June.

A little further along Main Street is Somerville, an 18th century house now listed as of architectural interest. It is believed that this is where the young Jedediah Strutt served a seven year apprenticeship with a wheelwright. He found lodgings with a family of stocking makers and here he met his future wife, Elizabeth, the daughter of Thomas Woolatt. Jedediah went on to improve the stocking frame and became the partner of Sir Richard Arkwright, who was engaged in cotton spinning. Together they established mills at Cromford, Belper and Milford but the partnership was dissolved in 1780, Jedediah Strutt taking over the two latter mills. Through his energy and enterprise, the town of Belper owes much of its prosperity.

On the top of the hill in Findern is Tower House. From its elevated position, on a clear day, can be seen 22 churches (including Lichfield Cathedral) and parts of the Peak District. Tower House is a converted windmill which used to supply flour to a wide area. One notable miller was Joe Lovatt, a somewhat eccentric character, who worked at his mill until he had accumulated sufficient money and then mounted his horse and departed to preach in the villages of Derbyshire, like John Wesley, until, his money exhausted, he returned to his milling again. The current occupier of Tower House is Edwina Currie, MP.

Findern has a legend which has caused much interest and questioning over many years. The story tells how Sir Geoffrey de Fynderne returned from the Crusades bringing with him some white flowers which he planted on his estate at Findern. They flourished and multiplied and eventually were to be found in many cottage gardens. The tradition was that though the family might die out, the flowers would never become extinct. It was thought that the flower had perished, but it did survive, growing in several gardens. It was a short-stemmed, white, double narcissus with a very small amount of yellow in the centre. It has been identified as *Narcissus Poeticus Plenus Odoration* – a double form of narcissus known as Poet's Daffodil. Happily, there are a few plants still growing in the village, although they do not flower every year.

Flagg

Flagg is a small village situated between the market town of Bakewell and the spa town of Buxton. It lies in a true geological bowl, surrounded by gentle rises. It is interesting to note that some very beautiful cloud formations appear over the village.

There is a mention in the Domesday Book of the village, which was then known as Flagun. The name Flagg comes from the original word 'flag' meaning turf or sod. This could suggest that turf cutting was once the village's main means of support.

The village has a manor house dating back to before the Domesday Book. This today is Flagg Hall Farm. In 1086 William the Conqueror rewarded one of his barons, John de Finnes, with the honour of 'Warden of the Cinque Ports' and his descendants held this prestigious position for over 400 years. It is thought that the family of Fynney, who lived at the Hall for many years, were the descendants of the famous Fiennes. On the windowsill on the staircase of Flagg Hall is a skull. This has been there for many years, and is reputed to be that of one of the Fynney doctors. It is said the skull cannot be removed from the house without weird and unexpected things happening.

In the mid 19th century well dressings were held during Wakes Week, which was always begun the first Sunday after the 24th June. Flat point to point races were and still are held and are the high spot of Easter Tuesday, although they are usually guaranteed to bring bad weather. On one occasion King Edward VIII, the then Prince of Wales, rode at the races. The first race is started in the actual village and is over stone walls. The remainder are started on the course itself.

A Unitarian church built in 1838 is now leased to the Church of England and there is a Methodist chapel built in 1839. The Unitarian church was used as a village reading room until the village hall was built in 1931. There is one public house, the Plough, and a combined shop and post office. The village school was erected about the year 1895. The population is about 122. The main occupation is dairy farming but at one time quarrying and lead mining were also occupations.

Before water was piped to houses, farms and fields, all water was pumped up from a well and collected from stand taps in the village. Flagg water supply never failed and farmers from miles around would come with their tanks to collect water for their animals. Times have changed, but Flagg still remains the friendly village it always was.

Foolow 🦢

Foolow is a small, picturesque limestone village situated in the Peak National Park, two miles west of the plague village of Eyam, in whose parish it is. The name is said to mean multi-coloured hill or burial ground and is first mentioned as Fowlowe in 1269.

Since Roman times it has been a lead mining area and although this ceased some years ago, remains of the activities of 'the old man' can be seen today with mine shafts and spoil heaps still visible. Many of the waste heaps have now been removed for the fluorspar, which was in lead mining days, considered useless.

At the present time there are 53 houses and 125 inhabitants. As with many villages within the Peak National Park, new building is not allowed to extend outside the village bounds. Much of the village dates from the 18th and 19th centuries. At the eastern end stood the toll bar, which was demolished a long time ago and a bungalow erected on the ground in 1953. The manor house is a fine example of a gentleman's residence and was built in the 17th century. Overlooking the village green is the Old Hall which has been two residences for many years.

At one time there were five hostelries in the village. The 'Spread Eagle' survives today as a private house and the Bull's Head (now named the Lazy Landlord) is the only remaining public house.

The pond and green, with its cross (dating from the Middle Ages) and bullring, remain the focal point of the village. The cross bears the date 1868 on its plinth. This is the date it was removed from the site where the chapel gates now stand and it was placed in its present position. The church, which is dedicated to St Hugh, was built in 1888 and in 1928 the porch was erected with stone from the disused smithy across the road from it.

In 1966 the Wesleyan Reform chapel celebrated its centenary with a dedication service. Until a few years ago it was the custom to depart from the chapel at midnight on Christmas Eve to sing carols at each house around Housley (a hamlet half a mile away) and Foolow, to the accompaniment of a violin, usually ending around 5 am on Christmas morning. Many of the tunes to well known carols are original to Foolow. This was repeated Christmas Day in the early evening until midnight. Sadly, only the Christmas Day evening custom remains, ending with the singing of 'Diadem' round the cross.

Originally fresh water had to be collected by the inhabitants from a well (which still remains) at Piece End, half a mile from Foolow. In 1983 the dressing of the wells was revived. There are two wells dressed, one of which is designed and petalled by the children. This annual event takes place during the last week in August.

Until about 25 years ago there were six or seven mixed farms in the village. When the farmers collected their cows from the fields for milking, they all had a specific time to do this. This enabled the herd to drink at the pond without getting mixed up with a neighbouring herd. Now only one small, mainly sheep farm, remains. Today, most of the working people commute to Sheffield.

When the village was basically a farming community, the green was muddy and indented with hoof marks. Today, many of the farm buildings are dwellings, the grass is regularly mown, spring bulbs flourish and visitors picnic and watch the ducks swimming on the pond. The one thing that has not changed is the friendliness and community spirit of its inhabitants.

Fritchley 🌿

Fritchley was once a small industrial centre, where local lime quarries and railroads provided work. Cottage industry was common, making stockings, spinning and weaving, also hat making. Two mills existed, a cornmill at Millgreen and the other, a bobbin mill, was burnt down in 1885.

The Quakers formed a Society of Friends in Fritchley in 1864, and meetings are still held in the Meeting House on Chapel Street. On the green stands the Congregational church and adjacent schoolroom. Until 1989 there was a village store on the green. This has now closed down and become a house. The post office remains today on Chapel Street and sells groceries and supplies. The Red Lion public house on Front Street is open for business. Over the years the village has had three alehouses.

The Methodist chapel was built in 1829 and rebuilt in 1862. One Henry Sulley, a member of the congregation, was noted as an expert stockinger whose work was exhibited in the Great Exhibition. Queen Victoria is said to have ordered a pair of fine cashmere stockings after being impressed by the workmanship.

The surrounding countryside is very rural and the agriculture is mainly grassland – dairy herds and sheep. The fields are divided by stone walls and the village is built of sandstone and gritstone locally quarried. The oldest building is 'The Old Farm', situated just off the green and Bowmer Lane.

Froggatt 🌿

Froggatt is a small village with some 200 inhabitants; above it to the east is Froggatt Edge where many well-known climbers have gained experience. To the west the river Derwent winds through the woods and across it stands an interesting 18th century bridge, wide enough for single file traffic only but with inlets over the piers for pedestrians to step aside. The bridge is unusual in that it has a large central arch nearer the village side and on the farther side a smaller arch, the latter probably part of the original bridge which spanned the much narrower stream existing before the Derwent was dammed at Calver. In the 1930s the land on the far side of the bridge to the left used to attract visitors to the water's edge and has jokingly been called Froggatt Lido.

Froggatt was so-named not because of the presence of frogs but because there were originally 17 fresh-water springs in the village. The few remaining village folk remember the village wells; at least three can still be seen, one near the bridge, one along Hollowgate and a third called 'Top Spout' half-way up the green.

The village was originally owned by the then Duke of Rutland who some 200 years ago had 17 stone cottages built by local stonemasons. One of these, named Fletcher, eventually lived in the cottage by the bridge. Now named Bridge Foot Farm it is still inhabited by Mr Fletcher's great grandson's widow. There are still a few cottages in their original state, several listed buildings, but many have been modernised and others enlarged. Some new detached houses are built, but only where special reasons apply, and under the strict eye of the Peak Park Planning Board.

Originally the men of the village were stonemasons or small farmers and worked locally; now there are a few local businessmen, eg a garage owner and a landscape gardener, but most work in commerce or professions in the towns.

There is a Wesleyan Reform chapel in the village and a post-box in a pillar, but no street lights and only one lane has a name plate. All Saints' church, Curbar, serves Froggatt village too.

The highlight of village life is probably the Annual Horticultural Show. Originally there was only a 'Cow Club' but in the 1930s a Mr Carnall, Ernest Fletcher, John Morton Senior and Mr Hattersley met in Riley's Cowshed and Froggatt Show was born. First held there it has moved three times, now being held in a field on the far side of the bridge by kind permission of a local farmer who is Show President. August Bank Holiday Saturday is the great day – it used to be called Feast Day.

Gamesley

'Gamis Pasture' – a pretty rural place, consisting of farms, thickets and by-lanes. If you know Gamesley, you could close your eyes and visualize it as it must have appeared at the time of the Domesday Book.

Long before Domesday, the Romans, around AD 75 must have seen some strategic advantage here and established a fort on the road connecting Manchester with Brough and Templeborough (Sheffield). This fort was named Melandra and the site it occupied is now designated as an Historic Monument. It is still visited by archaeologists from time to time although the fort itself has long since disappeared. It is supposed that local people used the dressed stone from it to build houses in the area.

Gamesley enjoys an enviable situation. It is located on the old turnpike

The Old Bakehouse, Gamesley

road that linked Glossop with Marple Bridge and is now called Glossop Road. The woods situated between Dinting Vale and the village shield it from that very industrialized area. Fortunately the woods are covered by tree protection orders to keep developers at bay. West and north-west is Longdendale with views across green fields to Hollingworth and Mottram. The fine old Mottram church on War Hill can be seen clearly. To the south are the Derbyshire hills and to the east Simmondley and the Dark Peaks can be seen. The railway between Manchester and Glossop, with its now disused marshalling yard, separates Gamesley from the rapidly growing village of Simmondley.

For many years Gamesley consisted of houses built along Glossop Road and Cottage Lane with a few farms dotted here and there. There were several small shops and one public house. There was industry around the turn of the century in the form of a bedspring manufacturer but this factory is now converted into a row of cottages.

An isolation hospital for infectious diseases was built just to the south of the village in the 1880s. It was well administered and served the borough without losing a single patient until closed by the Ministry of Health around 1950. The hospital, a collection of odd buildings, was returned to the care of the borough but they did not succeed in selling it and it became derelict. In its 125 years of existence, Gamesley House has seen many changes from a family home, to a garden centre and at the present time it is a restaurant. It is not impressive for its architecture. Some of the stone cottages are much more attractive and interesting. The relative tranquillity of Gamesley, compared to other parts of Glossop,

102

was literally shattered in 1966 by the arrival of bulldozers clearing the way for the building of an overspill estate for Manchester Corporation. Since the estate has become populated, it has brought certain benefits along with the increase to the number of homes. Gamesley is now connected with surrounding towns and villages by frequent bus services, the number of shops has increased, and we have our own post office, pharmacy and library. There are also two junior schools, two churches and two new public houses.

Glapwell 🌿

Glapwell is a small village situated on the A617 Mansfield to Chesterfield road, approximately two miles east of Junction 29 of the M1, just inside the Derbyshire border with Nottinghamshire.

In the Domesday survey, the hamlet of 'Glapewelle' is listed with Bolsover, and by the 13th century it was owned by the de Glapwell family, one of whose heirs married into the family of Woolhouse, who resided at Glapwell Hall in the 17th century. The Hall, which was allowed to fall into disrepair in the early years of the 20th century, was demolished in the 1960s. The remains of the conservatory, the stables and a small building thought to have been the coachman's cottage, still stand on the site, and in very dry weather, the foundations and carriage drive can clearly be seen on what is now the village football pitch.

During its heyday, the Hall was the main focus of the village, providing employment for most of the residents. One lady who worked as a maid at the Hall recalls that she had to clean out 16 firegrates before going to church on a Sunday morning!

In the 1880s, the Sheepbridge Coal and Iron company sank the first shaft of what was to become Glapwell Colliery, and together with the coming of the railway, this resulted in an increase in the population of the village (99 people in 1851; 1,680 today). It is said that the colliery was sunk on its site because the Hallowes family, who lived at Glapwell Hall at that time, refused the company permission to sink where they originally wanted to because they did not want to have the outlook from the Hall spoiled by pit chimneys, smoke and pitheads! The colliery finally ceased production in 1974.

Many local residents today can remember the 'Village Treat', given annually by Mrs Georgina Jackson of Glapwell Hall. All the local children were invited, and there was a fine tea, and lots of games and races which took place in the park opposite the Hall (a park now, alas, converted to farmland). Children from neighbouring hamlets were brought in by means of high-sided haycarts, and a great deal of fun was had by all. When Mrs Jackson died in 1932, the children of the parish raised money by collecting empty jam jars, etc, and helped to pay for a window to her memory in the parish church of St John the Baptist, at Ault Hucknall.

Although there was originally a chapel at Glapwell many years ago, this is now just a ruin, and the village is now served by the parish church of Ault Hucknall, about one mile to the south. The famous English philosopher, Thomas Hobbes, author of *Leviathan*, is buried in the church. He was, for many years, tutor to the Cavendish family at the nearby National Trust property of Hardwick Hall, also in the parish of Ault Hucknall. A piece of the old Hall acts as a lintel over the fireplace in the village pub in Glapwell – the Young Vanish, named after a famous racehorse of the early 19th century.

Despite the closure of the colliery, the village remains a busy and active community. It has a post office, a village shop, a mobile provision merchant, a dairy and a garage, besides several farms. There are a number of flourishing local organisations, including youth organisations, village football and cricket teams, horticultural association, etc. There is also a Well Dressing Association: the first wells were dressed in 1976, and it is now an annual event which takes place each July. All profits made by the Well Dressing Association are put back into various village organisations.

Grassmoor

Grassmoor is situated three miles south of Chesterfield in North Derbyshire. Originally the name, according to parish records in 1568, was Gresmore, the origin of the name being 'Grey Copse'. When it became Grassmoor is not known.

The main employment in the village was coal mining when about 90% of the men worked at the Grassmoor Colliery. The first shaft was sunk in 1846 and officially opened in 1880 by Mr Barnes. An explosion occurred on the 19th November, 1933 when a number of local men lost their lives. The colliery closed in 1970.

In 1935 the coke oven by-product plant was built by a firm called Simon Carves which brought more employment to the village and also the coking plant at Wingerworth, which replaced the old coke ovens in the 1950s. After the closure of the colliery a training centre was opened in 1972 with recreational facilities. Most of the young boys going into other mines in the area were trained there.

Two rows of houses were built for colliery workers, the longest named East Street, but commonly called 'Sluggards Row' because the miners living in these houses, although they were nearest the colliery, were always the last to arrive. The second row named Grasshill was for colliery officials and was known as 'Four Bob', the reason being that the rent was only four shillings per week.

Barnes Park, so named after Mr Barnes, the colliery owner, was opened in 1920. At that time there were tennis courts, bowling green, football field, cricket field and swings for children. The tennis courts and bowling green are no more, but the cricket, football field and swings still survive and are used frequently.

There are three public houses and a Working Men's Club and Institute. The oldest of the pubs, situated at the far end of the village, is called the Boot and Shoe, but commonly known as the 'Slipper'. This is situated on the corner of the Main Road and the west side of Birkin Lane. On this side, still visible, a window has been bricked up. This window was used in earlier years as a turnpike and a toll had to be paid for transport passing through.

The cinema which was also at the far end of the village, was opened in 1936 and was called The Electric Theatre. This was later known as the Roxy, but like so many buildings this has 'bitten the dust' and in its place there is now a garage and forecourt. Apparently there was another cinema in the village situated at the top of New Street. This was made into a billiard hall (named the Drum) and then into a betting shop, which has also been demolished.

The Grassmoor Country Park on the old colliery site is very pleasant. The interesting Five Pits Trail takes you along all the old colliery sites in the area.

The building programme in Grassmoor has developed rapidly over the last 15 years. There is no church in the village as even this has been demolished and two bungalows stand on this site. However there is a wide variety of shops in the village which cater for almost all needs.

Great Hucklow 🦃

Great Hucklow is a former lead mining village, which although small – only 100 or so inhabitants – has always been a very active one. It now has a thriving Women's Institute and a group called 'Community Spirit' formed a few years ago by the youngsters, mainly teenagers, who arrange social events and a Well Dressing during August.

In 1927, although no longer active, Great Hucklow had its very own theatre company, created by Dr L. Du Garde Peach, a local author/playwright, whose father was the local minister. He set about forming this company called 'The Village Players' from residents in and around Great Hucklow. They were allowed use of the Holiday Home in the early days – a place where children from deprived areas were brought during the summer months for holidays arranged by the Unitarian chapel. During the winter months the plays were staged there and planned to coincide with the full moon, so that players and audience would have a 'guiding light' to and from performances – for most had to walk!

Their first production was *The Merchant of Venice*, and this proved so successful that many more classics were staged over the 40 years they were performing. Many more in fact were also written by Dr Peach himself, and acted in the Derbyshire dialect. So successful were the players that it was decided perhaps they should have their own theatre. An old Cupola barn at the other end of the village was purchased for £200 – and the land adjoining it for £100. People came from miles around to this small village theatre and in the early days used to bring their own refreshments and even cushions to sit on, and rugs for warmth. Unfortunately when its creator died, so did the theatre. The building is now used as a Scout centre for visiting groups.

Great Hucklow school was built in 1873 outside the village on what was called a sand hillock but was more precisely a spar hill, ie the remains left behind when the lead had been washed.

Memories of schooldays 70 years ago are still fresh. 'A very old cart track ran by the side of the school which veered towards Camphill Farm – this is now the Lancashire & Derbyshire Gliding Club. To the right of this old lane we came to a grassy lane called The Silence – very eerie – in autumn the hedge sides were covered with juicy blackberries. In times past these old lanes were the lead mining roads leading to the Old Cupola and the miners carted the lead there for the smelting. This area was called the Mill Dam. On our way to school we would drop stones down through the cracks in the boarded-up openings to hear the hollow rattle as they reached the bottom of the old Cupola, sending shivers of fear through us. A good start to the day!'.

Great Longstone 🐿️

In the Domesday Book Langes Dune or Tune, is recorded as the name and means Long Settlement. One can possibly assume that Longstone Edge, which is now called Longstone Moor, was the long settlement to which this refers.

The most famous inhabitant of Longstone must be G. T. Wright Esq, belonging to the Wright family of the village. He compiled the 'Longstone Records', which is the authoritative document of both Great and Little Longstone alike. This is a wonderful piece of work, considering that he was a sick man when he started what must have been a monumental task in those days, around 1800.

More recent characters included Jack Holmes, a small man of vast joviality, always happy, singing and continually whistling. Always neatly dressed in knee breeches and leggings, one could, as the saying goes 'set one's watch by him'. He always appeared at certain points in the village at certain times each and every day. Another was a relation of his, Bill Holmes. Bill was mine host of the Crispin inn in the days of the horses and traps. But his main fame was in poultry shows, for he excelled in breeding Black Leghorns. At one of the poultry shows held in the Longroom at the old Bull's Head, which is now the Monsal Head Hotel, Bill decided that the legs on the birds he was showing were not black enough, so the black lead pot came out, and the hens' legs were well and truly blacked. Well, you can guess the outcome when the judge held the birds by the legs.

The village has several important buildings, including the church of St Giles, which is the mother church of Hassop, Rowland, Wardlow and of course the two Longstones. Longstone Hall is the centrepiece in the village, and admired by many visitors. The school was built in 1862 and is still in use.

Another building of great interest is the Shackly Building or Mary Fernihough's yard. This dates back to around 1600, and is being renovated into living accommodation. It is believed to have been the home and farmhouse of the Earl of Shrewsbury around the 1600s.

Grindleford

Grindleford. A strange name you may think, but a long way back in time grindstones were fashioned from the local stone at quarries in the area and carried across the ford of the river Derwent. The setting of the village is absolutely beautiful; surrounded by hills with differing vegetation, with the wooded Padley Gorge and the river Derwent running through its centre.

For a village that has a small population compared with other Derbyshire villages, Grindleford straggles some one and a half to two miles from the Padleys to Stoke Hall.

In the area known as Upper Padley is Padley Chapel, the only remaining part of Padley Hall, and the wide mouth of Totley railway tunnel. Exactly 300 years separates important happenings at these places and first of all we go back in time to the year of the Spanish Armada, 1588.

The Fitzherberts who lived at Padley Hall were staunch Roman Catholics, so of course they had priests under their roof in order to conduct the Mass. The then owner, Sir Thomas, was in prison in the Tower of London, and through domestic treachery, on the 12th July 1588, a raid took place during which Sir Thomas' brother John and two priests, namely Nicholas Garlick and Robert Ludlam, were arrested and taken to Derby Gaol. On 23rd July, the two priests were tried, found guilty of high treason and condemned to death by hanging, drawing and quartering. Sir John was also found guilty but allowed to live by paying £10,000 and living out his life in the Fleet Prison. Today Roman Catholics make a pilgrimage every year to the restored chapel on the Sunday nearest to 12th July in memory of the two priests, who are known as the Padley Martyrs.

Moving ahead 300 years, the building of the Totley railway tunnel began in September 1888. It runs from Totley in Sheffield to Grindleford in Derbyshire and is the gateway to the Peak District by rail. It is a remarkable feat of engineering, being three miles 950 yards long. After much hard work, and of course some troubles, the tunnel was completed in 1893. Five years later in 1898, Grindleford had its own passenger station as this was part of the railway company's contract to build one at or near Grindleford bridge for the benefit of the Duke of Rutland of Haddon Hall. Inevitably the fortunes of the village began to change, with horse-drawn buses at the station to transport passengers to surrounding villages and the arrival of the first commuters, who in many cases were the wealthy steelmen of Sheffield, living in large houses up the steep hill to Nether Padley above the Maynard Hotel. Today, of course, because of the increase in leisure, large numbers of walkers and tourists use the train.

The best example of life today was the building of Bishop Pavilion; this is a community hall for the village and named after Eric Bishop, a local resident whose generous bequest enabled the building to be completed and also provided funds for any future extension which might be required. It is in use practically the whole of the time and has become the centre of village life and activities.

Hadfield

Hadfield was known as Hetfelt in the time of the Romans, which means 'heathy open land'. There is a hill called Mouselow, which is supposed to have been a stronghold of the Ancient Britons.

Legend has it that a Saxon chief called Alman fought and killed the Prince of Mouselow and took his title. He wanted to marry the daughter of the Lord of Woolley (Woolley Bridge and Woolley Lane), but she hated him, so he took her prisoner. The Prince of Melandra came to her rescue, and there was a great battle. So great was the bloodshed that the place was afterwards called Redgate and still bears that name today. The place where Alman died was called Almansdeath. On the map it is shown as Almans Heath, a name which still remains (the place where the cemetery stands today).

There are tales also of King Arthur himself journeying through the valley and it is possible that he could have passed through the small village at the foot of Mouselow Hill. Robin Hood is also supposed to have visited the area on several occasions.

In 1140–1148 Mouselow Castle was built but was demolished by Henry II. The Castle School in Hadfield Road still uses the castle emblem on its badge.

The Old Hall in the Square shows a date of 1646 over the door. This makes it one of the oldest houses in the district. It is a Stuart house built in the reign of King Charles I and it was rumoured that there was treasure buried under the floor. One occupier had the flagged floors taken up but found nothing.

In the past the early settlers were mainly farmers. They hunted, kept sheep and cows and grew crops around their homes, but in 1780–1790 the mills came, the first one being Waterside Mill on the river Etherow. In 1867 the Longdendale valley was flooded to make reservoirs for Manchester's water. From then on the village became mainly concerned with textiles and more mills were built. The millowners changed the face of the village, building more and more houses for their workers.

In 1868 the first Baron Howard of Glossop built St Charles' Catholic church and his family are all buried there. Then a member of the Howard family married the Duke of Norfolk and took the lands around Glossop and Hadfield as her dowry. The present Duke of Norfolk, who is Earl Marshall of England, is a frequent visitor. Members of his family are also buried in the church that his forebears built.

Hadfield today is a successful blend of the old and the new. The Old Hall, the ancient cross and the old gritstone cottages bear witness to antiquity, whilst the modern shops and large housing developments show the new face of the village. Although the mills have all gone and the people now have to travel outside for work and pleasure, the community spirit still lives on.

Harpur Hill

Harpur Hill's only pub waited many years before it had any 'locals'. A coaching inn, The Parks was just a stop on the way to somewhere else and until 1820 that was a fairly accurate description of Harpur Hill itself. Before that date The Parks, now the oldest building in the village, as well as seeing to the needs of travellers, must have been a croft or parks, the old name for a smallholding.

The opening of the quarries brought rapid changes to the once quiet Hill. Quarrymen and their families moved into the rows of limestone cottages built for the growing workforce. Some who were less well off lived in caves they hollowed out of the lime ash dumps, they were known as Limers. The Cromford and High Peak railway carried away the limestone and the village was dominated by the Hoffman kiln, with its 170 ft high chimney. The kiln was reputed to be the biggest of its kind in the world. Blasting, stonecrushing and lime burning must have made Harpur Hill a very busy and noisy place to live.

The village expanded quickly and before the end of the 19th century a school and Methodist chapel were built. St James' church was built in 1910. All of them were built of local limestone and they are still in use today.

Life must have gone on in this way until the First World War, which took many of its men away to fight, some of whom never returned. A memorial to those who lost their lives was erected in the centre of the village. A rough-hewn piece of limestone from the quarry in which so many of them worked, stands on a pedestal of random limestone blocks. A monument not only to the men who died but to the origins of Harpur Hill.

The scientists arrived in 1927, and using land on the outskirts of the village began work on the dangers of fires and explosions in mines. The station is run now by the Health and Safety Executive and the research has broadened out to include disasters other than those in mines, such as the fire at Kings Cross Station.

The football team played a part in the life of the village and for many years their greatest 'fan' was Granny Askey of Burlow Farm. She never missed a match and used her umbrella to spur on her players, shaking it at any opponent who dared to tackle a member of 'her' team.

The life of the village changed again when it played host to the RAF during the Second World War. RAF Burlow was built on Burlow Farm and at the other side of the hill a maze of tunnels were dug in which they stored bombs. The RAF stayed for 25 years before the unit was closed down. The storage tunnels were converted to peaceful uses and because of their constant temperature, mushrooms were grown there for several years. They are now used to store cheeses. The buildings were reopened as the High Peak College of Further Education, Derbyshire's only residential college.

The occupations of the inhabitants have changed and each passing industry has added more people and further housing around the original limestone cottages. Modern developments have reached the outskirts of Buxton, joining Harpur Hill to the town. Still surrounded on three sides by farms, Harpur Hill has not been swallowed up and much of its life is still centred on the heart of the old village.

Hathersage ✒

Situated in the Peak National Park at the entrance to the Hope valley, Hathersage is the first village on the A625 after leaving Sheffield and marks the division between the Dark and White Peaks. There is some controversy about the origin of the name Hathersage but anyone looking up from the village to the surrounding moorlands in late summer will understand why it is commonly believed to be a corruption of 'Heather's edge'.

The village boasts seven old houses or 'Halls' said to have been built by a member of the Eyre family during the Middle Ages for his seven sons. People who have lived there claim that at least three of these – Highlow, Northlees and Moorseats, are haunted. Northlees and Moorseats are also well known for their association with Charlotte Bronte who wrote her novel *Jane Eyre* after a visit to her former school friend Ellen Nussey, the sister of the vicar of Hathersage. She used the two Halls as models for the homes of Mr Rochester and St John Rivers. The building which is now the butcher's shop is said to have been the original of the shop where Jane Eyre tried to barter her gloves for 'a cake of bread' and the Bronte link is carried further in that the landlord of the George Hotel at the time of Charlotte's visit was called Morton – the name she gave to the village where Jane sought help.

Traditionally Hathersage was the home of Robin Hood's companion

Little John and the cottage in which he is supposed to have lived was standing up to 100 years ago. His grave is in a prominent position in the churchyard. A bow supposedly belonging to him was once kept in the church but seems to have disappeared after being removed, ostensibly for safe-keeping, some 250 years ago.

In the past Hathersage was an industrial village well known for making needles, heckle pins and millstones – large numbers of which can be found abandoned where they were made on the hillside above the village. Other activities carried on in and around the village included lead smelting, paper making, a mill making saws and farming. Today only farming survives. Many residents now travel to work in Sheffield or further down the valley but the growth of tourism provides work for increasing numbers in catering, retailing and craftwork.

Hathersage is one of the biggest villages in the Hope valley and its shops and other amenities make it a focus for people in the surrounding area. It is situated on the Sheffield to Manchester railway line, a facility increasingly used by both local people and visitors. There are three active churches and six public houses. In the summer the sports facilities, given to the village in the late 1930s by G. H. Lawrence, a wealthy Sheffield businessman who lived in Hathersage, and now run by the parish council, are popular with local people and visitors.

Older residents still remember the fair which used to be held in the village on 13th October during potato picking week, when the school was closed and stalls were set up all along the main street, but nowadays the highlight of the year is Gala Week, usually the second week in July, when the village is decorated, a gala queen is crowned and the whole village takes part in a week of activities including fell racing, tug of war, treasure hunts and sports competitions. The Blessing of the Crib on Christmas Eve is another event which generates a sense of community and is much loved by the children, when a 'stable' with life size figures is erected on the grassy bank of the stream which runs alongside the main street.

Hatton

Hatton is an ancient village extending one and a half miles along the busy A50, west of Derby.

Travelling south we enter the village at the Salt Box junction. Many years ago this area was thought to be an important stop on the 'Salt Run', carrying salt from one end of the country to the other. It is referred to as the Turnpike. Unfortunately, it is well known as an accident 'black spot' but also now serves as an oasis to many truck drivers who find adequate parking and refreshment at the Salt Box Cafe, which won an award of 25,000 tea bags in 1989 for the 'Best Cafe Cuppa'.

The Turnpike was the origin of Hatton village, where a river once ran and was redirected to avoid flooding. There were a few cottages, the 'Old Cock Inn' which is now a private residence, and the first Church school which was held in the old mission room at the back of the Wesleyan chapel, the arch of which can still be seen overlooking the main Uttoxeter Road. All Saints' church was built by Mr Gould of Tutbury in 1886. The Methodist Prince Memorial church was built in 1912. It is said that John Prince, Foston farmer and local preacher for 50 years, could be seen riding from one chapel to another on Sundays and that his horse knew the circuit so well that he could indulge in 40 winks on the homeward journey!

Many of the inhabitants commute to nearby towns and cities but others are employed by very successful local industry. The most notable is the Nestle factory, which draws 76% of its work force locally. The factory was built in 1901 in a dairy farming area where the essential ingredient, milk, was available for the production of sweetened condensed milk. It had a side line in those days of a piggery, housing over 100 pigs at the Marston end of the factory.

The Nestle's 'Bull', a steam whistle, was used at the onset of the Second World War as an air raid siren for the district until the more familiar 'Wailing Winnie' was installed and later transferred to the local fire station. Since 1959 the factory has concentrated solely on producing various blends of instant and ground coffee, the delicious aroma of which can be scented wafting all over the village. Another important source of local employment is Clayton Equipment Co Ltd, formed in 1931 and now part of the Rolls-Royce organisation. They produce locomotives for mines and export to 40 different countries.

Just beyond the railway line is a fine stone bridge over the river Dove, and linking Hatton and Tutbury. The land along the river Dove was once described as 'the stinking marshes north of Tutbury' by Mary Queen of Scots when she was imprisoned in nearby Tutbury Castle. In 1831 workmen removing gravel from the Dove found silver coins, and working upstream they discovered a hoard of coins of various currencies; apparently a scramble commenced and people flocked to the area with their spades. The treasure of over 100,000 coins was said to belong to the Duchy of Lancaster, but only 1,500 coins were forwarded to officials.

The village cannot be classed as quaint, or even pretty, but the natives are friendly!

Hayfield 🌿

Hayfield, with a population of 3,000, is an ancient village nestling at the foot of Kinder Scout. It sported several industrial works such as cotton manufacturing, paper-making and textile printing, together with over 100 shops. In fact, the village from the early 1900s was practically self-supporting. The first mill in the village to be worked by a steam engine was situated at Phoside, often called 'Foxholes'. The church, St Matthew's, dates back to 1386, built at river level, and the existing church was rebuilt in 1818 on top of the first church. There was an earlier church too, at Kirksteads, Bowden Bridge, Kinder. St John's Methodist church, erected in 1782, is one of the oldest still in use in this country.

Hayfield was the venue for two cattle and sheep fairs each year, one held on 12th May and the second on 10th October. Shepherds met at the Pack Horse inn on the 12th July each year and one shilling was paid for each lost sheep returned to its owner. After a lapse of several years the Sheep Dog Trials and Country Show was revived and is held at Spray House Farm, Little Hayfield in September.

The village was very popular at Easter and Whitsuntide when train and bus loads of hikers and ramblers came in their hundreds to walk over the moors to Edale and to the Downfall. Sadly, the railway station closed in January 1970. There was a Mass Trespass of the moors in 1932 which was organised by keen ramblers to enable them to retain their freedom to walk over Kinder Scout, and a plaque was erected in the quarry at Bowden Bridge, Kinder, to celebrate the 50 years in 1982.

Over the years Hayfield has experienced several serious blizzards and floods; on some occasions these have isolated the village for several days. One such flood from the Kinder side of the village took the large cast-iron roller from the cricket field down to New Mills, three miles away, such was the force of the water.

In 1983, when Hayfield held its first Jazz Festival, the event was sadly marred when a run-away lorry careered down the steep hill into a crowd of spectators, killing three people. A memorial garden in the centre of the village is a permanent reminder. In May 1969 another loaded lorry, out of control, knocked down the walls of Livesley's chemist's shop, killing two ladies inside the shop. The present bypass is the result of this tragic accident.

A legend in Hayfield is that in 1745 hundreds of bodies rose out of their graves to the great astonishment and terror of several spectators. They, oddly, left a most fragrant and delicious odour behind them! At Highgate Hall or Boggart House there is a sealed well. Apparently a Scottish pedlar was murdered near it and his bones were found in a nearby garden. These bones were interred in Hayfield churchyard in 1770. As long as the well remains sealed the ghost will not haunt the area.

Hayfield has some very old pubs. Whilst the Royal is not the oldest, it certainly has a history. It was built as a parsonage in 1755 for Rev J. Badley. He died in 1765. His wife discovered that the deeds had been made out in her husband's name, so she sold it and it became the Shoulder of Mutton. Restored as a vicarage in 1805, there was controversy over the new incumbent. He was turned out of the vicarage and the building became the present Royal Hotel.

Hazelwood 🌿

Lying at the southern end of the Pennines some seven miles north of Derby, the village of Hazelwood commands delightful and varied views.

Two archaeological digs have revealed that the Romans had kilns in Hazelwood, where they had on hand the essential materials, fuel, water and clay and were only half a mile from the Roman road on the Chevin immediately to the east of the village. The finished articles would have been taken on mules or packhorses across the Derwent at Mule Ford (a name later changed to Milford). In 1958 pottery, identical to that found at almost every Roman military station in the Midlands, Northumberland and Hadrian's Wall, was discovered in 'Jenny Tang' wood. A later search uncovered a lead smelting hearth and a round stone, possibly from the terrace of a Roman villa.

The Victorian church of St John the Evangelist lies at the crossroads. Built in 1846, the church was severely damaged by fire in 1902 and rebuilt in that same year. Colonel Colville of Duffield Hall provided most of the £1,000 required to build the church, school and master's residence.

The Knowle, built in 1848 and presently the base for Lubrizol International Laboratories, was for some time in the first part of this century the home of Mrs E. M. Hull, the author of the novels *The Sheik* and *Sons of the Sheik*, both of which were filmed with Rudolph Valentino in the leading role.

Chevin House was the home of the Alleyne family from 1880 to 1973 and Sir John Gay Newton, who bought the property in 1880, was the engineer responsible for the design and construction of the roof of St Pancras Station, London, at the time the largest single-span roof in the world. Stone from Hazelwood Quarry was used in the facade at St Pancras.

In Spring Hollow the spring, which has never been known to dry up, was surrounded by stone work to commemorate Queen Victoria's Jubilee in 1897. It was in Spring Hollow that the late Mr Sam Land had a very strange experience. Driving into the Hollow in an empty trap his pony stopped, sweating with fright, and refused to go on. Mr Land saw three top-hatted men, arms linked together, who just melted away. He had to lead the pony home and later learnt the tragic news that a brother had been killed inspecting pit ponies in a Lancashire coalmine.

The 17th century Puss in Boots inn was formerly a millowner's house. The remains of the mill on the river Ecclesbourne, the boundary between Hazelwood and the parish of Windley, disappeared when the inn car park was built.

The Blue Bell inn is just as old and is associated with Padge Barber, who lived at the bottom of the Depth o' Lumb. Padge, who apparently spent much time in the Blue Bell, was a bitter and jealous woman whose fabricated and cruel stories are reputed to have driven one young couple to their separate deaths. Following her own death in a violent thunderstorm she has been supposed to haunt the district riding her shaggy pony.

Heage 🍂

Heage or High Edge is described in Woolley's *History of Derbyshire* as 'lying scattered all about'. The village is in two main parts, Heage itself and Nether Heage (or formerly High Heage and Low Heage). Neither village has a centre and consists of houses and cottages scattered along the roads and lanes, with some small estates of modern housing. The name is from the Anglo-Saxon 'Heegge' meaning high, lofty or sublime.

Situated in the Amber valley area, the main occupation of the original inhabitants would have been farming. There are still many family-owned farms today, rearing sheep and dairy cattle and growing cereal and root crops. In the early days of the industrial revolution coal mining and the ironworks at Morley Park and later at Butterley were major employers. There was a drift mine in the village (now a small housing estate) and coal was mined at nearby Hartshay and taken on horse-drawn barges along the Cromford Canal. Village folk also gained employment at the cotton mills and hosiery factories in Belper.

In modern times the villagers find work at L.B. Plastics in Nether Heage, once the site of a POW camp, or Bowmer & Kirkland, the builders, in Heage. Heage is also home to many small businesses including builders, painters and decorators, but also boasts Derbyshire's only full time professional falconer and an etching and printing studio.

Heage Windmill

115

The Yew tree studio owned and run by Charlie Downes is in one of the oldest houses in Heage. It was once owned by Joseph Spendlove, who was responsible for bringing piped water into the village. Previously water was drawn from numerous wells and springs in the area. Mr Spendlove was also the founder of Bowmer & Kirkland which was then a builder's, joiner's and undertaker's.

The oldest building in the village is probably Heage Hall, situated in Nether Heage, which is now a farm. Parts of the Hall date back to the 15th century. There have been many stories concerning the Hall over the centuries. One of the ghosts is said to be of the wife of George Pole, an eccentric dandy and owner of the Hall during the 17th century. George so ill-treated his wife that when she died he paid for the rebuilding of Heage church in penance. His own ghost is supposed to have been seen either with his dogs in the fields or driving his coach and horses in the lanes.

Later occupants of the Hall were the Shore family, who also owned and worked Heage windmill and water mill (no longer in existence) at the bottom of Dungeley Hill. The windmill has six sails and is a landmark seen from miles around, especially from the west.

The parish church, dedicated to St Luke, was originally built of wood, but was destroyed by a violent tempest in June 1545. Rebuilt in 1661 and enlarged in 1836, it has no square tower or spire, but an unusual octagonal bell tower on the north side of a barn-shaped structure, with the oldest part of the church at right angles to this.

In 1842 three men from Heage were involved in criminal activities which must have caused quite a stir at the time and gave rise to local sayings such as 'They 'ang 'em in bunches in Heage', and 'You can tell a man from Heage by the rope mark on his neck'. The three men Samuel Bonsall, William Bland and John Hulme, a tinker born in Leek, went to rob a house at Stanley Common one September night. The dwelling was owned and lived in by spinsters Martha and Sarah Goddard. Both were beaten by the robbers, Sarah survived but Martha died.

The post box in the wall of the village post office in Brook Street is of particular interest. It is one of a few in the country that is embossed with the initials of Edward VII.

Heath ✍

At the time of the Domesday survey of 1086 there were two settlements here, the two Lunts, which is a Danish word for a clearing in the woodland. The major settlement was in the valley below the old church, which was built in 1162. In 1088 Robert de Ferrers had given the manor to the monastery of Geronden, which was to hold it for more than 400 years. The Cistercian monks were famous for their farming skills, particularly in the management of sheep, whose wool was later to become the main source of the country's wealth. Over this period the name of the village was to change from Lunt to Lund, to Lound alias Heth, and finally to Heath.

After the Dissolution of the Monasteries by Henry VIII, the Savages of Stainsby became lords of the manor. Their manor house was near the site of the old Stainsby school. The fish ponds are still marked; a dead yew tree on the corner of Hawking Lane shows where the chapel was; the water mill is still there and field names indicate the park. Heath has the site of the gibbet on the common.

At the end of the 1500s the Savages sold their manor of Heath to Bess of Hardwick and the Cavendish connection began which was to last to the present day. For the next 300 and more years the village was to slumber on. 'Dozey Heath' was an appropriate name for it. A church school was built in 1687; open fields and common were enclosed; three pubs – the Elm Tree, the George and Dragon and the Horns flourished; vicars came and went and a new church was built in 1852.

After the calm of the preceding decades came the winds of change of the 20th century. The mining village of Holmewood was built on the western boundary, to house the workers of Hardwick colliery, sunk 20 or so years before. The parish population increased from 756 in 1901 to 2,132 in 1911. The opencast mining in the 1960s destroyed the old field patterns, mature trees, hedges and ponds. The construction later of the M1 motorway and junction denuded the village of several hundred acres of good farmland.

Heath is no longer a village of farms, farm labourers, estate workmen and village craftsmen. There is a church and a vicar, a pub and landlord, a post office, a school but no schoolmaster, no village bobby and no shop; a smithy but no smith. Gone too are the times when the village was in charge of its own affairs, as it was in the days of the manor courts and later the parish vestry.

Higham & Shirland

Although Higham and Shirland are one parish, they are two villages, both situated on the A61 Derby to Chesterfield road. Higham branches off from the A61 and its main street follows the line of the old Roman Rykneld Street. Strettea Lane also takes its name from Roman times.

The parish was in existence by the time of the Norman Conquest and by 1220 the foundations of Shirland church had been laid. This imposing gritstone building was refurbished to make room for the poor parishioners; the old box pews had only room for the gentry.

The famous industrialist John Smedley built a Wesleyan chapel in the village of Higham. He thought it too far for his workers to travel to Shirland in bad weather and so arranged for them to worship nearer home. Later he also built a school for 70 children. These buildings have been converted into private homes.

Both Higham and Shirland were agricultural settlements. The former belonged to the Turbutt family of Ogston Hall until the properties were sold off in 1952. The parish was quite self sufficient. Craftsmen and journeymen such as weavers, cobblers, wheelwrights, farmers, butchers, saddlers, herb growers, a mason and a blacksmith all lived and worked in the villages.

A charter to hold fairs and markets was granted to Higham in 1243. Indeed Higham held an annual cattle fair on the first Wednesday of the new year until the beginning of the Second World War. On this day the children had a holiday from school and helped to mind and drive the cattle, sustained along the way by mugs of hot tea or cocoa from the householders. Any stray cattle caught were held in pounds (small walled enclosures) one of which can still be seen at Well Farm. Goodwives would gather around the ancient stone cross to sell their butter, eggs and herbs. One such character was a Mrs Bradley. She had 21 children and often walked to and from Chesterfield on market days. She lived on Well Lane, which used to be the local rubbish dump.

The cross at Higham was repaired in 1755 at a cost of three shillings and sixpence but the steps are still the original. The whole cross was moved to a safer position when road traffic became heavier.

Higham Farm Hotel houses in its foyer one of the three wells left in Higham. At one time were were as many as 23 wells in the village but most of these have not survived. The other two are at Well Farm and Bull Farm.

Bull Farm used to be the Black Bull inn and was the entertainment centre of the area since it had its own theatre. Legend has it that the infamous highwayman Dick Turpin once stayed at the Black Bull. There were no such places of entertainment in Shirland which had turned into a place of industry with the sinking of Shirland pit in 1864. By the end of the century the colliery employed 500 men and improvements in their working conditions led to amenities for the village in the form of a bowling green and a Miners Welfare. After more than 100 years Shirland pit was closed. The site of its spoil heap is now a golf course and little evidence is left of the old mine workings. However Shirland Miners Welfare Band is probably the successor to a band begun by the mineworkers.

In recent years most of the village of Higham has been designated a conservation area thus preserving its character and charm.

Hilcote 🌿

The opening of 'B. Winning' colliery in about 1890 brought Hilcote into existence although, now the colliery has closed 'B. Winning' has again disappeared. It was named 'B. Winning' due to the fact the owners of 'A. Winning' at Blackwell were also the owners of 'B. Winning'.

The colliery company had to provide houses for the workers so they built some rather fine semi-detached homes in New Street for the officials. The workers' terraced cottages were built in Cokefield Terrace and Pasture Lane. Hilcote Arms Hotel was built and also a Co-operative store and beer house known as 'Daltons' in Berristow Lane. The post office was opened in 1906. A school was built about 1990, children previously going to Old Blackwell. That school was closed in 1972 and is now used by the Methodist church.

There appears to have been a building on the site of Hilcote Hall since the 16th century, if not before. It was classed as being in Blackwell. The Wilkinson family occupied the house for some 200 years. It has been used as a farm of late years.

Hilton 🌿

Hilton is situated on the A516 Derby to Uttoxeter road, eight miles from Derby and five miles from Burton-on-Trent. It is not a pretty village; the older buildings are on or near to the Main Street.

The Wesleyan Methodist chapel situated in the Main Street (known as the High Street before the 20th century) was built in 1841 and is still a thriving place of worship. A Primitive Methodist chapel (now a private residential cottage) was erected at a later date and is still known as 'Tell Me Why' by those who recall the words shown on a window facing the road.

Older members of the village can recall when the Americans had their camp on the outskirts of Hilton during the Second World War. They

Wakelyn Old Hall, Hilton

remember the large Ministry of Defence Camp of more than 300 acres, with an internal system of over six miles of roads. This was where the first sewerage system in the village was installed. This depot is now closed with plans for further development of housing and light industry.

The present newsagent's in Main Street used to be a charity school-room and has been used for many village activities before the present village hall was opened in 1962. A small stick bakery once stood on the main road. The baker used to blow a brass bugle when the oven was hot; the locals would then take their food to be cooked.

On entering Hilton from Derby, you pass the Old Talbot public house, a 16th century cruck building. Further down on the left is the Hilton House Hotel, once a private house which was owned by the Massey family, the first people in the village to own a car.

The oldest building in Main Street is Wakelyn Hall, built in a style that places it among the principal houses of the county in the 15th century. It is reputed once to have been an inn and to have hosted Mary Queen of Scots on her journey to imprisonment in Tutbury Castle. Whilst being restored in this century, a font, almost certainly Saxon, was discovered below a pump. This presumably came from the chapel of ease which existed in Hilton during the 13th century and during the 1500s was dedicated to Sir John Port of Etwall.

At one time there was a smithy which was part of the King's Head public house. A large gritstone boulder used to stand on the corner and an old seafaring man of the village used to sit making ships in full rig, out of a fowl's breast bone.

The old mill, over 200 years old, was modernised in the 19th century and the water wheels dismantled some 40 years ago. In the early 1800s it was used for grinding corn for the famous 'Derby Dog Biscuits' sold as far away as Leeds and London. Sir Oswald Mosley of Rolleston was a firm advocate of wholemeal bread. He opened a shop to sell his bread, the flour for which was ground at the mill. It closed as a corn mill in 1936, but reopened to process damaged corn from the blitz on the London Docks.

The old Hilton gravel workings are now owned by the Derbyshire Naturalists Trust and are a bird sanctuary and nature reserve.

The Derby-Stoke link bypass should greatly improve the environment in the village by taking away the majority of the heavy traffic which has been plaguing the inhabitants for many years.

Hognaston

Although it sounds as if the village name has some association with hogs or pigs, it was probably based on an 8th century Anglo-Saxon community – 'Hocca's pasture farm', and was referred to as Ockenavstun in the 1086 Domesday Book. Phonetic spellings across subsequent centuries has resulted in today's version.

A settlement grew up and flourished on this south-facing slope because of the many water sources – at least six wells and springs, although, surprisingly, the tradition of well-dressing has passed Hognaston by.

The settlement grew during the early 17th century because the road through the settlement was the 'main' road from London to Manchester, via Buxton, even though it would have been nothing more than a rough cart-track, and nearly impassable during winter months. The road would almost certainly have seen activity from the Royalist and Parliamentary armies during the Civil War of the 17th century. It would also have been used by many a packhorse – hence the name of one of the three inns at that time – the Packhorse. The other two were the Red Lion and the Bull. Only the Red Lion survives today, and offers bar meals and a small camping/caravan site. Business and prosperity declined with the opening of the road through Ashbourne in the late 17th century, when the settlement reverted to a mainly farming community.

Hognaston can boast at least one famous son – John Smith, founder of John Smith & Sons, Clockmakers of Derby. The three bells in constant use in the parish church-tower, together with the clock, were given to the church by John Smith & Sons as a memorial to their founder, and the clock is maintained by them each year. The lovely parish church, dedicated to St Bartholomew, is on a raised site in the centre of the village. The doorway, tympanum and font are Norman (late 12th century).

There were, until the early 1970s, three bakeries operating and employing local people, both baking and delivering bread, etc. Occupations in the village before 1914 were many and varied – hawker, monumental mason, wheelwright, draper, blacksmith, corn factor, tailor, grocer, baker, carrier, postmaster and farm work. All have now gone, with the exception of the last two, and Webster's Bus Company still remains in operation.

Sadly, Hognaston lost its village school in 1983. The building, erected in 1871 as a school, is now a field study centre which is used by groups of city children to study the local environment.

Severn-Trent Water are building the infamous Carsington Reservoir on our doorstep. The reservoir has faced many problems and setbacks, but it will give Hognaston a much needed bypass. Unfortunately, a lot of trees, hedgerows and agricultural land were destroyed during the building of the reservoir.

Hognaston parish has only 300 residents, but the community is alive and growing.

Holbrook 🦡

Holbrook is a village on a hill, with many beautiful views. The Saxon name for it was Hale Broc meaning Badger Hill. There is a Roman road running through it called Portway, and a Romano-British kiln of circa AD 350 has been found near to Holbrook Hall (1646).

The village church of St Michael, built in the 18th century, is a typical example of classical Italian architecture. There is a Methodist church dating from the 19th century, also being a classic example of its kind.

Before the First World War, children could play football and cricket in the streets as the traffic was very scarce, just an odd horse and cart would pass by. At Christmas time the children would go guising and perform plays in public houses and any house that would allow entry. Dancing bears used to pay a visit and perform in the village. Travelling fairs, with round-a-bouts, hand-driven, would set up in a field near the centre of the village.

Damson trees were very plentiful and the first Sunday after the 29th September was called Damson Sunday, when damson pie was eaten. They were a special variety, said to have been imported, and bore large juicy fruit. Dye was made from this fruit, and used to dye stockings.

Frame-work knitting was done in houses and small workshops. Stockings were made for Queen Victoria and a member of the Spanish Royal family was married in a pair of silk stockings made in Holbrook. The roads were rough tracks. Turnpike roads were later made and toll houses were built; one still stands on the turnpike road, now renamed Makeney Road.

Before the Second World War the village had a good football team and cricket club. The tennis club played on the vicarage courts. The Boy Scouts had an excellent drama group and entertained the villagers to well-directed concerts. There was also a Girl Guide group. The Duchess of York's mother was a member when she lived as a young girl in Holbrook Hall. The Allotment Association had a thriving membership and the annual show was a great event.

Today all houses have piped water, electricity and gas. The streets are well lit and the roads are fairly good. New houses have been built and the old ones have had a facelift. Villagers can now go to a Sports Centre for recreation. Still it is a very friendly village to live in.

Holmesfield 🦡

The village of Holmesfield lies halfway between Sheffield and Bakewell, with easy access to Chesterfield. Holmesfield consists of 14 hamlets, and each has its place in the story of the village.

To the north of the village is the hamlet of Norwoods where G. B. H.

Ward lived; he was well known as the 'King of Ramblers'. In 1900 he formed The Clarion Ramblers. At the summit of Lose Hill near Edale an area of 54 acres was presented to him by his fellow ramblers; this was handed over to the National Trust in 1954.

The beautiful valley of Cordwell lies below the centre of Holmesfield. Here for over 100 years the Barlow Hunt has resided. The Late Major W. Wilson was Master of the Hounds. Fox hunting was the main sport in Holmesfield and the opening meet was usually held outside the Angel inn, where hot punch and sandwiches were served. Of course hunting was reserved for the 'gentry', the lower orders followed on foot and this was not always encouraged.

The hamlet of Millthorpe took its name from the grist-mill where the local farmers brought their corn to be ground. Sadly this was demolished in 1971. Mr Gilchrist and his family lived up the hill at Cartledge Hall. He was well known in Sheffield as a gifted preacher. Opposite the Hall are two small cottages, at the side of which can be found a file and nail making forge. Former inhabitants of Holmesfield were grinders, miners and farmers.

At Cowley Bar is the Rutland Arms, almost in its original state. It has an old skittle alley, discovered with the original skittles intact. A famous personality was Charlie Wheat – a not so simple donkey. He was also known as the 'Cowley Buzzer', having an uncanny knack of knowing when it was twelve noon (summer or winter). This he advertised with a loud 'Hee Haw'. Charlie was often present at the Barlow Hunt, and having a penchant for cakes he'd follow the meet into the Angel inn to partake of the hospitality provided. His greatest claim to fame was that he won the Cowley Donkey Derby on 2nd August 1920 and the silver cup twelve inches high was suitably inscribed. He departed this world when he was 29 years old and was sadly missed.

Much of the social life of the village stems from the church. The present St Swithin's was built in 1826, though it is recorded that a chapel had stood on the site from the 7th century. It is 850 ft above sea level.

The local village school 'Penny Acres' takes its name from the land it was built on. Money was obtained from the letting of this land enabling a trust to be formed to provide for two poor widows of the parish. The trust is still in operation but now 'food parcels' are dispensed to the old age pensioners around Christmas time.

Like most small villages, there was a village store – you name it and it was sold there. This was a blessing during the winter months when often the village was isolated for weeks. It had a huge 'Yorkshire Range'. Customers loved it on cold days and there was always a chair or a box available; no one was in a hurry, besides one needed to know the local gossip. A set of chandler's scales hung from the ceiling; yes, they sold bran, corn and wheat too, they also weighed newly born babies – that's service.

Holmesfield is a lovely village, surrounded by wide spaces and fields with their own names: Hob fields, Gorse, Nine fields, the Cragger. There are woods to the north known as Holmesfield Park. There is a profusion of holly trees, perhaps that was why Holmesfield was once Hollyfield? Also to the north is the site of a motte and bailey castle, though unfortunately the site is badly mutilated. The motte has been used to partly fill the moat, providing a flat and accessible surface for cattle to graze. Originally there was an easily defended dwelling for the local tax collector to lodge while collecting his dues.

Holmewood 🌿

Holmewood is situated four miles south of Chesterfield and one and a half miles from Junction 29 of the M1. It has a population of approximately 4,000.

With the modernisation of the local colliery there was need for a larger workforce, so a colliery village was built. Between 1901 and 1911 the Williamthorpe Wood opposite the railway station, which was on the Great Central Railway (later LNER) on the route between London and Aberdeen, was gradually turned into the village of Holmewood, hence its name. Holmewood was dominated by the pit, residents being mainly miners and their families.

Due to lack of resources the colliery was closed in 1968. This closure, together with four other local collieries, and the withdrawal of railway services, left a legacy of derelict land. This has been carefully reclaimed by the County Council to provide, together with associated woodland meadows, the 'Five Pits Trail' which includes very pleasant walks and a haven for wildlife. In the case of Holmewood there are also two sites for light industries, bringing much needed employment into the area.

In earlier days there was a church mission, two chapels, a Salvation Army hall and a cinema in the village. Sadly all these have closed due to lack of interest, with the exception of the church mission, which is still used today for worship.

Holymoorside 🌿

Some say 'Holy', some say 'Holly', and some just say 'Moorside', but they all refer to Holymoorside, a village about three and a half miles to the south-west of Chesterfield. 'Holy' is supposed to refer to the fact that in the Middle Ages, monks from Beauchief Abbey near Sheffield were sent via Holymoorside to Harewood Grange, a tiny hamlet on the moors nearby. But as these were the erring members of the fraternity, and Harewood Grange was a monastic 'house of correction', they would hardly have acquired a reputation for holiness.

It is more likely the name is derived from an Anglo-Saxon word meaning 'hill-clearing'. It is quite easy to see the reason for 'Moorside';

even today the purple expanses of Beeley Moor and Eastmoor are only a few minutes drive away, and, before some of the area was enclosed during the 18th century, the heathery slopes came right down to the centre of the village.

The chief assets of the village are the small recreation ground and the large village hall. The latter is in almost constant use and caters for most of the indoor activities of the community.

Today most people earn their living outside the village, travelling daily to Chesterfield, Sheffield or even further afield. A hundred years ago things were very different. Self-sufficiency was the motto and there were tradesmen and craftsmen of all kinds in the community. Farmers were predominant, but there were also miners, quarrymen, lead miners and smelters, blacksmiths, butchers, grocers, joiners, basket-makers and besom-makers, even a taxidermist! There is still one besom-maker left.

Many people, particularly women and girls, were employed at Manlove's cotton thread mills. These were large buildings, three storeys high, built towards the end of the 18th century and acquired by the Manlove Brothers about 1840. They were prosperous for about 50 years but closed in 1902 and now hardly a trace remains. After 1902 they were gradually demolished and in 1928 a pleasant avenue of 15 houses, known as Riverside Crescent, was planned for the site and completed in the 1930s. Cotton Mill Hill and Dye Mill Yard remind us of this era and one of the dams remains, a beauty spot and the meeting place of the local anglers.

There are some attractive names in the village. Water comes from the 'Whispering Well', Wellspring House is close by, and Pennywell Drive reminds us of the days when piped water was not the norm. An annual Well Dressing has been revived. Cornmill Cottage, Laundry Yard, Cathole and the Pinfold evoke times past, but Sewerage Lane is hardly an inspired choice! Hipper Hall, a 16th century farmhouse with an even older tithe barn, is probably the oldest building in the village.

The village school was built in 1874 largely at the expense of the millowners, the Manloves. There are five shops, two pubs, the Bulls Head and the Lamb, and three churches, St Peter's, the United Reformed church and the Methodist chapel. All tastes are catered for. It is not a really beautiful village but people who come to live here usually stay.

Hope 🌿

The name Hope means an upland valley, which description accurately places this Peak District village. To the north stand Win Hill and Lose Hill and the heather moors of the Dark Peak, to the south the limestone dales and quarrying areas of the White Peak, and in between lies the Hope valley running down towards the larger valley of the river Derwent.

From Anglo-Saxon times until the reign of Charles I, a large part of north Derbyshire was reserved as a royal hunting forest: wild open country sparsely populated. In Hope church can be seen 13th century memorials bearing the symbols of forest officers, or woodroffes, a term which survived as a family name figuring in local affairs for a further 500 years or so, and is perpetuated in the Woodroffe Arms public house.

Hope was mentioned in the 1086 Domesday survey as having a church, though the present St Peter's dates from about two centuries later. In the churchyard stands a 9th century preaching cross, headless alas, thanks to Oliver Cromwell. Inside, features of interest include a carved oak pulpit dated 1652 and a schoolmaster's chair of similar date. But this ancient church is no museum; it can be seen at its best between 9.30 and 10.30 on a Sunday morning!

The green hills around Hope are grazed by many sheep. Cattle are also reared, and a few small dairy herds help to supply milk for neighbouring towns. Hope's sheep and cattle market, which takes place twice weekly for a good part of the year, attracts farmers from a wide area. In past days, any animal straying from its owner's field could be impounded by the appointed pinder, and released only on payment of a fine. In Hope, although this custom has died out, the pinfold exists for all to see, and was once featured on television. The highlight of the agricultural year is Hope Show, held on August Bank Holiday.

The coming of the railway in 1892 made it possible to travel daily to Sheffield or Manchester, and opened up for many residents alternative interests to the pastoral occupations which had predominated down the centuries. In 1928 Earle's Cement set up their works here to take advantage of the limestone and shale needed for their product. This offered employment for many local people, and still flourishes under the name of Blue Circle.

All basic family needs can be met in Hope shops. There are also two banks, a post office, garage and hairdresser. The oldest business is the butcher's, which has been in the same family since at least the mid 19th century.

The village hall was given to the community in 1904 by Mr Edward Firth, a Sheffield industrialist, in memory of his son Loxley, and so is called Loxley Hall. Newer acquisitions include a complex of flatlets for elderly people. This was brought about by the perseverance of Miss Evelyn M. Wilson MBE and was named Caroline Court after her late sister. An attractive building, completed in 1990 opposite the flatlets, was named the Evelyn Medical Centre to honour Miss Wilson's achievement.

Horsley 🦋

Horsley is a small village five miles north of Derby, with a population of around 500.

The village consists of a main street lined with mature trees, a church and chapel, a village green complete with 'spreading' chestnut tree, a school, pub, post office, shop, village hall, and a golf course on the outskirts of the parish. This is a sign of the times; a farm converted into a leisure amenity.

The most important, certainly the oldest, building in Horsley is the church of St Clement and St James which serves Horsley and the neighbouring parishes of Coxbench and Kilburn. A church has existed in the village since Saxon times, but the present building dates from around 1200, though it was enlarged and altered during the following centuries. The distinctive broach spire was built in the 14th century.

Horsley chapel, a Wesleyan Methodist church, is a small attractive stone building facing the village green, not far from St Clement's church. It was opened in 1845.

Horsley also had a castle, situated about a mile away in the next parish of Coxbench. Although few traces of the building now remain, it was a royal stronghold from the time of King John until the reign of Queen Mary Tudor. Legend has it that a tunnel runs from the church to the castle, but there is no proof of this.

A small school existed in French Lane before the present Church of England school was opened in 1828. This was enlarged in 1874 and, thankfully, is thriving. Horsley has one surviving pub, the Coach and Horses, but another, the Ship inn, once existed on the Kilburn side of the village. This building, which dates from 1625, is now an attractive private house.

The village possesses two rare features. One is the stone pillar box on French Lane. This is believed to be unique to Derbyshire and possibly the whole country. The second feature is the three fountains, given to the village in 1864 by Rev Sitwell. He was a relative of the Sitwells of Stainsby Hall in the nearby village of Smalley and he arranged for spring water to be piped from the Old Hills to the village. The fountains are named Blanch, Sophie and Rosamund after his daughters.

A local legend concerns a stone carved with the letters L.L., which is set on Lady Lea Road, the lane leading from Horsley to Horsley Woodhouse. One version of the legend says it commemorates a Lady Lea, who was thrown from her horse and killed at that spot, but no one knows who Lady Lea was, if she ever existed. Another version says that years ago coal was brought by horse and cart from Mapperley Pit to Coxbench station. A cutting with a bend in it was made in what is now Lady Lea Road to make the journey easier for the horses. A local 'lady' was supposed to have bestowed her favours on the navvies building this, and they placed the stone in the road in her memory.

Once most people in Horsley were farmers and farm workers, miners or stockingers, but now, though it is still a rural village, few people work on the land and the local mining and hosiery industries have declined.

Villagers are employed in all walks of life, travelling away from Horsley to work. This does not mean the village is a 'dormitory', but it is a flourishing community with a bowls club, over sixties club, a horticul-

127

tural society and, of course, the Women's Institute. Another popular activity locally is walking. The surrounding countryside is beautiful and co-operation between farmers and walkers means that footpaths are open and well used.

Hulland Ward 🐾

'Dog Lanes' – now there's an odd name! For its origins we must go back nine centuries or so when a vast tract of land, including that on which Hulland Ward now stands, was the Royal Duffield Forest or Frith. Here in 1372 came John of Gaunt to hunt as did also Kings Edward I and III and King Henry IV. And in Dog Lanes the hunting dogs of the forest were kept. Even today older folk remember Hulland Ward as Wardgate – possibly Woodgate – one of the gates into the forest.

The old packhorse road between Manchester and London ran along the ridge here and this was the route used by Bonnie Prince Charlie on his way to Derby in 1745.

But Hulland, or Hoillant as it was called in the Domesday Book, really began on low lying land south of the ridge road where, in 1485, a chantry chapel was founded by John Bradbourne and his wife Anne. The moated mound where their manor house stood can still be seen in the meadows close to the two remaining medieval fish ponds. It is said the house was destroyed in the Civil War, and much of the stone used to build the 'Old Hall' on higher ground just south of the ridge road at what is now Hulland. Here also are to be found the Primitive Methodist chapel and the newer Hulland Hall.

Christ church, in the Diocese of Derby, was built in 1837/8 and stands on the highest point of the area. Until 1853 Hulland formed an outlying chapelry of Ashbourne. In 1863 a school was built next to the church.

Meanwhile Hulland Ward had become the main village. It had grown up along the ridge road about five miles east of Ashbourne and just north of Hulland.

The main occupation in the area has been mixed farming and in years gone by several small businesses flourished. Among them were a milliner's and draper's, a saddler, two butchers, a joiner and wheelwright, shoe repairer, threshing machine proprietor and two blacksmiths (the last of which closed less than 20 years ago) and, in the 1930s, Hulland Gravel Works opened.

Today there is a general store, garden shop, saddlery and post office. There are two garages, a cabinet maker, a doctors' surgery and two public houses. Hulland Gravel has become English China Clay and, covering a huge area, is one of the biggest concrete works in the country. Twenty eight council houses were built at Hulland Ward in 1950, and 15 years later a large housing estate and modern primary school on the north side of the main road, thus increasing the population to around 1,000.

The Smithy, Hulland Ward as it was about 1900

The whole area is criss-crossed by numerous footpaths which, in the past, were in constant use by all.

Upper and Nether Biggin, Biggin Mill and Millington Green lie to the north of Hulland Ward and are included in the district. Here also is a network of footpaths. In the 1940s an old lady of 90 said these paths were very necessary in her childhood, when the narrow winding lanes were dangerous for walking due to the heavy-laden packhorses going to and from the water mill. This is now a private house, the weir gone and the mill pond silted up.

Biggin House at Nether Biggin was built in the reign of Queen Anne. Opposite stood a medieval chapel attached to St Oswald's church, Ashbourne.

Many wells were in use in this area until 1953 when piped water was brought. Two wells on higher ground gave water containing iron. Two lower down, both in woodland, gave sulphur water. One of these was buried in a landslide following tree felling in the Second World War. The other, still used, has never been known to run dry or freeze. It steams in frosty weather. Tea made from it is strong and of very good flavour so the wartime ration went a long way.

Ilam

The village of Ilam lies in the Manifold valley just inside the Peak District National Park. It is a small place, about 150 people, and many of them live on scattered farms.

It is one of those confusing places on the border – officially in Staffordshire, but in reality looking very much towards Derbyshire. The nearest easily accessible town is Ashbourne. Just to complicate things even more, the houses in the village centre are built in a very unusual Alpine style, and a visitor is quite likely to hear the sound of the local Scottish pipe band practising their music, so you could be forgiven for wondering if you are even in England.

The village was a part of the estates of Burton Abbey until Henry VIII gave it to three squires – the Ports at Ilam Hall, the Meverells at Throwley (the ruined medieval hall is the oldest of the three houses) and the Hurts at Castern Hall, who are the only family still in residence.

Ilam changed a great deal in the first half of the 19th century. Jesse Watts Russell bought the estate from the Ports and started to improve it. He built a new Hall, renovated the neglected church and added an imposing family mausoleum, moved the whole village further from the hall, and provided a new vicarage for the Rev. Bernard Port and a new school and school house. The Hall has now become a large youth hostel and the vicarage is Dovedale House, diocesan Residential Youth Centre. Both attract a large number of young visitors to the village.

The church is mostly a Gilbert Scott building but it is noteworthy for its Saxon font and Saxon crosses, a Tudor chapel with the medieval tomb of St Bertram and a lovely 17th century tomb of the Meverells. A pair of maidens' garlands keep us all guessing. No one can be sure which young woman was commemorated this way but one possible suggestion would place it in 1834. A claim to fame is the large marble sculpture in the Watts Russell chapel by Francis Chantrey.

Thousands of visitors come to the village each year, visiting nearby Dovedale, and Ilam country park with its Paradise walk and the underground river. The local rivers are famous for fishing – after all this is Izaak Walton country.

The legend of St Bertram is well known. He was a prince whose wife and child were killed by wolves in the forest. He retired from public life to a hermit's cave in this area. His tomb is in the church (although he is not buried there any more), and there is a well named after him, as well as the old bridge over the river Manifold.

Ilam hosts two important events each year, Dovedale sheep dog trials followed by shepherds' service in the church, and the Manifold show. The majority of local people work in the village – in farming, haulage, hotel work, bus driving and of course many work for the National Trust, who now own the estate. The village may seem a bit quiet to some visitors – the shop closed some 30 years ago, there is no pub except for the Izaak Walton Hotel. There must be many times when visitors staying in the village outnumber the locals, but those who live here love it so much that they simply do not want to leave.

Ilkeston ✺

Ilkeston, the Queen of the Erewash Valley, stands proudly atop a substantial hill. Mentioned in the Domesday Book, Ilkeston was originally an Anglo-Saxon community as is borne out by parts of the ancient church of St Mary, which was originally served by the monks of nearby Dale Abbey.

A former mining community with a number of pits in the surrounding areas, all now disappeared, it has seen many changes over the years. The railways came and went, and there were at one time three stations bearing the name, one being a link-line to the Erewash Valley main line served by the push-pull local. Ilkeston has seen many differing trades and industry apart from the mines, the manufacturing of lace being one of these, still being created.

For all its industry, and nearly 600 businesses operate within its boundaries, Ilkeston is a very green place as is most evident if you should climb the 99 steps of the tower of St Mary's and look around. Trees are everywhere and greenery abounds. The parks and flower beds are a feature of the community and reflect great credit on the local authority. It enjoys one of the finest cricket grounds in the county with wide views of the surrounding countryside, presented to the people many years ago by the Duke of Rutland, who at one time owned a great deal of the land here.

There are fine schools set in pleasant surroundings, one of which was opened by George V, and the local library was one of the many presented with funds from the literary benefactor Andrew Carnegie. Its thriving and colourful markets on Thursdays and Saturdays attract eager shoppers from a wide area, all seeking the latest bargains and anxious to be kept abreast of the local gossip.

Every October most of the streets in the centre of Ilkeston are closed to allow the Annual Charter Fair to come into being. Created over 700 years ago the Ilkeston Fair is now perhaps one of the largest street fairs in the country and is well worth a visit.

Ilkeston might well at one time have become a spa, for about 100 years ago a natural spring produced waters beneficial to certain ailments. The Bath House was a haven of relief to many in the late Victorian age. However, sadly the properties in the water were not maintained and the spring dried up. The main street is known as Bath Street and is the only reminder of what might have been.

Ilkeston is blessed with its own local dialect, recently put into print in a series of booklets, and there are still pockets of the community where the rich character of the former mining tongue can be heard although it might not easily be understood.

The people of Ilkeston are the honest hardworking backbone of the working men and women of this land. They know what they want and will let you know if they don't get it. Many a trader has been heard to say that if you can sell your wares in Ilkeston you'll sell them anywhere. For a community proud of itself and with heart, Ilkeston has got a lot going for it.

Ireton Wood & Idridgehay

Ireton Wood and Idridgehay are in the parish of Alton, Idridgehay and Ashleyhay. Idridgehay is situated on the B5023 three miles from Wirksworth, and ten from Derby. It lies in the beautiful valley of the

Ecclesbourne river which rises near Wirksworth and has its confluence with the Derwent in Duffield.

Wallstone Farm which is in the parish is mentioned in the Domesday Book. This area was in the Appletree Hundred, part of the Duffield Frith (Royal Forest). This may be the reason why there is no evidence of ancient industrial development. Agriculture now, as in the past, is the main industry with a strong emphasis on dairy herds, cattle and sheep.

One mile south of Idridgehay lies Ireton Wood; it is suggested that its name was simply derived from Ireton's Wood – a neighbouring village is Kirk Ireton. In the days of the stage coaches the village boasted two hostelries, one of which was called the Pig and Whistle, but today there are few inhabitants and the village is well off the beaten track.

Idridgehay is the larger of the two villages. The oldest house, a thatched timber-framed building now called South Sitch was built in 1621 by George Mellor, whose initials with those of his wife are still to be seen in the fabric. Much later the then owner of South Sitch, Robert Cresswell, was a principle benefactor with James Milnes of Alton Manor when the church of St James was built in 1855. Shortly after the church was built a parsonage was erected at the eastern end of the village but this and another house was destroyed by a land mine which fell in 1941.

The parochial school was built near the church in 1866 and thrived for many years as school and social centre but closed for lack of pupils in 1988. It is now a private house – the facade, clock and bell have been preserved in the conversion.

The railway came to Idridgehay in 1867, built by the London Midland who were intent on having their own line to Manchester. With this in mind, although it was and still is a single track, all the bridges were built double width. In the event another route was found. It became a very busy branch line carrying commuting passengers and milk from local farmers who converged on the station from far and wide every evening at 5.0pm. Although the line is occasionally used to carry stone from the Wirksworth quarries the station was closed some years ago and is now a private house.

The village shop and post office on the main road, which was also damaged by the land mine, has been trading for well over 100 years. The local pub, the Black Swan, is an attractive old building which according to a plaque at the entrance was used by George Eliot as the original for 'The Waggon Overthrown' in her novel *Adam Bede*.

The Derbyshire artist, George Turner, whose works are nationally renowned, lived in Idridgehay for some years at the end of his life. He was a prolific painter of local rural scenes. He died in 1910 at the age of 67 and is buried in the churchyard.

Idridgehay is now largely a commuter village but must once have been nearly self supporting with its own church, two shops and post office, a butcher, inn, railway, smithy, threshing contractor, brickmaker, corn miller, boot and shoe maker, timber agent, agricultural implement maker, a lengthman and even an itinerant clog maker. There are tales of a ghostly white dog drifting across a lonely lane, of a headless highwayman hurrying who knows where, and witches who met in bygone days – take a walk up Windley Lane to Cliffash some dark night – you may believe them!

Ironville 🌾

Ironville derives its name from the ironworks established there in the mid 19th century – 'The Iron Village'. It is the best example of a mid 19th century company model village in Derbyshire, entirely the creation of one company, the Butterley Company. It was built between 1834 and 1860 on a tract of land which previously had been used for meadow and pastureland. The partners in the Butterley Company were concerned about the physical and spiritual welfare of their employees. They built a church and a school and provided a complete range of public services.

The Cromford Canal, which is adjacent to the ironworks, was built in about 1795. A man-made reservoir in a picturesque setting now provides excellent fishing facilities for the keen angler.

At the highest point in the village is the Jessop Memorial standing in extensive grounds, until recently open to the public. Here on Whit Monday every year members of the Band of Hope met. A procession of highly decorated maypoles was led by local brass bands.

The village now has a large church hall where many activities are enjoyed by the residents. Until quite recently there were only two council houses, but now there are also one-bedroomed council bungalows for the elderly.

Killamarsh 🌾

Killamarsh is in the north-east corner of the county on the border with South Yorkshire and has recently avoided being taken over by Sheffield.

Killamarsh was mentioned in the Domesday Book as Chinewoldmaresc, which is believed to originate from Chinewold's marsh – Chinewold being the lord of the manor. It was a scattered agricultural community, but coal has been mined here for more than 500 years.

With the building of the Chesterfield Canal which passed through the centre of the village, and the railways – there were once three stations – it became an important trading place. From the 19th century, coal mining was the most important industry. There were several coal mines in the vicinity and when boys left school they automatically followed their fathers into mining. In his book *Colliers and I*, F. J. Metcalfe, a former rector of Killamarsh, tells of his affection for the colliers and his efforts to keep young boys from bad influences and to stop them from swearing.

He appears to have been a remarkable man and his influence was felt for many years on the people of Killamarsh.

Around the 1830s Killamarsh was notorious for bull, bear and badger baiting and also cockfighting. A reminder of these is the naming of the newest public house – the Bull and Badger. However, all was not bad.

In St Giles' church is a rare stained glass window depicting the crowned Madonna and child. This escaped the ravages of Cromwell's Puritans. An interesting item on the outside wall of the church is a stone tablet which records the fact that John Wright, a pauper, died in 1797 in his 103rd year. The Methodist church too has a beautiful stained glass window which shows a miner at work. The Congregational church in High Street is known as 'The Church on the Hill' and the Ebenezer gospel hall is sometimes called 'The Church in the Field'. Close to the church in the 1850s lived and worked the village clock maker, George Turton.

The scattered communities have been joined together by housing estates. The population has therefore increased so that it is now a 'town sized village' with an infinite variety of occupations amongst its inhabitants.

Rother Valley Country Park, which caters for all kinds of water sports, is partly in Killamarsh. National competitions are sometimes held here. There is also a lake for fishing and one which is a nature reserve where many species of birds are to be found. There is a grass ski slope and scope for model gliders.

There has been a Doctor Lipp in Killamarsh for nearly 70 years. Doctor George and Mrs Isobel Lipp came here in the early 1920s and their two sons carried on the practice, as Doctor Charles and Doctor Donald.

Kirk Ireton ✍

Kirk Ireton, with a population of 400, nestles on a hillside 700 ft above sea level four miles to the south of Wirksworth. Many of the older buildings date from the 17th century and most are built from gritstone quarried locally. The name Ireton is unique to Derbyshire and Kirk Ireton is believed to mean the 'Church of Irish Enclosure', probably where Celtic missionaries settled.

Like many rural villages the occupations of Ireton residents are no longer based on agriculture; within the last 25 years the number of working farms in the village has dropped from nine until only one remains. The farmhouses and buildings have been converted into desirable residences.

The village still boasts a primary school, church, chapel, pub and shop cum post office. The Barley Mow pub is one of the oldest buildings, with real ale and a unique atmosphere – it has never been modernised. Indeed it was one of the last premises in the country to accept decimalisation – the 87 year old landlady Mrs Ford did not hold with the new money.

Kirk Ireton still celebrates its traditional Wakes Week, which starts on Trinity Sunday, the church's patronal festival, with a procession of villagers led by a local brass band and the Oddfellows banner from the Barley Mow to the church for a service of thanksgiving.

Holy Trinity church dates from 1120, and has an interesting custom known as 'roping' for weddings, when village children put a rope across the road and bride and groom cannot leave the church until a toll is paid in silver by the bridegroom. Also centred on the church is the village ghost story; one day a passerby heard a voice from the graveyard enquiring 'What time is it?'. No one could be seen, and the startled passerby hurried on; a few seconds later Luke the gravedigger emerged from the bottom of a newly dug grave to look at the church clock.

The village once rejoiced in the nickname 'Sodom'; this came about because the village boys used to throw sods of grass at any strange young men who came courting a village lass. They used to 'Sod-'em'!

There are still some village charities extant. The Slater-Cooper pays pensioners a twice yearly payment of around £20 and the Anne Downing Clothing Charity now pays for school trips, while the School Endowment Fund buys each child a bible when they leave.

The village has been home for craftsmen and artists and boasts many amongst the inhabitants today. Kirk Ireton had an illustrious visitor in the 1930s when the then Prince of Wales came to visit the workshop of Mr Sherwin, who was famous for his linenfold carving; on leaving the Prince left his Panama hat, which is still in the ownership of the Sherwin family – after they offered to return it to him.

Kirk Langley 🌿

Situated on the A52 four miles north-west of Derby and nine miles from Ashbourne is the village of Kirk Langley.

The church, dedicated to St Michael and built about 1320, is largely in the Decorated style of architecture and is a fine example of a village church. It is believed to have replaced a much older building, there being traces of a Saxon wall near the west door.

Some thirty years ago the village suffered a great shock when the lovely old rectory built in 1662 by Rev Thomas Meynell was sold, demolished and houses built on the site. Also lost to posterity was the tithe barn where former rectors received their tithes in kind.

Adjacent to the churchyard stands the Leeke Memorial Hall, the village school until 1879, and now a listed building. The headmaster, who with his family is buried in the churchyard, resided in the south end of the building. Named after a much loved rector, the Rev W. M. Leeke, it is the centre of village activities.

There were at one time several forges in the village. Now one only remains on Moor Lane, where Tom Lee, blacksmith and farrier for many years until his death in 1962, would stand clad in leather apron, horse's hoof between his knees, watched by a group of fascinated children as they made their way to and from the village school. In 1932 Edward VIII, then Prince of Wales, paid a visit to the forge whilst on a tour of Derbyshire village crafts. On Church Lane Wheelwright's Cottage, still in the possession of the Brown family, was once the home of Alf Brown. Son and grandson of wheelwrights, he was a great character with a rare sense of humour. Passers-by would stop to chat in his shop doorway and children, their feet making patterns in the sawdust, would watch eagerly as carts, wheels and even coffins took shape (for he was also the village undertaker).

After the Second World War a small and well designed council estate known as the Cunnery (the name taken from the field on which it stands) was built close to the A52. Many of the houses are now privately owned.

For many years there was on the Town End a bakery and grocery shop run by the late Samuel Clarke. Today the post office run by Mrs Unwin incorporates newspapers, grocery and confectionery and serves the village.

Of old customs one only seems to have survived: the School Treat, now known as the School Party. In former days the whole school would walk in crocodile formation up the mile long drive to Meynell Langley, there to be entertained to tea in the stable yard (weather permitting). Later games were played on the lawns and on departing each child received an orange.

A feature of interest to visitors is the ancient Mapple Well which until mains water came in 1952 had served generations of people living on the green, who with yokes and buckets came to fetch their daily supply. Another feature is the pound on Church Lane. Thanks to the parish council both these monuments to the past have been restored and are regularly maintained.

Linton ✺

Linton is a bit like Topsy, it just growed and growed. The original village was confined to what is now Main Street and High Street where a few old houses still remain, although none of any architectural interest. It was noted by William the Conqueror's agents at the time of the Domesday survey, being named as Linctune, meaning the farmstead on the hill. This could be where the manor house stands. The principal landowner at the time of the Conquest was Henry de Ferrers.

Every village has its ghost, and Linton's is said to be that of 'Old Doll Bath', more correctly known as Lady Dorothy de Bath. Rumour has it that a paving stone in the back passage of the manor house is still stained by her blood after she was murdered by her lover. Now her restless spirit walks through the manor drive and spinney on moonlit nights. It's a brave man who walks down Linton Hill alone at such a time.

She could not be buried in Linton churchyard because that was not there until 1881, the church being built mainly due to the generosity of the owners of the manor, the Beard family, to serve the increasing population.

The majority of the villagers would have been employed by the local farmers before the discovery of coal in the mid 19th century. The village rapidly grew with the opening of the Netherseal Colliery and the Coton Park and Linton Colliery, with many terrace-type houses being built to accommodate the men who came from the surrounding area to find employment.

Much of the farmland was lost with the building of a council estate in 1946. With more council-built property, including accommodation with a warden for the elderly or handicapped, and at least four privately built estates during the last 30 years, the village has spread considerably.

The first school in Linton was held in the 'Iron Room' and was opened on 26th May 1873. This building was also used as a night school, for church services and Sunday school meetings, but numbers grew so fast that it became necessary to extend, and the foundations of the 'New Room' were laid on 25th March 1877. This is now a church hall, known as the 'Brick Room', and was the only hall in the village apart from the school hall up until 1972, when a modern village hall was built.

The village has three old public houses, now refurbished, one of which – the Square and Compass – was the old toll house for the turnpike road (a term still used by many of the locals). This was renamed Cauldwell Road when new houses were built. The travelling showmen brought their swings and round-a-bouts to the field next to the Square and Compass for Linton Wakes week which was held in November.

In spite of the closure of local collieries, Linton is still a thriving village with the local workforce commuting to nearby towns. The church and school are still the centre of many village community activities for both young and old.

Little Eaton

The origin of Little Eaton is Anglo-Saxon and simply means 'Little Town by the Water'. The village is situated three and a half miles north-east of Derby and is surrounded by moors and woodland where bluebells bloom in abundance in the springtime; their beauty has inspired local artist James Preston to recapture it in water colours and oils, and his paintings are now sold worldwide.

It was in 1793 that Benjamin Outram of Butterley invented the flanged rail and laid one of the earliest railways from Denby to Little Eaton, on which four horses hauled eight trucks with wooden wheels, laden with coal. For over a century until its closure in 1908 villagers saw these coal trains being hauled along the 'gang railway' to be unloaded onto barges at the Derby canal wharf in Little Eaton. In winter ice-breakers were regularly needed when the canal froze; the story goes that one Little Eaton bargee set off for London in bitterly cold weather and that his journey took so long his barge was found to be empty on arrival because he had used his load of coal to keep warm.

The canal clockhouse, standing defiantly amidst 20th century industrial units, is the only reminder of past transport; the clock still ticks and is wound daily by tenant William Marshall (a condition of his tenancy).

Mills also brought prosperity to the village; the old bleach mill on Mill Green, where tape was bleached as early as 1636, and Peckwash paper mill. The latter was recorded in 1851 as one of the greatest paper mills in the world. Peckwash Mill chimney is still an industrial landmark beside the Derwent, but it hasn't smoked since 1905 when an injunction was obtained against it emitting smoke. Paper making then moved to Brooke Mill in the village centre.

The Little Eaton hermit, Alice Grace, was born in Derby in 1867 and came to Little Eaton with her parents around 1888 to live in a cottage (now demolished) on the 'gang road' behind the Queen's Head public house. After the death of her parents, Alice was evicted for non-payment of rent and until 1908 spent her time lodging in sheds, barns and disused buildings, until finally residing in her famous box homes at the pinfold on Th' Back o' the Winns in Coxbench Wood. The last 19 years of her life were spent in the Union Workhouse at Shardlow where she was forcibly taken for her own good after spending some 20 years as a hermit. Alice died in 1927 and is buried in the churchyard behind the church hall although there is no stone to her memory.

During this period the working classes were beginning to have spare time, and Little Eaton became a favourite resort; in fact it could have been called the Matlock of that era. A train trip or a twopenny canal ride to the woods, quarries and tearooms were popular Sunday and Bank Holiday outings and Alice Grace became extremely well known, which resulted in many postcard views of her.

Modern housing has been slotted in where cottages once stood, and meadows and hedgerows have given way to housing developments thus increasing the population. Yet the community spirit still prevails and is demonstrated on Sports Day, organised by the Sports Day and Carnival Committee, and held on the first Saturday in July for almost 70 years.

Longford ✍

Longford lies at the centre of a triangle joining the towns of Ashbourne, Derby and Uttoxeter. It is situated on an old Roman road, Long Lane, which joined the camps of Derby and Rocester. The village consists of scattered homes and farms, described by planners as a linear layout.

At one end of the village is St Chad's church, set in magnificent lime trees, Longford Hall, cottages and farm buildings. Sir Nicholas de

Longford settled here in the 12th century and the church was built at this time. It still has its Norman arches with extensions added in the 15th century. There are effigies in the church of three de Longfords in their Crusader's armour and the last of the de Longfords and his lady in 16th century costume. As you leave the public road to the right you can just see what remains of the almshouses.

The original Hall was rebuilt in the 16th century and extended 200 years later. In 1942 a fire caused serious damage and it lost its top floor, but was otherwise restored. The Cokes, related to the Earls of Leicester, took over the estate after the de Longfords, and they owned it until the beginning of the 20th century.

In the village is the Pump House, on the corner of Long Lane, which was once the main source of water for the village. It has also been a school, a canteen and a reading room. In 1973 it was given to the WI by the Manners family.

There is still a village school in Longford and children come from the parish, comprising Hollington, Alkmonton and Rodsley. It was originally built by the Coke family and there is an Education Charity set up by Dame Katherine Coke which gives grants to young people to help in their careers.

A mill was built along the road in the 11th century and there is still one there which is used as a private home, but this was built in 1837 by Arkwright. It was in working order until 1956 but the machinery has now been handed over to the Arkwright Society in Cromford.

Opposite the mill is the first cheese factory built in England in 1870 by a Dutch-American named Cornelius Schermerhorn, with local support, including Lord Vernon and the Coke family. It is a wooden structure and it is boarded outside and plastered inside with an open space between for the circulation of air. The factory was a co-operative and produced 20 cheeses a day and butter. It was eventually overcome by competition from imported cheeses and larger factories and is now a farm store.

There is still a post office/shop in the village and a pub called the Ostrich. Its name is taken from one of the figures in the Coke coat of arms. The village thrives – it is now a mixed community; there are still many farms but Longford is not so dependent now on agriculture for its survival.

Loscoe ✒

Loscoe is situated between Heanor and Ripley, and, according to the Assize Roll of 1281, was originally called Loftskov. Earlier this century it was a small pretty village surrounded by fields, woods, natural wildlife and lovely walks, some of which still exist today.

The main industry was coal mining, with three collieries, Old Loscoe, Ormonde and Bailey Brook, all of which have now closed. Before the mines opened there was an ironworks near Loscoe dam. The road leading to the ironworks is now called, appropriately Furnace Lane. The cottage at the dam is very old. A Mr Gillot, who lived there, had the responsibility of looking after the dam and the woodland for a large landowner. There was a boat that could be hired for a small fee and, when it was frozen in winter, skaters regularly enjoyed skating on the dam during the cold winter months.

There are still a few old buildings left in Loscoe. The Baptist church was built in 1864 on the site of an older place of worship, dated 1722. A new Church of England church was built in 1937 on land given by the squire of Loscoe.

At the top of Furnace Lane, there once stood a very old building called the Golden Ball, probably built in the early 1600s which was a public house and coaching inn. The building was demolished and a Memorial Garden was made in honour of those killed in the Second World War. Recently the garden has been made smaller and a new block of flats built. The memorial garden is still used for friends to meet, particularly the elderly residents of the flats.

Loscoe hasn't been without its eccentrics; for instance, the old postmistress. In the days before the Second World War the post office with its thatched roof and stable-type doors was in the middle of the village. The thatch has now gone but the cottage is still there, although the post office is now in another part of the village. On the upper half of the old post office door was a large wooden knocker which you would bang to gain the postmistress's attention. The old lady, with white hair and piercing eyes, would open the door, after moving a couple of bolts to let you in. It was rather dark, but very clean, the smell of paraffin and vinegar which was in a barrel met you as you entered. All she said was 'What do you want?' and, knocking at the knees, you would ask for a penny stamp, or perhaps a pennyworth of yeast, and almost fall over yourself to get out!

On the opposite side of the road to the playing field was a field belonging to Granfield Farm which extended to where the Loscoe Welfare stands today. The cart road from the house to the road was lined with quite a few walnut trees. Houses were later built here, in 1927 the vicarage was erected and a bowling green nearby was used regularly by the local community.

Denby Lane in the village has not changed much on the side where the school stands but the opposite side was once all fields. There were lovely oak trees and walks over the 'Dumbles' to Smalley and Denby. The present homes were built in these fields just over 30 years ago and the other part of the estate some 40 years ago.

Lower Hartshay 🎋

Old maps of the Ripley/Pentrich area show that the Roman Rykneld Street passed through Lower Hartshay to a Roman garrison at Pentrich. Today two old trees standing by the footpath to Pentrich mark the route.

The Hartshay brook flowed between two heavily wooded hills on which stood the manors of Ripilie and Pentric, to join the river Amber at Buckland Hollow. Three mills were sited on the brook, which was described as the workhouse of Pentrich/Ripley cornmilling. The area was Royal Forest and deer hunting was common. The names of Hartshay and Buckland were from the forest and the deer.

The Cromford – Langley mill canal brought new life to the area. Started in 1791 by William Jessop and his team of navvies, it passed through Lower Hartshay and under the 3,063 yard Butterley Tunnel to Golden Valley to join the Erewash Canal at Langley mill. Goods and minerals were transported along the whole length of the canal until the 1890s when the tunnel collapsed and was closed.

The Hartshay and Pentrich collieries provided work for the community and beyond. Coal was brought down from the Hartshay colliery on a narrow gauge line to the canal wharf. Many a child has stood on the footbridge watching the trucks pass underneath. There were spillages when loading the barges and the womenfolk would be out with their buckets. At a wharf further along the canal, trucks were unloaded from the Pentrich colliery.

The Cromford – Langley Mill turnpike road, later the A6610, was built around the time of the canal. It passed through the village and up the notoriously steep Hartshay Hill into Ripley – a difficult climb for the horse pulling his load and often impassable in bad weather. When the first buses ran in the 1920s many failed to make the steep gradient and passengers had to get out and walk. On descent brakes would fail and there were accidents.

The Ambergate – Pye Bridge railway built in 1875 gradually took over the role of the canal. It passed along the boundary of the village and mineral lines connected it to both collieries. It also provided a passenger service linking the London – Manchester line at Ambergate with Nottingham.

The village once boasted four pubs; the Wilmot Arms has been demolished and the Queen's Head is now a private dwelling, only the Gate inn and George inn remain. When the canal was in full swing they opened all hours providing refreshment for the bargees and thirsty miners.

There were several shops in the village, the last to close being the general shop and post office in 1966 when the owners retired. In the 1850s a tobacco factory operated next to the shop. A brass foundry stood on the site of the present recreation ground. The tall chimney was demolished in 1900, and many pieces of brass have been found in the area.

Great changes have taken place over the years. The mines and spoil heaps have disappeared. The mineral and railways lines have all gone. The A38 Ripley bypass cuts off the Hartshay Hill and access to the village is from a new stretch of the Ripley – Ambergate road.

Mackworth & Markeaton 🌿

Just off the main Derby to Ashbourne road, two lanes run down to the villages of Mackworth and Markeaton, which are linked through historical events and their geographical positions. The busy A52 straddles an old Roman road, originally constructed to take the traffic from Rocester, through Alkmonton, to Derby. This road probably served Saxon settlers, who developed this area at a later date.

In the 14th century the local Touchet family were linked through marriage to the Audley family. About the same time, Lord Audley, acting in the service of the Black Prince at the Battle of Poitiers, was so indebted to one of his esquires, he rewarded him with a gift of land at Mackworth. Styling himself 'de Mackworth' he had a castle built in the village, of which only the south gateway now remains.

The Hall at Markeaton was acquired by the town and demolished in 1964 because of its deterioration. Now, only the orangery and a few outbuildings remain, but the gardens and park are beautifully maintained for the enjoyment of the general public.

One church has served the villages of Mackworth and Markeaton since Domesday times, and although there may have been a separate church at Markeaton, its site is unknown. The present church of All Saints was probably built on the site of a former place of worship, and lies on the course of the Roman road. The tower was probably built for defence and is of a design rare in ecclesiastical architecture, having no outside door, slots in the stonework for barricading a door, and with crossbow loopholes on three sides. There are several interesting tombs of members of the Touchet and Mundy families, the earliest commemorating Thomas Touchet (rector 1381–1409).

The beautiful old church stands back from the lane in the most tranquil of settings, and is approached through a gate and by following the field path. A gate in the field-hedge indicates the direction the path continues to take for about a mile, until it joins Markeaton Lane. Ahead on the line of the Roman road, lies the tiny hamlet of Markeaton clustered around the park gates. The cottage which was once the blacksmith's shop, and now known as The Old Forge, is at least 300 years old, and looks across to a nursery garden and to a neatly preserved cottage. This was once the village alehouse, named after two racehorses, Nimrod and Hotspur.

Mackworth Castle

Returning along the full length of Markeaton Lane, Derby Crematorium in its wooded setting stands to one side, on the other is the Old School House.

On the southern side of the A52 lies Mackworth estate. Before 1950, this was mainly land of Humbeton Farm, of medieval origin, and a golf course, of which the club house still remains. The estate is now a busy housing complex with a population of several thousand. The main thoroughfare is Prince Charles Avenue, in recognition of the Royal birth in 1948. All the other roadways are named after districts of London.

Mapperley

Mapperley is a small village which stands on the edge of Shipley Country Park. It is thought that the name derived from the number of maple trees which grew in the district. A copy of a charter dated 1267, granting the village a fair and market, can be seen in the library at Ilkeston.

Holy Trinity church can be seen as you enter the village on the right at

143

the top of the hill. It was erected in 1851, but was badly affected by mining subsidence in 1964 causing it to close for rebuilding on more modern lines, reopening on 2nd April 1966. Lychgates were built at the entrance to the churchyard in 1922 as a memorial to the fallen of the First World War. Through these gates in springtime can be seen a carpet of crocuses and snowdrops.

A Methodist chapel was built in 1874 and opened on the 8th June 1875. People still talk of the Good Friday Teas, when Methodists from all over the district gathered and a special speaker was always invited. Sadly, the congregations became depleted and the building was sold in 1969 and is now a private house.

Mapperley colliery provided work for many of the men until it closed in 1966. A mystery that still surrounds the pit is the disappearance of Thomas Severn on 5th June 1918, never to be seen again. Much speculation has always surrounded this event.

The Old Black Horse is the remaining public house in the village. The other one, known locally as the 'Candle Stick', closed several years ago due to a methane gas leak at the property.

The only development in the village has been the building of Scandinavian houses in 1946, and in more recent years bungalows for the elderly and a few councils houses have been erected.

Mapperley was a little known village until part of Shipley Park was developed as the American Adventure Theme Park. Whilst this was welcomed by some, many preferred the Park as it was with its abundance of wildlife and quiet walks.

Marston Montgomery 🌿

Marston Montgomery takes its name from the Montgomery family who owned the lands of both Marston and the neighbouring village of Cubley at the time of the Domesday Book, and this distinguished it from Marston-on-Dove, only a dozen miles away.

The small village lies off the main road and so is lucky to avoid through traffic. Many houses have attractive views across pastureland towards the Weaver hills in Staffordshire. It is regarded as a pleasant spot, particularly in the spring when the damson blossom is out, making a froth of white all along the narrow lanes. There is a church, school, post office, village hall and public house, all of which help to give a feeling of community spirit. Once mainly a farming village, now few of its residents are involved in farming. A number of new homes have been built during the past 15 years, but not so many as to swamp the older ones. Several of the new dwellings are converted barns and other agricultural buildings. One was a creamery where cheese was made until early this century, taking milk from the local farms, and it continued to provide a meeting place for village activities before the Second World

War. Another new home was formerly the smithy, horses being brought for shoeing from many miles around until about 30 years ago.

The church of St Giles is said to have the oldest ecclesiastical masonry in Derbyshire, with a Norman font and Saxon and Norman arches, but much of it was rebuilt in the 19th century. It has a low sloping roof and a bellcote, and nestles into its surroundings with some old tombs and an ancient yew. The organ was enlarged in 1894 and was played for many years by a resident of the village, who retired from the job only in 1990 at the age of 95.

At one time there were four public houses in the parish, but now there is only one. The Crown inn has recently been enlarged and refurbished, making it a comfortable place for both locals and visitors to call in at. Perhaps the most notable architecture in the village itself is the manor house, an impressive black and white 17th century house with a massive external chimney stack. There is also a fine Georgian-fronted house in the village, the rear part being a century older. But probably the oldest house is in the attached hamlet of Waldley. This is a farmhouse with the date of 1632 engraved in the timber, though parts are believed to date from 1512. In fact the village is surrounded entirely by dairy farms, several with interesting 17th century houses.

The small school celebrated its centenary in 1972, and takes children from Cubley as well as Marston. It is at the centre of the village; indeed school, village hall, church, post office and pub are all within 200 yards of each other.

In 1987 the Derbyshire tradition of well-dressing was revived in Marston Montgomery, after a lapse of 49 years. This was done to celebrate the 50th anniversary of the erection of the village hall, called the Coronation Hall as it was put up in King George VI's Coronation year.

Marston on Dove

Marston on Dove is a hamlet lying nine miles south-west of Derby and two miles north-east of Tutbury.

Evidence from the site of the present parish church of St Mary, together with the name which means 'marsh settlement', suggests that the original community was Saxon in origin. It lay on a loop of the river Dove which was cut off when the Derby to Crewe railway line was built in the middle of the 19th century. A tendency to flooding seems to have given the impetus for another settlement to be founded on higher ground nearby at Hilton but despite this, the parish church has remained at Marston. It is believed to have the oldest bell in Derbyshire – cast by John de Stafford of Leicester in 1360.

In the Domesday Book, the manor is mentioned as being under the control of the monks of Tutbury, although Henry de Ferrers was the area's new Norman master.

The church organ was bought from Sudbury Hall in November 1827 at a cost of just over £74 and is the only one the church ever possessed. Before this, singers were accompanied by an orchestra of brass, reed and string instruments.

In the 1970s a new vicarage was built at Hilton and the original building in Marston became a private house which, together with three farms and five cottages, make up the present day hamlet.

Matlock

The Domesday Book recorded old Matlock as 'Meslach', one of six hamlets forming part of the large manor of Metesford, named after Matlock's original ford. Meslach became Matlac, Matloc and finally Matlock, meaning 'an oak where was held the local moot or parliament'.

During the Second World War a German plane, thought to be lightening its load to aid its escape over the hills, peppered this area with tracer bullets and shells. RAF planes often screech through here now, their pilots practising flying through the valley, sometimes so low that from high ground, it is even possible to look down on them.

It is a steep climb up Bank Road and Rutland Street – unfortunately the last tram has left. Cable-hauled and the steepest tramway on a public highway anywhere in the world, trams ran safely for 34 years, until 1927. One tramcar, soon pensioned off, had seats running not from side to side, but lengthways. Try as they may, passengers simply could not avoid sliding downhill again! Children adored the trams. They took free rides, played a version of 'Pooh sticks' in the rain-filled wheel grooves, and what better in wintertime than to hitch your sledge to the rear of an ascending tram, for a leisurely return to the top of 'the slopes'.

The tramway was built when the railway, together with plentiful spring water, had brought prosperity, fine shops, new homes and fresh employment to the area. There were old hydros all around, more than 20 operating at the turn of the century.

Local mill owner John Smedley spearheaded the growth of hydrotherapy in Matlock. His 'mild water cure' used all manner of showers, bathing contraptions, bandages and towels, together with copious amounts of spring water at varying temperatures. 'Nay, it's not to drink – ay, tha's reet now – tha sits int Sitz bath'. His own purpose-built palace was the hydro, famous nationally and internationally, visitors coming to 'take the cure', or simply to be cosseted in his opulent surroundings. Noel Coward and novelist John Wyndham came. Dame Clara, mother of Ivor Novello, lived there. At afternoon tea in the Winter Garden, Violet Carson played the piano.

Most local children today eventually attend the new comprehensive school, but there are fond memories of Wyvern House Hydro, which became the Ernest Bailey grammar school. Ernest Bailey, benefactor, had many mills. One day he moved out of his home and 34 boys moved in. Over almost 40 years, 450 of 'Bailey's Boys', waifs and strays, were fed, clothed and educated, many eventually finding work in his mills. The house carried on as a children's home; nursery nurses came to train there and were a familiar sight with their huge prams and tiny charges.

Water has many times been the bringer of disaster; hopefully the modern flood prevention/containment scheme will change all that, when heavy snow and a quick thaw always meant anxious times.

Matlock Bath

Matlock Bath's distinctive name is due to the discovery of thermal water, which led to the formation of baths. These springs contain lime and salt solutions. Over many years the solution hardened to form beautiful open-work forms of rock. Spread over the ground for a third of a mile, beds from one ft to 20 ft deep became known as tufa, or to locals as marl. Objects left in the water were 'petrified' or turned to stone. The rock was quarried and sold all over the world for rock gardens. When the road known as Temple Walk was cut, the antlers of a moose were found embedded in the rock and they were sent to the British Museum.

In 1696 a Bath was formed in the tufa, the waters being thought beneficial not only to drink but also in which to bathe. This led to the first commercial bath being built in 1698 and was the main reason for people visiting the locality. The Wishing Well built from tufa can still be seen, with its date '1696' above, within the Temple Road car park. The water is piped under the car park and reappears to tumble over the rocks into a pool. For generations youngsters with jam jars tied with string have fished for tadpoles and minnows in its warm waters.

The Old Bath Hotel (and the Royal Hotel built later on the same site) was frequented by the country's elite and famous authors, poets and artists found inspiration there. Set in the hillside above this hotel was the Royal Pavilion, a palatial building with its glass frontage and the setting for lavish entertainment. What a sight it must have been lighting up the valley and with the music echoing around. Sadly these buildings have long since disappeared and the sites are now occupied by a Theme Park and car parking to cater for today's tourists.

The white edifice on the Heights of Abraham overlooking the valley has enticed visitors for over a century to wend their way up the steep wooded hillside to venture into the depths of the Masson and Rutland Caverns (lead mines once worked by the Romans) and still fascinating the curious. Today visitors are whisked through the air by cable car from the banks of the river Derwent to the Victoria Tower, but from these heights and looking along the hillside, one's imagination can easily slip back to the days of the coach and horses bringing the gentry to take the waters.

Over the years, for the enjoyment of residents and visitors, enthusiastic bands of locals organised events such as the Floral Fete, the Carnival, the Music Festival, the Miss Derbyshire Contest and the Venetian Fete. Sadly, the latter is the only survivor. The Venetian Fete originated as a one-night event in 1887 to celebrate Queen Victoria's Jubilee. There was a procession of decorated boats and Chinese lanterns were hung in the trees. That same year the Jubilee Bridge was erected as a lasting memorial. A few years later the Venetian Fete became an annual event and in those early days the boats and set pieces were illuminated by candles in jars lit with tapers by village youngsters.

The heyday of Matlock Bath came with the advent of the railway in 1849. Being a cheap form of travel it brought in thousands more visitors. Today people have their own transport and although the line is still open, the station built in the style of a Swiss chalet is now a wildlife centre.

Melbourne & King's Newton

Situated in the south of the county, eight miles from Derby, Melbourne contains within its parish boundaries the picturesque village of King's Newton. Having around 4,000 inhabitants, it is known today chiefly for its market gardening and the manufacture of shoes, but in the Middle Ages it was a place of some considerable importance, to which the size of the church and castle bore witness. The earliest historical mention of Melbourne is in the Domesday Book. Several theories exist regarding the derivation of its name, but the most popularly held belief is that it came from the presence of a mill by its stream (burn) – Mileburne.

The church of St Michael with St Mary, believed to be on the site of an earlier Anglo-Saxon building, is acknowledged to be one of the finest examples of Norman architecture to be found in a parish church, and visitors are often curious to know why such a magnificent building should be found in a relatively small Derbyshire village. The fact is that in the middle of the 12th century, when the church was built, the river Trent formed the boundary between the civilised south of the country and the more barbaric north. In 1133 Henry I granted 'the rectory of Melbourne, together with the manor' to Adelulph, first Bishop of Carlisle, so that he had a refuge to which he could retreat, out of reach of the marauding Scots. This proved to be a wise precaution because, within three years of taking office, the Bishop had to flee Carlisle and from then on conducted a great deal of his business from Melbourne.

The great castle was visited by King John on several occasions when he came to hunt in the royal park, and a drawing of 1602 shows it with many turrets and chimneys. However, little remains of the castle today, above ground, and what there is lies within a private property. In contrast, Melbourne Hall is very well-preserved and is open to the public each year for the month of August (excluding Mondays but including the Bank Holiday). It was built as a rectory for the Bishops of Carlisle, was leased from the Bishops in 1628 by Sir John Coke whose family later

The Pool at Melbourne

acquired the freehold, and subsequent generations of the family have altered and enlarged the Hall. The present residents are Lord and Lady Ralph Kerr, son and daughter-in-law of the 12th Marquis of Lothian.

One man who has had a lasting influence, both during and since his lifetime, was born of humble parents in Quick Close, Melbourne. In 1841 a temperance meeting was to be held in Loughborough and he arranged for the Midland Railway to run an excursion train, carrying 570 people from Leicester and back for one shilling per person. From this he began to arrange excursions for pleasure, taking a percentage of the sale of the railway tickets. And so began a world-wide travel business: the man's name – Thomas Cook.

The Quick Close house has now been demolished but at the top of High Street, close to the site of his birth, stands a row of 14 cottages built in 1891 by Thomas Cook, to be occupied by 'poor and deserving persons belonging to the general Baptist denomination'.

Like Melbourne, King's Newton has Saxon origins. Its principal building is the Hall, built in 1910 by Cecil Paget in the style of the

Elizabethan Hall on the same site which had been destroyed by fire in 1859.

Across the road from the Hall stands the Hardinge Arms, and it was from here that one William Taylor sold his home-brewed ale to the local people. Finding an apple seedling growing in the thatch of his roof he decided it was worth removing it carefully and growing it in his garden. It proved to be a winner and, increasing his stock by budding and grafting, he introduced the 'Newton Wonder' to the horticultural world.

Steeped in history as Melbourne and King's Newton are, it would be very wrong to imply that the community lives in the past. There are many flourishing societies and clubs, an active Community Care group providing help and transport to the sick and disabled, and each summer a large fete and carnival, with procession of decorated floats, raises considerable sums of money for local charities.

Mickleover 🦢

This Saxon village was originally called Ufna meaning high bank, later becoming Mickle Ulfa to distinguish it from another village on a smaller bank.

In 1556 Joan Waste is said to have been tried under the Witchcraft Act for saying that the Communion was only symbolic and that the bread and wine did not become the body and blood of Christ. She was the blind daughter of a baker and was burned to death at the corner of Chain Lane.

Henry VIII gave the manor house to his Secretary, Sir William Paget, and it was later given by Elizabeth I to George Travell. In 1648 Edward Wilmot bought the estate but sold it in the 18th century to the Newton family, who completely rebuilt it. The Newton family lived there into the 20th century when it became a boarding school, before being annexed to Pastures Hospital.

The oldest building in the village must be the Old Hall. It is a beautiful and well preserved property with a date over the porch, although it is thought this is the date of alterations. A captain in Cromwell's army is believed to have owned it and Oliver Cromwell is thought to have stayed there when he stormed Tutbury Castle.

The first record of schooling in the village was in 1765 and was probably held in the church. Schooling was given in other locations over the years before in 1881 the junior school on Uttoxeter Road was opened. Recent years have seen the building of housing estates around the village with new schools being built. The old school has become a community centre with many varied activities taking place there.

All Saints' church was built between 1310 and 1330, an earlier church on the site having been destroyed by fire. The church has been renovated over the years, with major work taking place in 1858 when a Victorian font was installed. However, in 1945 the 14th century font was found and is used to this day. As well as All Saints' there is the Anglican St John's built in the 1960s, the Catholic church of Our Lady of Lourdes and the Methodist chapel on Station Road.

Mickleover, even though it is an urban mass of modern houses, is still known as the village. The old market place still remains, and the green, the Hollow and Orchard Street still give the area around The Square lots of character. Western Road, once known as Poke Lane, still has two of the original cottages. Although Mickleover lacks many amenities, it is surrounded by fields and farm land.

Middleton by Wirksworth

Middleton, meaning Middle Town, is a small industrial village situated between Wirksworth and Winster, and is about 1,000 ft above sea level. In earlier years it was noted for a place of correction for lead miners, and Jail Yard still remains.

One notable character was George Buxton; though living in humble circumstances, he had great musical talents both as a performer and composer. His works were composed of psalms and hymn tunes, etc. A headstone in Wirksworth churchyard records his death at the age of 67.

D.H. Lawrence spent one year at Mountain Cottage overlooking Via Gellia. In his book *The Virgin and the Gypsy* Woodlinkin was based on Middleton by Wirksworth.

The Congregational church is the most important building. It was built by Jonathon Scott who was the minister of Glenorchy chapel at Matlock Bath, as the lead miners had no place of worship. In 1785 the Congregational church at Northampton was altered and enlarged, and the pulpit and reading desk of the famous Dr Dodderidge came to Middleton, where the pulpit still remains. There are two other chapels and the parish church of Holy Trinity.

At Middleton Top there is the well known Engine House, an industrial monument built in 1829 to haul waggons up the 708 yards long, 1 in 8¼ gradient incline. The railway closed 134 years later but is now preserved by Derbyshire County Council – the engine being renovated by the Derbyshire Archaeological Society. The main occupations were lead mining and quarrying for the men, some of the women working at Masson Mill about two miles away.

A Hall is said to have existed at the top of the village and nearby a barn where cocks were trained in the brutal sport of cock fighting.

There are a number of stories told. One day, a farmer and his servants were in the harvest field, leaving his wife and infant son at home, when a strange phenomenon occurred. The infant was asleep in his cradle and his mother left him for a moment. On returning she exclaimed 'Oh God, my child has changed!' No-one knows if the child was substituted for another, or whether it was the work of the fairies, but he grew up to be a comely man and was known as Fairy Robert. When 90 years had silvered his locks, he still had the bloom of youth on his cheeks.

When there were very few taps in the village, people collected water from the Basin. Women assembled there with their cans. Often there were quarrels, but there was an individual who had his eye on these encounters, and he assumed the right to be King or Emperor over the water. He was known as Old Tom Bevy. He would leave his house at 2 am and remain until 9 am sitting on a three-legged stool, and would not allow anyone to have more than one can until all had been served. There was a woman who helped Tom Bevy. She considered herself Prime Minister and was known as 'Polly Wag'. She would say 'Na ya two hussies, yon big fahling aht abaht that drop o' watter. Yo shanner ha'it – I'll tak it mysen.' Many surnames were the same, mainly Spencer, Doxey and Slack, most of them having family nicknames, some of which remain to this day.

In those days Middleton was a self-sufficient village, nearly every other building a shop or business of some kind. Social life revolved round the churches. There was little money but good fellowship, and above all, good family life.

Middleton-by-Youlgreave ✺

This is a small hamlet nestling above the river Bradford about a mile from Youlgreave. There are two large houses in Middleton, Lomberdale and Middleton Hall, where one of the village's most famous eccentrics lived.

Squire Bateman lived during the late 1700s/early 1800s and many stories are told about him. He was a public benefactor, an historian, an archaeologist and perhaps most endearing, he was the owner of a fire tender! He had his own fire engine and it was pulled by a magnificent team of matched greys. It is said that he was responsible for comfrey being planted down in Middleton Dale as this plant is very good for horses.

On one occasion there was a fire in Matlock at the Olde English Hotel and Squire Bateman set out to deal with it. On his arrival he started to fight the fire, when up dashed the Matlock Fire Engine. Unfortunately, they had forgotten their spare hose and applied to the Squire for the loan of his. This request was curtly refused as he said this was *his* fire and *he* would deal with it!

The Post Office at Milford

Milford & Makeney

In olden days, Milford and Makeney were nothing more than part of a large game forest, where the lords of the manor of Beaurepaire (Belper) shot a deer or three when they felt in the mood.

The fast flowing Derwent gave a few far-sighted men the idea that those waters could be utilised. In time an iron foundry and a flour mill were set up on its banks and the fertile valley land began to be farmed.

Then along came a certain Jedediah Strutt who built a huge factory, the machinery of which was driven by the same fast-flowing river. Of course, this was no good without people, and there was nowhere for people to live. So he built himself Milford, or most of it. And people came from miles around because he had built good houses.

Time went by and cotton boomed and cotton slumped. And cotton boomed and cotton slumped again. And one day it slumped never to recover its former glory. These were bad days indeed for poor Milford and Makeney. The factory closed. The shops closed. Many young people of the once thriving villages moved away.

The old house of the builder of Milford was turned into homes for the elderly as was the mansion in Makeney which had belonged to one of his descendants.

Milford had been known as Treacle City in days of yore. The story goes that a tub of treacle being delivered to one of the many shops burst open when it 'fell off a lorry' and the inhabitants gathered like bees round a honey pot to scoop it into any old containers but now that Milford was on the map again, the locals decided that in no way were they going to let the legend die.

Now every year the villages of Milford and Makeney go slightly mad, dress up in outlandish gear – anything from a Viking to a Duck or a Robin Hood – and, accompanied by a band, tour the village with a maypole, decked in all its glory, which the children dance around. Not to be outdone, the grown-ups display their skill at morris dancing and the day ends at the village school with all the fun of the fete. The Hollybush, the King William, the Strutt Arms and the New Inn do not complain about their trade on that day.

Millers Dale

Millers Dale is a hamlet in the parish of Tideswell. It stands on the left-hand bank of the river Wye, two miles from Tideswell and eight from Buxton, sharing its name with the dale in which it lies.

During medieval times two corn mills were built, the river powering their machinery. Ancient upland trackways, which converged in the dale, gave the mills their names. The Wormhill mill, probably the older of the two, stood in the upper reach of the Wye, with the Tideswell mill lower down.

In recent times the flour mill has undergone some alteration and change of use, to a craft supply centre, with world-wide connections. Twenty years ago the derelict Tideswell mill was demolished, making a site for a pumping station feeding the Chapel-en-le-Frith area. Stone from the original walls was used to house the bore-hole and its machinery. The 150 year old water wheel was restored and placed adjacent to the pumping station. Stone walls enclose the whole site.

Closure of the quarries and railway in 1967 changed life considerably. The post office, which was in the booking office closed, the stationmaster being also the postmaster. The last postman covered a round of twelve miles on foot and cycle. He did this as a temporary job for 25 years, having originally retired as a gardener. Today the Peak Rail Society has high hopes of opening a single-track line to Matlock. This would be an added attraction for visitors to the Peak District.

Richness of flora and fauna along the dale sides has resulted in the area being designated a Site of Special Scientific Interest. The reserve, which is managed by the Derbyshire Wildlife Trust, is part of a disused limestone quarry.

Due to industrial expansion and development of the railways, a growing population needed new homes, which the Dakins supplied, and church authorities cared for their religious and social needs. On land adjacent to the 1740 House, one of the three oldest buildings in the hamlet, the School Church of St Anne was built. Designed by Canon Samuel Andrew, vicar and rural dean of Tideswell, St Anne's is of Victorian Gothic style seating a congregation of 100. Examples of carving executed by Advent Hunstone, a noted ecclesiastical wood-carver of Tideswell, enhance the furnishings.

In the past, the church and public houses were centres of activities. Harvest Festivals, with the sale afterwards in the public house, were supported by all the village, as was the unique event in 1952, when the railway authorities allowed a restaurant car and coach to be shunted into a siding so that the whole village could partake of a celebratory Coronation meal.

Milton 🍃

Milton – a dot on the map, a village sign on an empty road, a curving street of assorted houses, with two pubs and a village hall but no church. A hamlet of some 60 dwellings, Milton is to be found in the Trent valley, between the village of Repton (ancient capital of Mercia) a mile to the north-west, and Ticknall two miles to the south-east. It would seem that little has changed in 900 years.

Having been owned by several local influential families, Milton passed in 1602 to Thomas Burdett, who came from Bramcote, near Nuneaton, to marry a local heiress. (This may explain why the property now known as the Coach House inn was previously called Bramcote Lodge.) His descendant, Sir Francis Burdett built St Saviour's church on his estate at Foremarke in 1662. Milton still retains a link with Foremarke church, many villagers regarding it as their parish church. The Burdett Foremark estate sold out to the Prudential Assurance Co in 1943, and Prudential then sold to the Church Commissioners, who still own much of the land around Milton today.

The common denominator of Milton's history was agriculture – milk and arable farming. John Farey, in his *General View of Agriculture*, published in 1817, says that sheepfarming was prevalent at that time. He also remarked on the number of dovecotes or pigeon houses in Milton, amongst only 16 in the whole of Derbyshire. One of these dovecotes or pigeon houses is still in existence on a three-storey barn at Brook Farm, which has for some years, together with the farm houses and other substantial properties, been a listed building. The dovecote is empty but its weathervane still provides a clear indication of wind direction to the local inhabitants.

Perusal of old county directories and census returns gives some idea of

155

the life of the village over the years. In 1827 there was a shopkeeper, a wheelwright, a corn miller and the proprietress of a ladies' boarding school. By 1857, the shopkeeper, cornmiller and school had been joined by a butcher, a tinner and brazier, a carpenter, and a beerhouse as well as the Swan inn. The 1881 census shows Milton consisted of 39 households, 194 people. There were seven farms, one inn, a shop (and four dressmakers!). The major occupation was that of farm labourer.

Milton's only claims to historical or archaeological interest are the Ice Age stone outside one of the farms, and a Roman coin found in 1934. The stone stands just beyond the post box and the red telephone box and is believed to have been brought down in the last Ice Age.

As recently as the mid 1950s, Milton was still predominantly agricultural, its population comprising farmers, farm workers, estate workers and their families. Today agriculture is no longer the main occupation, with only two working farms and one resident farm worker among the population of approximately 150 people. The old mission room which was provided by the Burdett family is now the village hall. Like many other villages and hamlets, Milton has become a commuter community.

Morley

Morley is situated approximately five miles north-east of the city of Derby on the A608 and is essentially a rural area with four working farms, Broomfield Agricultural College and a newly constructed golf course. It is mentioned in the Domesday Book and the name is derived from a meadow on the moor. The village is comprised of a series of detached settlements: Brackley Gate and The Croft, Almshouses Lane, The Smithy and Brick Kiln Lane, and the Church Lane area.

The name Brackley Gate may originate from the Brackley family of Horsley Park Gate who lived there in the 17th century. This area includes disused stone quarries which were a source of employment for Morley men until about 1917. Brackley Gate's elevated position affords panoramic views over undulating country to the foothills of the Pennines.

The Croft is an unadopted road, originally leading to Moor Farm, at the end of which is a cluster of 17th and 18th century cottages.

The 17th century almshouses in Almshouses Lane, built with monies provided by Jacinth Sitwell, lord of the manor of Morley, consisted of six dwellings under one roof, each containing two rooms, half for the poor of Morley and half for the Smalley parishioners. They were originally intended for 'six poor, lame or impotent men'. The Lane also includes several farmworkers' cottages and a small stone-built Methodist chapel. The Lane lies on the route of the ancient Portway which continues as a footpath over the fields towards St Matthew's church.

Halfway between the two, the track deviates to avoid Morley's mysterious mound. Several eminent historians have put forward theories as to its original purpose; namely, a defensive position, an obstruction of the

Portway to encourage new roads to be built or the possible site of the 'Morlestone' mentioned in 1086 and still a meeting place in 1300. The mound is now covered by trees and stands about 20 ft high topped by a five ft diameter platform and was once surrounded by a moat.

The Smithy, as its name implies, was the area where the blacksmith plied his trade in what is now the Three Horse Shoes public house. His income was derived from both smithying and innkeeping. On the opposite corner of Brick Kiln Lane was a toll bar cottage which was demolished in 1929. Also in this area is Morley primary school built in 1881. The disused brick works on Brick Kiln Lane are now in the keeping of the Derbyshire Wildlife Trust and are an attractive haven for various plants, birds and animals, and managed as a nature reserve.

Church Lane was probably the original centre of Morley as quoted in the Domesday Book. It was here that the lords of the manor of Morley lived. The original Hall no longer exists, the only remaining evidence of this building being an archway inside the churchyard and adjacent to the mausoleum. The present Hall dates from 1837. Also within the church grounds is an old butter cross.

Behind the church stands the tithe barn, which became a regular venue for village festivities including Harvest Suppers, drama productions and dances. Many a village romance blossomed within its ancient walls.

St Matthew's church is a gem of early medieval architecture well worth seeing. It contains supreme examples of medieval windows and tiles which, in all probability, were rescued from the defunct Dale Abbey in the 16th century. The tombs of the Stathums, Sacheverells and Sitwells, erstwhile lords of the manor of Morley, are magnificent examples of their type.

The ancient ceremony of 'beating the bounds' has been reinstituted over the past few years, without the digging of holes into which youths were deposited head first! Now it is just a gentle walk.

Morton

The village of Morton is situated about one mile from the main Derby – Chesterfield road. Morton itself is a small village of just over 1,500 inhabitants, the oldest part clustering around the church, whilst new housing estates have sprung up on the Stretton Road, Evershill Lane and Pilsley Road.

The stone building which is now the old school room was erected from voluntary subscriptions and served the village as a school for many years until the present Morton school was built in 1884.

Holy Cross church stands at the top of the village. It has a low church tower capped by eight crocketed pinnacles. In the old part of the village against the churchyard was an ancient pond, filled in in 1950. Trees and shrubs were planted on the site by the Morton Women's Institute in commemoration of the Coronation of Queen Elizabeth II in 1953.

Round the corner, now Church Lane, was the former village inn, the White Horse. The licence was later transferred to Sycamore Farm, and in 1841 this alehouse was open six days a week, the granary used as a club room where weekly meetings were held.

The lime tree planted in front of the Sitwell Arms was to commemorate the marriage of the Prince of Wales in 1863, and the chestnut tree now standing on the triangle was removed from the church yard and replanted there. It has always been a lovely tree, always the first in the village to bud, and to shed its leaves in autumn.

Yew Tree Farm was the residence of the local doctor, Dr Oldham, and the mounting steps for getting on his horse can still be seen inside the former gateway. He was killed by lightning down Higham Lane when returning from a visit in his pony and gig. Yew Tree Farm brings to mind the fact that six or seven yew trees still stand within a three quarter mile radius of the church.

Mosborough ✎

The village of Mosborough had its origins as a Roman settlement and the name is derived from 'Fort on the Moor'.

As a hamlet in the parish of Eckington it was mainly agricultural with a scythe and sickle works. Sites of the cottages of the charcoal burners may still be located.

Its situation in an elevated position in a natural hollow could account for the weather, which seems to be peculiar to Mosborough. Often escaping from the severe elements around us, plants not really recommended for the region grow quite happily.

From vantage points one may see across the countryside 20 miles in one direction and about 30 miles in the other, 17 churches and some quite spectacular views. As a village it has the reputation of having a very friendly atmosphere, though whether this would account for some of the odd characters that there have been over the years it would be difficult to say.

One worthy, Fab Ashley, a poacher who was offered the job of gamekeeper for obvious reasons, has had many stories attributed to him. With his friend Bucket Newton, he stood watching a passing funeral cortege – 'Who's dead?' says Bucket. 'Him in't box' says Fab.

The church started in a dame school, a building still standing as a private dwelling house, dated 1680. The church of St Mark standing today, across the road from the dame school, was built in 1887. It is very well looked after, has an excellent organ and a spectacular brass lectern.

Many small gin pits were sunk in the area and so miners were added to the community. Superstition was rife and any collier on his way to the pit and meeting a woman would be afraid to go further and would turn back towards home, grousing at the woman for being abroad so early.

Mugginton 🌿

Mugginton is predominantly a farming village and is thought to have Saxon origins. It was spelt Muginton in the Domesday Book.

When, a few years ago, Kedleston church was declared redundant, the parishes of Mugginton and Kedleston became a united parish. The parish church of All Saints Mugginton with Kedleston, as it is known, stands on a hill giving extensive views over the surrounding countryside. It is thought that Mugginton has been a site of Christian worship for over 1,000 years. A little remains of the original Saxon building. The present building is mainly 14th and 15th century but the lower part of the tower is Norman. The oldest part of the nave is the west wall in which there is an 11th century window above a late 12th century arch. The hollow yew tree in the churchyard is over 1,000 years old.

There is still a Church of England (Controlled) primary school near to the church. This serves children from a large rural area. The date 1840 is on the outside of the building, but it is thought that the original school was established in 1746 as a church school, funded by charity money given by Samuel and Ann Pole 'for teaching poor children the English language and the catechism of the Church of England'.

One of the houses in the village was formerly a mill where locally grown corn was ground. The former smithy is now used as a garage for a private house, but the bellows and old tools are still there.

The village has local cricket and football pitches situated slightly out of the village, at Mugginton Lane End.

Richard Lees Ltd, manufacturing concrete beams, the Cock inn, a restaurant and public house, local farms and a fishery give local employment. A number of the residents commute to nearby towns.

Netherseale 🌿

It was a mild May evening in 1674 and the members of the two families staying at Netherseale Hall were preparing for a party. Maids hustled and bustled about as they fetched and carried for the ladies of the house, rushing backwards and forwards from one room to another.

Suddenly the house was filled with screams and shrieks of anguish and terror coming from the sitting room where the youngest members were gathered waiting for the party to begin. Imagine the horror when the door was flung open and the young people were seen frantically trying to dowse the flames engulfing two of the girls – their pretty party dresses now ablaze.

The doctor – on the scene almost immediately having been summoned by a distraught servant – sought to bring relief to the unfortunate young ladies. Sadly there was nothing he could do for Miss Isobel and Miss Agnes, the daughters of Mr and Mrs Sergeson.

Later, when Mr and Mrs Sergeson were able to come to terms with the loss of their children, they made a gift of jewellery belonging to Isobel and Agnes to St Peter's church. Arrangements were made for the lovely stones to be set in a Communion Chalice and Plate and these beautiful pieces are still used on special occasions.

Sometime later the Hall was pulled down and the site left to nature. Recently, however, a Leonard Cheshire Home has been built where the Hall once stood – perhaps a very fitting replacement.

Nigel Gresley was the rector of Seales at the time of the fire. He was the father of Sir Nigel Gresley, the famous railway enthusiast who is buried in the old churchyard under an oak tree supposedly a granddaughter tree of the Boscobel Oak, in which Prince Charles hid when escaping from Cromwell and the Roundheads.

Newton 🎕

There is little recorded for Newton until the 16th century, but it is believed coal mining by the 'Bell' principle, where a hole was dug and the coal taken out then infilled from another hole, was taking place in the lands known as 'Dimmy' in the Newtonwood Lane area, Tommy Nooney's in the land between Main Street and the present mineral railway line, and the land at the rear of Red Barn Farm bordering Huthwaite.

In 1554 Lady Scheffielde issued a lease of a pit to Richard Richardson. It is believed this was on the Red Barn Land, where for the first time in this district a footrill type was opened where they went underground and shored up the roof. Richard Richardson was at that time said to be of Newton 'Old Hall', which indicates the Hall was there then. It is believed it was built from local stone at the behest of Elizabeth I for the Earl of Carnarvan, then owner of part of the Blackwell manor estates.

There were five cottages in the 1700's about where the old folk's bungalows are now in Main Street. In one of these lived Jedediah Strutt in 1754, who is reputed to have invented the 'Derby Rib' machine and later joined his brother-in-law at Belper cotton mills.

An old building adjoining the Hall was used as an inn. This was rebuilt in 1916 as a station hotel, it being accepted at the time that the LNER railway which was to be brought from Nottingham to Sheffield would provide a station at the railway bridge in Alfreton Road. The station was in fact eventually built at Tibshelf. The George and Dragon then became a white elephant until about 1920, when a cinema which had been built in Hall Lane started to have variety shows and drama sketches. The artists who were travellers stayed at the hotel.

A colliery sunk at Tibshelf in about 1880 and known as 'Bottom Pit' brought a considerable expansion in the Newton development. Houses were built in Bamford Street and New Street and Sherwood Street to house the influx of miners. In addition there was a brick works and coke ovens.

The closing of the local collieries in the 1930s brought some decline to Newton. Opening of industrial sites in adjoining areas has assisted and during the 1950s expansion of new buildings with an estate of council houses and in 1970s with a private estate, has almost doubled the Newton population.

The LNER railway and Newton station was closed under the Beeching axe but the Newton-Sutton line was retained as a single mineral line.

A one-time occupier of Newton Hall, William Downing, was some-what of an oddity. He is said to have married the sister of his wife when she was on her death bed, but she recovered and it is reported they all lived together. He had both buried in the grounds of the Hall and stated he wished to be buried there. The graves are still there, and rumour has it his wife's ghost still walks.

Newton Solney 🎐

Niwantune, the New Farm, was a small agricultural settlement in the year AD874 when the Danes sailed along the Trent and captured it along with its neighbour, Repton. Since then it has seen a succession of ruling families, possibly the most famous being the de Solneys and latterly the Ratcliffs. Recorded in the Domesday Book as being the property of Henry de Ferrers, Earl of Derby, it was, under the feudal system, passed down until in the reign of Henry III it became the possession of Sir Norman de Solney. Solney being a corruption of Sulney, the village is now known as Newton Solney – the New Town of the Sulneys.

Standing on the southern bank of the beautiful river Dove at its confluence with the river Trent, this small and picturesque village nest-ling in the Trent valley may give visitors the impression of being a quiet, sleepy village which time passes by. Not so!

Today, with so few villagers being employed in agriculture, it has become a commuter village, with many residents being employed in the nearby town of Burton-on-Trent and having easy access to Derby, Birmingham and the M1. Of course Burton-on-Trent is famous for its breweries and Newton Solney was once the estate of the Ratcliffs, a notable brewery family, for whom most of the villagers worked either on the estate itself or by cycling three miles to Burton-on-Trent to the brewery of Bass, Ratcliff and Gretton.

The Newton Park Hotel, once the Ratcliff home, was built around 1800 for a local solicitor. His son built Bladon Castle – a large red brick folly. Built on a high wooded ridge at the western end of the village it presents a majestic sight when viewed against the sunset. During the early 1940s it was occupied by allied soldiers and later by prisoners of war. It is now owned by a local farming family. During the war an incendiary bomb hit the vicarage, sadly destroying all the village records. In this same era the Home Guard, using the ancient ford, crossed the river Trent on foot to reach the pillboxes, which are still in existence, on the opposite bank.

The octagonal Beehive Cottage, built from bricks made locally, stands at the entrance of a tree-lined lane leading to the 12th century church of St Mary. Two of the three church bells were cast just before the Civil War and have the inscriptions: God Save Our Church, 1615, and God Save The Church, 1638.

Village friendliness and well kept cellars attract clientele from far afield to the two village pubs built in the mid 19th century. The Brickmakers Arms, recently renovated, was once the village bakery and takes its name from the brickyards, the remains of which can still be seen at the rear of the pub. The Unicorn inn gives its name to the local football team who can be heard replaying the latest game on a Sunday lunchtime over a pint. Every Bank Holiday Monday teams from each pub compete for a cricket trophy, playing on the recreation field overlooking the river where the many fishermen enjoy the peace and tranquillity of the river bank.

The village hall, built by Colonel Robert Frederick Ratcliff, one time High Sheriff for Derbyshire, has a rifle range used by several rifle clubs. Christmas sees villagers of all ages joining in the village shoot when everyone is supposed to bring a prize to win a prize!

A strong community spirit runs through the village and this is shown through the many events which take place during the year. During the Ratcliff era every child who visited Newton Park on Shrove Tuesday was given one pint of milk towards the making of pancakes (needless to say there was usually a queue). Although this custom died out many years ago we now celebrate with a Pancake Race through the main street.

To complete the village there is a real country shop-cum-post office, attractively styled almshouses left by benefactors from the past, several farms border the village and lovely country walks for the energetic. Pride in the village was rewarded in 1990 when Newton Solney became the winner of the past winners award for the Best Kept Village in Derbyshire. Who said Newton Solney was a quiet sleepy village?

Newton's Walk, Derby ✤

The Women's Institute of Cedars is not in a village; it is part of the city of Derby, but what is a city but a 'village grown'? Certainly the area of Derby which is bounded by Kedleston Road, Duffield Road and Broadway has a character all its own, and local people still speak of 'going down the village' when they go to the shops.

The headquarters of the Derbyshire Federation, officially on Sherwin Street, is actually situated on Newton's Walk, and was once the social heart of this area. The superb hall had humble beginnings. Until 1880 there was little building development on the north-east side of Kedleston Road, Derby.

Then building began in Cedar Street, and the top house of the street was authorised for use for church purposes on Sundays, and as a day school during the week. It is likely that the mission school continued to provide week-day education until around 1910, when the new Kedleston Road schools opened.

By 1907, with the completion of the Sherwin's Field estate (Sherwin Street, Longford Street and Bradley Street), and the commencement of the development from Bromley Street to White Street, the mission house had to be greatly enlarged. The Men's Institute met in a corrugated hut at the rear, and the Mission House was the centre of social and church activities until 1920.

The numbers attending afternoon Sunday school were so great that classes had to be transferred to the Kedleston Road infants school. By 1923 the need for bigger accommodation was desperate. There was little or no sanitary provision, and the Mission House was a potential fire trap.

It had been hoped to build a church, to be known as St Aidan's, and that the area would become a parish in its own right, but now it was decided to postpone the church, and to concentrate on the provision of a new church hall. St Aidan's church hall, Newton's Walk, opened on 15th November, 1930. The Cedar Street Mission closed, and the house was sold.

Parkfields Cedars grammar school for girls was close to the Kedleston Road block of council schools, and as time went on there was need for more accommodation at the grammar school, particularly for PE and dance on a regular basis and for a quiet room for external examinations. It was during the 1950s and 1960s that the church hall provided that extra space.

When the grammar school was moved to its new Mackworth site and St Aidan's joined with St Alkmund's, the church hall was bought as WI Headquarters, and modernised.

Norbury & Roston 🦡

Norbury and Roston have always been in the ecclesiastical parish of Norbury. They are closely knit villages with many families going back several generations. Farming predominates and there are the constructional engineering works of Deville and Lear and Weston's slaughterhouse.

Norbury appears in the Domesday Book as Norberie or Nordberie, the 'norther' defence on the Dove, while Sudbury was to the south. Today Norbury is a scattered community and visitors may be surprised to find the church, dedicated to St Mary and St Barlok, tucked away out of sight with only two houses to keep it company. The 14th century chancel, with stained glass windows that predate the Black Death, is dominated by the great east window. This was restored over a period of ten years in the 1970s.

The 17th century manor house beside the church was the home of the Fitzherbert family for 700 years, and the stone building at right angles to the church is all that remains of the Norman house. The National Trust now owns the manor, and the stone hall may be seen by appointment. The Fitzherberts sold the Norbury estate to Samuel Clowes in 1872 and he built a big new house on higher ground to the right of the church. This was pulled down in 1959. Norbury shares its rector with Snelston and Clifton, where he lives.

The mill-stream which flows behind the station produced the power for the now ruined Norbury Mill. This was mentioned in the Domesday Book. Flour was ground there until 1890. It was then used as a builder's yard and then as a sawmill.

Anyone familiar with the works of George Eliot will know that Norbury is Adam Bede country. He was born on Roston common in the house bearing his name, and Bartle Massey's school, where he went, is the original village school on Green Lane, once the old turnpike road.

Half-way between Norbury church and Roston in Lid Lane are the school and village hall. These are the social centre of the community. When the Green Lane school became overcrowded the present one was built, in 1894. The children walked to their new classrooms in a crocodile, carrying their books. In those days it was thought necessary for boys and girls to have separate entrances, and the words are carved on the door lintels. Break time was also segregated, and a wall used to run across the yard at the back from the cookhouse, where the girls were taught cooking. This wall ran to the outside toilets. The old pump on the lane side, although long blocked up, has been restored, and the children dress the well in the summer.

Roston, spelt Roschintun in the Domesday Book, centres on the area known as the Bullring. Whether this was once associated with bull baiting or the cattle market, which was held in Shields Lane near the existing public house (the Shant) is unclear. The village never had a church of its own but there are now two disused Methodist chapels. The story goes that there was once disagreement as to where the chapel should be built and the building materials would disappear from one site to be found on the other in the course of the night. No agreement being reached, two chapels were built a few hundred yards apart. They were both supported by congregations until the 1940s and the 1960s. One chapel is now derelict but the other has seen the successful start of two small engineering businesses which have now moved onto bigger premises.

Water can still be drawn from the spring which supplied the whole village, and which has never run dry. A well-dressing was held annually until the time of the First World War. The Wakes, run by Gipsy Smith and held in a field behind the Shant, stopped shortly afterwards. They were held in the first fortnight in September when the damsons were being picked. These were taken to the cotton mills in the nearby Churnet valley for use as industrial dye.

Roston Hall, parts of which are very old, is reputedly haunted by the ghost of the 18th century squire who is said to have shot himself after wrongly accusing a servant boy of theft, for which he was hanged. Female voices chattering on the stairs have also been reported.

The village is fortunate to still have its small post office store, and although the population of Norbury and Roston may have dropped from about 500 in 1840 to around 300 today, the community is flourishing.

Normanton ᨇ

Little more than half a century ago Normanton was a pretty little hamlet gazing remotely on green fields towards the town of Derby.

The old church of St Giles, which bore many traces of Norman origin, survived until 1861, when it was replaced by the present attractive edifice. The last ordinary meeting of the Parish Council took place on 23rd March 1928, and so after a thousand years the township of Normanton ceased to exist.

In Village Street, eastwards, ancient cottages in front of the churchyard were demolished in 1920. Today the village has simply been engulfed by the march of progress, and a visitor would spent much time searching for signs of Old Normanton, which is lost forever.

North Wingfield ᨇ

North Wingfield has a population of 7,590 and was originally a farming community with some small scale coal and iron-stone mining. It grew to its present size to accommodate the development of large collieries in the area. The Great Central Railway opened a new line in 1892–93 to serve these collieries and provide means of transporting coal to London. The miners were generally brought in from outside the village and were housed in colliery company terraced rows. These houses have now disappeared and the mines worked out, with the population travelling to more distant places of work.

North Wingfield has many old and interesting buildings, including its village church where the roof still has much of its original 14th century tracery beamwork. A Norman arch leading to the chapel, a font of either Saxon or Norman times, a 12th century window and an ancient wooden chest can be seen here. The 80 ft high tower, some 500 years old, boasts an even older great bell. A small stone coffin lies in the porch, probably of a Norman child, and in the recesses of the chancel lie knights in chain armour believed to be from the 13th century and of the local Deincourt family. A very old sundial can be seen in the churchyard.

At the road junction a short distance from St Lawrence's can be found the remains of what is believed to be a medieval village cross. It was used in 1702 as a guide post and has three sides of its base engraved with fingers pointing the way.

Close to the church is the 15th century Blue Bell inn. It was originally the chantry house and is now a public house and restaurant. It is rumoured that a tunnel leads from the inn to the church and the inn is also believed to be haunted.

The old rectory house was greatly extended in 1690 and contrary to most Elizabethan buildings has the middle arm of the letter 'E' missing. A plaque on the front wall of the old rectory bears the inscription 'Nunno deficiente plus ultra' which roughly translated means that the cash ran out before the extension could be built.

The closing of the pits and the withdrawing of the railway service left a large amount of derelict land. This has been reclaimed by the County Council and the Five Pits Trail created giving miles of traffic-free pathways for walking, cycling and horse-riding with picnic sites and magnificent views across the Derbyshire countryside. Woodlands, ponds and meadows have been created making the Trail a haven for wildlife.

Born at the beginning of the 20th century, Harry Hopkinson, later to be known as the 'Great Torrani', filled the village church with his pure soprano voice. He travelled to many parts of the world, even receiving a large jewelled ring from an Empress of the Middle East who was much impressed with his yodelling act, indeed his yodelling records have become much sought after record collectors' items. For all his fame, Harry's character never changed. He always kept in touch with his native village and kept a horse near his father's house, allowing the local children to ride upon it.

Alice Barnett ran the local fish and chip shop for 35 years and had such a good reputation for her value for money food and kindliness that the local council decided to name a development of bungalows for the elderly after her, calling it 'Alice's View'.

Oaker 🌿

Will Shore's Lane, Oaker leads up to Oaker Hill, a prominent landmark. Will Shore, one of the brothers in a poem by William Wordsworth called *A Tradition of Oker Hill* was a forbear of the great Florence Nightingale. He changed his name to Nightingale in order to inherit the family estate. The village of Oaker is now well known as the home of Pollyanna Pickering, an internationally acclaimed wildlife artist, who runs a registered bird hospital, which cares for many injured birds of prey.

Following the road which eventually leads to Matlock, the hamlet of Snitterton appears, where, after passing the attractive Elizabethan Manor Farm, embedded in the road is one of the only four remaining bull rings in Derbyshire. Hidden from the road is Snitterton Hall, Pevsner's 'gem of

an Elizabethan manor house'. Here in Civil War Days lived Col Mill-
ward, a Royalist Colonel. His grandson, Rev Charles Jennens, was
responsible for the selection of the passages of Scripture used by Handel
in *The Messiah*.

Footpaths from here lead through Northern Dale and Wensley Dale to
the village of Wensley, 650 ft above sea level. The Wendesley family are
thought to have had their manor house on land now known as The
Green. A badly weathered Wendesley slab dated about 1500 is now in
Darley church.

Before 1939 most families had someone employed in the nearby Mill
Close mine – which was one of the world's most productive lead mines.
The mine closed due to flooding.

In 1829 two houses in Wensley were demolished to make way for the
Methodist chapel. In 1849, Francis Pearson, the lay preacher, was
distressed to learn that a previous local preacher, John Turner, had died
from starvation after existing on the few turnips from his garden after
the failure of the harvest. This motivated Mr Pearson to set up the Local
Preachers' Mutual Aid Society, to assist members in need. The Society is
still active today. Each autumn, members and friends fill the chapel at a
Pilgrim Service; a great day for the tiny village. A plaque in the chapel
gives thanks and commemorates Mr Pearson.

Coming down the hill, St Mary's church stands at Cross Green, South
Darley. This church built in 1841 is modelled on the parish church of
Troyes, France, where Henry V and Catherine de Valois celebrated their
betrothal after the Battle of Agincourt in 1415 and the Treaty of Troyes
1420. It is the only church in Derbyshire whose altar is in the north.

Three ancient inns serve the village, one just over the beautiful bridge
over the river Derwent – the parish boundary.

Ockbrook ✧

Ockbrook is two villages in one. There is the old settlement which Occa,
an Anglo-Saxon, established along the banks of the brook around the 6th
century and from which the village derived its name. Alongside it is the
Moravian settlement, one of only three in the country, which sprang up
in the second half of the 18th century. Nowadays the village is a united
community but when the Moravians arrived in 1750 they were regarded
with suspicion and some hostility which occasionally exploded into
violence.

The church of All Saints became the parish church around 1600.
Before this it was a chapelry of Elvaston. It has two notable features, one
being the tower which was built in the 12th century, to which the
prominent broach spire was added sometime later, and secondly the
Norman font which was not appreciated by the Victorians and thrown
out into the garden of the former rectory for many years. This was
restored to its rightful position in 1963.

In the 1700s life in the village changed. Coal was mined at Stanley and men from Ockbrook walked over the fields to work at the mine. Coal was carried from Stanley to Ockbrook along the Ridings to Coal Lane as it was called then, where it was transferred to small trucks which ran along rails on top of an embankment on the right side of Coal Lane. Part of the embankment may still be seen. At Borrowash the coal was put on the barge. Later residents in the large houses along Coal Lane objected to how the name was spelled and had it changed to Cole Lane. It looked more superior.

Following the arrival of the Moravians there was a great change in the village. Large houses were built and the community increasingly attracted the middle class and more affluent members of society. Work also diversified. There were four silk glove makers, four shoemakers and someone who made straw bonnets. Up to quite recent times it was possible to see a number of long framework knitters windows in upper storeys of various cottages. The Cross Keys inn, where stockings were made for Queen Victoria and her court, still has its window.

The jewel in Ockbrook, viewed on its hilltop site from the west as travellers pass along the A52, is a terrace of red brick Georgian buildings, the Moravian Settlement. From here one has a magnificent view across the village and the valleys of the Trent and Soar to the hills of Charnwood Forest.

A local landowner Isaac Frearson invited the Reverend Jacob Rogers to preach in his own barn after hearing him deliver a sermon in the open-air by the market cross in Nottingham. Ten years later Isaac Frearson sold his estate and in 1750 the settlement was founded. Settlements were strictly run. Single men lived in a choir house. There was also a choir house for the single ladies. Even when entering the church the single brothers and sisters entered by separate doors. When they began their building work they were hampered by some villagers who first tried to cut off their supply of bricks and then removed those already laid. Despite this local suspicion the church was opened in 1752. The bell in a striking cupola has long since replaced the blowing of French horns for summoning the faithful to prayer. A clock made by Whitehurst of Derby has just been renovated and paid for by local collections. The flagstones were brought from Dale Abbey and laid when the church was built.

The routing of the new A52 dividing Ockbrook and Borrowash resulted in many new homes and an increase in local traffic and population. Ockbrook is a very attractive village and convenient for commuters to Nottingham, Derby, Long Eaton and Ilkeston. Ockbrook still retains a cricket ground, two conservation areas, four pubs which all supply good food and drink and is the centre of many walks to Dale and the surrounding countryside.

Old Brampton

Old Brampton is a village with a long history of occupation. It is mentioned in the Domesday Book and some of the sites undoubtedly have Saxon connections. In shape it is linear, extending for some two miles from east to west on either side of the road which links Chesterfield and Baslow. There are no side turnings, and today the village is entirely residential, having neither post office nor shop.

The tree-lined road winds from Chesterfield up to the high moors. In the Middle Ages the road was used by packhorses to bring in produce from the outlying farms, lead mines and coal bell pits. Charcoal burning was also carried on in the vicinity. Mary Queen of Scots probably travelled this road as she was transferred from one to another of the big Derbyshire houses where she was imprisoned. The road became a turnpike road, and in 1815 was designated a Public Carriage Road. Because there is now an alternative wider and faster road from Chesterfield to Baslow, Old Brampton is not harassed by heavy traffic and it is fortunate in being served by a long-established local bus service, still run by a local family.

The centre of the village, and village life, is the parish church of St Peter and St Paul. It is believed that the church existed in 1100. The church clock celebrates the 1897 Jubilee of Queen Victoria and is amusing because of a mistake by the clock-face painter. He painted only four minutes between twelve and one, then six minutes between one and two – the result it is said of too generous a lunch. Subsequent painters have been careful not to correct the mistake. The George and Dragon public house stands just across the road.

Next to the church stands a small stone building built in 1830 to be a National school. There had been another school dating back to 1682. The school by the church was closed in 1918 when a larger one was built beyond the edge of the village up on Pudding Pie hill, to serve Old Brampton and the adjacent tiny settlements of Wadshelf and Wigley. Today the old building is used for church affairs, as a Sunday school, and as the monthly meeting place for the WI.

Across from the church stands Brampton Hall, recorded as a Saxon manor in the Domesday Book. Although it has been altered many times there is still a pair of cruck timbers inside, which were probably part of the original structure. There is also a coat of arms which is believed to be that of the de Caus family who lived in this building from the 12th to the 15th century, when it was known as de Caus Hall. It was the home of Matilda de Caus whose effigy is in the church. Today, Brampton Hall is the home of an internationally famous breeder of clumber spaniels, who is also the world authority on that breed.

Further west, up the hill towards Baslow, is a tiny Methodist chapel, built in the grounds of Hollins House in 1846. Bequeathed to Marsden

Street chapel in Chesterfield in 1957, it was closed in the 1960s and is now used as a workshop.

Unusually for the present day, this village on the edge of the moors can boast three herds of dairy cattle.

At the eastern edge of the village, two large old houses have recently been converted, one into a nursing home for the elderly, the other into a hospice.

Old Glossop ✣

Old Glossop nestles at the foot of the Snake Pass, with the wild hills and moors of Bleaklow in the background.

As the name implies, it was the original Glossop, the name being derived from 'Glotts Hop', meaning 'Glotts Valley'. Today's Glossop was then known as Howard town or Bridgend. The village originally formed part of the Duke of Norfolk's estate, but this was split up and sold off in 1924/25. There are many references to the Howards in the names of roads. The primary school is also named after the Duke of Norfolk. The grounds and gardens of Glossop Hall were given to the residents, and this is now known as Manor Park. Nowadays, the park is very popular with residents and visitors of all ages. The children ride on the miniature railway and feed the ducks on the pond, while the older generation can be found around the bowling greens or strolling in the gardens.

The houses and buildings are mainly built of the local grit-stone, though some of the newer property is built of more modern materials. Many of the 17th and 18th century houses that remain, cluster around the old market square and cross. A new base and new top were added to the cross in 1910 to commemorate the accession of George V. The oldest building in the village now forms part of the Bulls Head inn.

The church of All Saints is Norman in origin, though it has been considerably added to over the years. There was once a passageway – long since blocked off – that joined the church to the vicarage. It is alleged that the ghost of The Grey Lady can sometimes be seen in the area!

In the past, most of the inhabitants of Old Glossop would have been involved in agriculture, quarrying or the textile industry. Fast flowing streams from the surrounding hills ensured the area became one of the principal centres of the cotton industry. It was also conveniently near the commercial centre of Manchester.

With the collapse of the textile industry, so life in the village has gradually changed. Old Glossop is now mainly a dormitory village. There is now only one working farm left, and where once stood cotton mills, there are now engineering works. Most people go to Manchester, and other surrounding towns, to their work.

Shopping habits have also changed dramatically. Where once this was a self-contained village, with the advent of the car and supermarket it has gone the way of many other villages. Only the post office – a hive of activity on pensions day – the baker's and an antiques shop now remain. There used to be seven pubs, now there are three. Many residents take part in the quiz teams and dart teams organised by these pubs.

Walking is, of course, a popular pastime in this area, and Doctor's Gate, an ancient packhorse trace across the Pennines, is very much the gateway to the hills. The story is that Dr Talbot, who was reputed to be responsible for this track, had a Faustian confrontation with the Devil. To decide the issue they both agreed to a race along this rugged track. The Devil was in front as they came near to the winning post, but the wily doctor grabbed his opponent's tail and pulled him back, thereby making it first over the line.

Osmaston &

Osmaston at the time of the Domesday survey was called Osmundestune. The original name of the parish was Whitestone.

The old St Martin's church was built in the 15th century to replace an earlier building of wickerwork. In 1843 the foundation stone was laid for another church, opened for divine service in June 1845. This was also dedicated to St Martin and is still used at the present day. The village school was built in 1943.

The village hall was opened on Coronation Day 1937 to replace the old Victory Hut. The hall has a thatched roof and is used for various functions. The school use the kitchen every day for the preparation of meals, and the children dine there. Opposite the village hall are four thatched cottages which are known as Coronation Cottages.

Outside the Shoulder of Mutton public house there was a weighbridge, used to weigh stone which was being used to build Osmaston Manor.

The village pond stands at the bottom end of the village overlooked by the two oldest thatched houses in the village. At the back of these are two new houses, the first to be built in over 40 years.

Leading into Osmaston Park used to be an avenue of lime trees, but these were destroyed in February 1962 by a gale. The avenue led down to Osmaston Manor, which was built in 1849 and demolished in 1964 when Sir Ian Walker and family moved to Okeover Hall near Ashbourne and took the Okeover name. The smoke tower from the manor still stands today.

The polo field which once belonged to the manor now belongs to the village and is used by football clubs, weekend caravan clubs and the annual Ashbourne Shire Horse Show which in August 1990 celebrated its centenary.

Over Haddon 🪶

The village of Over Haddon is situated two miles south-west of Bakewell, in the Peak District. It clings to the sides of a steep valley, and overlooks the beautiful Lathkill Dale.

Lathkill Dale was the first National Nature Reserve to be so designated in Derbyshire in 1972, and the Nature Conservancy Council (NCC), who administer it, have recently moved into new offices in the village.

The Romans are the first people to have left evidence of having mined in Lathkill Dale. Mandale Mine is one of the earliest recorded mines in Derbyshire, and is mentioned in the 'Quo Warrento' of 1288, because it was producing and selling a lot of cheap lead and was therefore putting a lot of smaller mines out of business. By 1615 some of the Mandale workings were 300 ft deep. Many of the miners' paths up the daleside to Youlgreave are still in existence, one even having paving stones which, although covered in grass, can still be made out.

Although the lead was running out by the 19th century, a grandiose scheme was planned to erect a steam engine to drain the mines, which would be run by a waterwheel using surplus water from the Lathkilldale mine reservoir. In 1840 the Mandale aqueduct was constructed in order to carry water from the reservoir to work the waterwheel (which incidentally was reckoned to be the second largest in the country at that time). However, in spite of this modernisation, these workings were short-lived, and the machinery was sold in 1852. The remains of the aqueduct can still be seen, however, in the form of its stone pillars.

The story of mining in Over Haddon cannot be concluded without mentioning the extraordinary events of 1854. In one of the lead mines on Manor Farm gold was found in some lava. The owners had it investigated, and it was found that although gold did indeed exist it was deep down, and in such small quantities that no profit could be made. However, a company was formed, gold was extracted and sold for £25 per ton. It generated so much excitement that hundreds of people rushed to invest in the mine; discussions even took place to build a railway connecting Over Haddon and Bakewell to transport the vast quantities of gold that would pour from the mine. However, hardly any gold was found – even deep down, the company was liquidated and many investors were made bankrupt.

Until the mid 20th century most of Over Haddon was owned by Lord Lothian and his ancestors. In the 19th century Lord Melbourne, Queen Victoria's first Prime Minister, was the owner. Nearly all the village is built of limestone with slate roofs, but in the estate records of 1841 it was noted that most of the 45 houses belonging to the estate were 'generally thatched and in bad repair'.

The village has one pub, the Lathkill Hotel, and in fact a public house has stood on the same site for hundreds of years. It was originally known as the Miner's Arms, and only changed its name at the turn of the century.

Over Haddon has produced remarkable characters who have aroused national or international interest. The first of these, Martha Taylor, was born about 1649. She had apparently suffered a blow on the head in her early teens, but suffered no ill effects until August 1667, when she became ill, and ate her last meal for some time on 27th December of that years. Two years later in 1669 a pamphlet was published describing the 'celebrated fasting damsel', in which it was noted that two 'watchers' had been appointed, one by the neighbouring townships and one by the Earl of Devonshire, who took a great interest in the case. She was also attended by 40 to 60 women who watched her constantly day and night. She died 15 years later, but unfortunately there is no record of her life in final years, so we will never know if she recovered her appetite.

Over Haddon has changed greatly in the past decade. Only one dairy farm remains out of three, the others having changed to sheep, horses, and a craft centre. There is a tiny post office, two small tearooms, a Montessori nursery school, and the NCC will soon have a visitor centre. Although a tiny village with a population of about 250, it is a thriving, living village with lots of children and activities.

Padfield

Situated in the north-western part of Derbyshire, you can find Padfield by taking a left turn off the B6105 Woodhead road from Glossop. The village nestles practically on the side of the Longdendale valley and under the protection of Bleaklow.

Years ago Padfield held a Plum Wakes. This was one of the highlights of the year, when the fruits the valley was famous for, were eaten in cakes, puddings and pies.

In 1811 when the church register gave details about the numbers of inhabitants as 450 and 78 dwellings, it gave no indication of what was to come with the arrival of cotton in the valley. Families with names like Lees, Platt and Barber built their mills (today names still found on the streets of Padfield), vast buildings overshadowing the stone cottages.

With workers from Yorkshire to fill jobs in the mills, the inhabitants of Padfield swelled to over 2,500 and dwellings to 557. The ups and downs of the cotton industry show in the riots of 1831 when 500 rioters burst into Mill Brook mill, smashing machinery. The rioters were protesting about very low wages in the mill. Then again in the cotton famine, due to the American Civil War, men were set to work building roads in the area. Platt Street and Post Street were two of them – Post Street was nicknamed 'Pinch Belly' because once again wages were low and food hard to come by.

The primary school has been in use since it was opened in 1887. In those early days the children attended half a day and worked half a day in the mill, when a hundred children attended each session. Today they have around 75 children's names on the register.

The two churches and the Liberal, Conservative and Working Men's Clubs were the focal points for entertainment. The Sunday schools each had cricket teams, the Harvest and Cobweb suppers were eagerly looked forward to, as were the garden parties at Rose Bank, which were a real treat for the poor of the village. Also every Christmas morning after carol singing the Sunday school officials put on coffee, which was scarce at that time and therefore a special treat, and cakes for the singers.

There were also nine shops, inclusive of a Co-op, butcher's, baker's, hardware, post office and carpet shop. Out of all this great variety all that is left is the Peels Arms and the two chapels. There is still a Victorian post box in the wall where the post office once stood.

The Woodhead railway line provides one boundary to the village. This line is no longer in use after its closure to passengers in 1970 and then freight in 1981 after 136 years of operations over the Pennines. This once busy line to Sheffield from Manchester was a great loss to the area, giving an unforgettable journey to the passengers who were lucky enough to use the line.

Looking around Padfield, the oldest part of the old Glossop Borough, you would be hard put to find out where all this activity went on, except for one or two mill lodges, mill owners' houses, and part of one mill still standing. It all changed with the decline of the cotton industry in the valley. Many residents found work outside the village travelling to Ashton-under-Lyne, Manchester and Stockport, leaving Padfield in the daytime to settle down into the peaceful place it is now.

Palterton ✧

The village of Palterton stands between Bolsover and Glapwell, on the eastern escarpment of the Doe Lea valley, overlooking intersection 29 of the M1 motorway.

Until the beginning of the 20th century and the coming of the coal mines, Palterton was a farming village only. Four rows of terraces were built for the mineworkers.

Palterton colliery closed during the late 1950s, but as the mine was situated a mile from the village, this mine had never had much influence over the village. Mingled with the 140 houses, stands one public house, a Miners' Welfare, a shop cum post office and a small mission church, which houses a weekly Sunday school but has only one service a month. The school has three classes of children from five years to eleven years and around 90 pupils attend, some of these being bused in from nearby Hillstown.

Parwich 🦢

Parwich, a village of some 500 inhabitants, is named in the Domesday Book as Pevrewic and was a royal desmesne. You would not pass through this unusually compact village on your travels in the Peak District – you would have to seek it out. You would be rewarded by a picture postcard limestone village with an intricate pattern of small lanes, ginnels and greens. The sheepwash, now the village pond, has recently been taken over by an Aylesbury duck and several mallards. It previously provided the setting for the annual mating orgy of hundreds of visiting frogs. Will this survive the arrival of the ducks? Only time will tell.

The Sycamore inn, the only remaining hostelry (the Crown and the Wheatsheaf having been converted into cottages) competes for custom with the splendidly refurbished British Legion, and there is still a church, chapel, school, post office and shop. Cattle no longer meander through the village at milking time and inevitably many smallholdings have been turned into desirable residences, but in spring lambs still gambol in Farmer Lees' patch behind Dam Farm in the centre of the village. Many working farms surround Parwich, while local quarries provide employment for other residents.

Do not be deceived into thinking this a sleepy village; it buzzes with activity. Apart from church and school functions there are Brownies, Guides, WI, Youth Club, Mother and Baby Club, Over Sixties, Horticultural Society, evening classes, cricket and netball teams. A sports committee is busily raising money for an ambitious outdoor activity centre with bowling green and hard play area adjacent to the cricket field.

Architecturally there are many interesting buildings and in summer the cottage gardens delight the eye with their window boxes and hanging baskets. The church of St Peter replaces the Norman church more than eight centuries old when demolished in 1872. Fortunately the old north doorway and chancel arch have been preserved: over the doorway is an ancient tympanum of very early date discovered in the walls of the old church. Parwich Hall, with its magnificent terraced gardens, stands dramatically on the steep hillside, while even higher is the Care Centre built in 1914 as a convalescent home and used as a hospital during the Second World War.

Parwich's past is no less colourful than its present. Farmer Lees, now in his seventies, talks about village life when he was a lad. The highlight of the Wakes sports was obviously the ladies' race. A pig would be greased and let loose: whichever lady caught it, kept it. There were pigsties near the present sports field with a big heap of pig manure. One year the pig dived into the muck and a Mrs Pollitt waded in and caught it! The same Mrs Pollitt kept a sweetshop, reared turkeys, ducks and hens, ran a taxi service and cooked chips in her kitchen for the village lads.

The village was virtually independent of outside craftsmen. There was Leonard Lord, all-purpose joiner, coffinmaker and funeral director.

Village funeral processions would be led by this small man in a tall 'shiner'. He was also a wheelwright and would take his wooden wheels to William Bradbury, the blacksmith, to have the iron hoops fitted. Mr Bradbury, already a busy man, had a part-time job as a chimney sweep, which he carried out before he started up his forge, so a visit from the sweep meant getting up at six am in readiness. Village lads liked to help with the blow bellows. Forging was a thirsty job and William liked his beer. Many's the time he would tell the lads to nip down to the Sycamore and fetch him a quart of ale. The cobbler lost a leg in the First World War but plied his trade efficiently with the help of crutches.

The population has remained much the same. There are more houses but smaller families. The school which used to have 100 pupils now has only 49. At one time the former pub, Crown Cottage, contained two families with a total of four adults and eleven children sleeping toe to toe.

Peak Forest

Peak Forest is set amongst the limestone hills, an attractive village on flat ground in a green bowl, as seen from nearby Mount Pleasant, when indeed it can look very picturesque as the name suggests.

The Royal Forest was founded in 1100 and it was sparsely wooded in some areas, in spite of its name. Wild boar, roebuck and otters were hunted by visiting royalty who stayed at nearby Peveril Castle (in Castleton). In the 16th century, when deer were hunted by settlers and to preserve the remaining herds, a 'park' of about four square miles was enclosed and a house was built for the ranger, called the Chamber of the Peak. It was rebuilt in the 18th century and later it became and is now, Chamber Farm.

The then Chamber of the Peak was where Swainmotes (forest courts) were held, with a Steward and a small band of foresters, and it would be close by that a settlement and the present village sprang up.

In the 18th century and later, the area would be self sufficient, with farms and cattle and with belts of trees providing shelter. Weather conditions could be hard in winter at 950 ft, even with the surrounding hills. Until the 1950s the land and properties belonged to the Dukes of Devonshire, who in their turn helped to conserve the area, with more tree planting.

There were open lead mine shafts and lead-impregnated land, but mining provided employment as did the stone quarries. Eldon Hole, now one of the traditional seven wonders of the Peak, was said to be 180 ft deep. The mine shafts finish just north of the village and because of the dolerite beds, stone quarrying was done in the north and west of Peak Forest, saving the area from bare quarry faces and stone blasting.

The clusters of warm stone cottages and farms give a fine background to the church, which was known at one time as the Gretna Green of the Peak. Originally built in 1657 and dedicated to King Charles, King and

Martyr, the incumbent of the time was able to grant probate to wills as well as marriage licences. Between the years 1728 and 1754 anyone could come to Peak Forest, day or night, to be married without banns. It was a very busy time there when Bonny Prince Charlie was in the country and a separate register was kept recording these runaway marriages. But in 1804 this register was finally closed by an act of Parliament. People can still be married in the village without banns, providing that one of the couple has lived there 15 days prior to the ceremony.

The present church was built on the old site in 1880 and much of the original stone and the old Venetian window was used in the building of the reading room on the right of the church, which housed shelves of books and a billiard table.

The primary school was built in 1868 for a bigger population than the present, as it took in children from a wide area, including Sparrowpit, Tideswell Moor and surrounding farms. It has never closed and has 20 pupils.

The village shop, being a general store and post office, is an asset and the mobile County Library van calls regularly; also as in most villages there are local craftsmen who can 'turn their hand' to any job.

The Devonshire Arms, a comfortable inn, attracts locals and the tourists who come by car or on foot to see the wonders of the Peak National Park. Being on the A623 road, the village has to contend with a fair amount of traffic between Baslow and Barmoor Clough. For commuters who work out of the area, Chesterfield and Buxton are within easy reach.

Pentrich

Pentrich is a small village nestled along the side of one of the last hills of the Pennine chain. The Romans came here during the first century, followed eventually by the Saxons and the Normans. In 1152 Pentrich was granted to the Church and remained under canon law until Henry VIII claimed it for the Crown. The land subsequently passed to the Cavendish family who held it until 1950.

The oldest parts of the church of St Matthew date from the reign of King Stephen, 1152, but five Saxon crosses carefully built into the lintels inside the church would seem to indicate that there had been a Saxon church on the site at an earlier time.

The most infamous period of Pentrich history was June 1817 when the Pentrich Revolution made national headlines. Revolution is perhaps too strong a word for what happened when a group of misguided villagers, under the leadership of Jeremiah Brandreth, took up arms in an abortive attempt to overthrow the government. The uprising was meant to include several counties and thousands of men but the few who set off from Pentrich that night were the only ones on the march. They reached the Derbyshire/Nottinghamshire border by dawn the following day only to be routed by a detachment of Hussars. A much publicised show trial was held in Derby where the three ring-leaders were tried, found guilty of high treason and executed. Fourteen of the other prisoners were transported to Australia.

Pentrich had two social events peculiar to the village. One was the Snowdrop Tea, held on Shrove Tuesday and the other was a Damson Social, held at the end of September to coincide with both the ripe damsons and the patronal festival at St Matthew's church. In the past Pentrich was noted for its damsons. They were grown not for eating but for use as a dye in the textile industry. Many of the old trees still survive but severe winters and strong gales are taking their toll of these brittle old ladies of the hedgerows.

The last 50 years have been almost traumatic for this sleepy village. The post-war years saw the outskirts of Pentrich ravaged and destroyed by the Ministry of Fuel and Power in their relentless pursuit of coal. They had neither the skills nor the inclinations of their modern counterparts and the land which was devastated 40 years ago is only now recovering. Subsidence from deep mining also wrought havoc on the older properties. Cottages were held together with iron bands, gable ends were supported by huge wooden props and doors hung at drunken angles. Some of the cottages in 1950 were still thatched and these too were in need of repair. It was at this point that Chatsworth Estate, landlord for most of the village, decided that Pentrich was no longer economically viable and the land, farms and cottages were sold, in most cases to the sitting tenants. So ended over 400 years of feudal tradition and in one jump Pentrich was launched into redevelopment.

During the 1960s and 1970s many of the old cottages were sold, demolished and new homes built. However despite all of this there has not been a population explosion or growth of property beyond the boundaries of the village proper. The derelict village of 1950 is now a most desirable place to live, but with the closing of the school and the loss of the post office this sleepy village is at risk of falling into an even deeper sleep.

Pilsley

Pilsley, a pleasant hill-top village near Clay Cross, must not be confused with the village of the same name on the Chatsworth estate. Mentioned in the Domesday Book, it was originally nothing more than a collection of farms and cottages.

Mary Queen of Scots, whilst in captivity in Derbyshire, enjoyed riding 'through the leafy lanes of Pilsley', which name (formerly spelt Pilleslege or Pinneslei) is thought to mean 'a clearing in a forest'.

The river Rother rises here and near its source is a patch of ground known as the 'willow beds', formerly producing material for a small basket-making industry.

In the second half of the 19th century the Industrial Revolution demanded coal. Pilsley changed dramatically! On 7th November 1882 the area was shaken by a terrific explosion. Miners working at Parkhouse Colliery, by the light of a naked candle flame, had caused gas to ignite, resulting in 45 men and boys losing their lives.

How did this colliery, founded in 1867, gets its nickname – 'Cat-pie' or 'Catty'? A lady took in miners as lodgers. She, being a good cook, regularly baked meat pies, which she stored in her pantry. Just as regularly slices of pie disappeared, presumably consumed. When challenged, her lodgers denied all knowledge, invariably offering the same explanation, 'Cat must 'ave ett it'. She decided to teach them a lesson and made a 'special pie'. This time, when told that the cat must have eaten it, she retorted 'That's funny, cat can't 'ave ett it, 'cos cat were in it!'

Pilsley's other colliery came into being in 1873. From here, 'Pilsley Brights' were delivered to Buckingham Palace, as Queen Mary (Consort of George V) would burn no other in her drawing room fireplace. By the mid 1960s collieries, railway lines and passenger station had all disappeared and very little remains to show of their existence.

There are two schools – both now primary – about one mile apart. This rhyme illustrates the rivalry that existed between the two halves of the village:

> 'Parkhouse bull dogs fast in a pen,
> Can't get out for Pilsley men.'

The Wesleyan Methodist chapel, built in 1843, is the oldest place of

Pilsey School and Methodist Church

worship. John Wesley's rule for the division of the sexes was observed – the women to the right, the men to the left. One man was bold enough to sit with his family amongst the ladies and met with much opposition. He persisted and succeeded in breaking down the old custom. In 1868 the old chapel was replaced by a new one. During the sermon, at the opening ceremony, a child began to cry. When the mother got up to take it outside, the preacher called out, 'Never mind, mother, it doesn't disturb me.' Her prompt reply was, 'No, sir, it is you who disturbed the child ...'

Harry Reeve, a wheelwright, settled in Pilsley in the 1880s. His business flourished and is still in being. Just before 'D' Day in 1944, an important contract was received from the Admiralty – one hundred landing ramps for beaches were hurriedly required. These were delivered on time!

Sport has played its part too. At one time the village succeeded in fielding six outstanding football teams. The cricket team was more select, its captain being the Director of the colliery company! A former pit boy, born in the village, became a national football hero. Sam Weaver signed professional forms in 1928 for Hull City. He later transferred to Newcastle United.

For many decades the Whit Monday walk was the highlight of the year. Everyone stayed at home and absent relatives and friends returned 'en masse'. Wearing new clothes, members of each church formed a procession and, led by two brass bands, they toured the streets. At certain scheduled points everyone halted to sing hymns. Those too young to walk rode in decorated 'carts', drawn by shire horses.

Quarndon 🦢

Quarndon is a pleasant hillside village which lies about three miles from Derby and about two miles from Duffield. The hill rises steeply to over 500 ft above sea level and there are some beautiful views, especially over the Derwent valley and towards nearby Kedleston Hall. The commanding height of Bunkers Hill was utilised as a beacon point at the time of the Spanish Armada, and again for the Silver Jubilee of Queen Elizabeth II.

The original settlement was at the foot of the hill on the southern side and thus was the site of the now demolished Norman chapel. In Victorian times the heart of the village was moved half a mile towards the crest of the hill, which is where the church, church hall and village school are located.

Throughout much of its history Quarndon was overshadowed by its larger neighbours but in the 17th century it began to gain national fame as a spa. This was because of the properties of its chalybeate spring and of the salubrious air. The spa was highly praised by eminent people, including Daniel Defoe, author of *Robinson Crusoe*, in 1727. The spa became well patronised and some of the existing houses date from that period. Ambitions to rival Buxton as a spa were finally dashed when the chalybeate spring ceased to flow, about 1900.

Thanks to the elevation of the village and the direction of the prevailing winds, the salubrious air and the reputation for healthiness remain. Quarndon can boast of having had more than one centenarian. One of them, Mrs Annie Fowke, became famous when she walked from Quarndon to London in the winter of 1836/7, to give evidence at the trial of her son. She was in her nineties at the time and she lived to reach 102. Another centenarian, Miss Hampshire, was the last survivor of a family which had kept the Joiners Arms in an unbroken line for 300 years, ending in 1928.

Not only have some old customs vanished but so has the important stocking weaving industry. As recently as 1846, there had been at least 25 hosiery frames constantly at work. Nowadays, there is little employment available within the village itself and most of its employed inhabitants work in Derby or neighbouring towns.

The village cricket ground is located in a road called The Common. That name is the only memory of the once extensive commonland that used to surround the village. The cricket team has been very successful in recent years and in 1983 it gained national fame by winning the All-England Village Cricket competition in a thrilling game at Lord's. The cricket ground now has a copy of Lord's famous weathervane, 'Old Father Time', to commemorate the feat.

Despite the close proximity of Derby, the village is separated from it by a green belt of agricultural and parkland. The district has largely retained its rural character. Quarndon regularly enters the Best Kept Village competition, which it has won on several occasions. The annual Garden Fete, held each June in the grounds of Quarndon Hall, attracts visitors from a wide area. The inhabitants have developed a fiercely independent community spirit and there are several thriving social organisations.

Repton 🐚

The village lies on the south bank of the river Trent some eight miles from Derby and five from Burton. The Repton brook runs into the Trent here and the Saxon village was built on both sides of the stream, stretching back from the river for about a mile.

Its recorded history began about 1,400 years ago when the Mercian royal family established a principal residence at Repton. Following the arrival of Christianity in Mercia in AD653 a monastery was founded, for both men and women who desired to follow a religious life.

The parish church of St Wystan spans the period from the 8th to the 15th centuries, with some later additions. Beneath the chancel is the unique Saxon mausoleum and crypt dating from the early 8th century. King Ethelbald of Mercia was entombed here in AD757, King Wiglaf in

AD840 and his grandson, St Wystan, who was brutally murdered, in AD850. The crypt then became a place of pilgrimage. In the winter of AD873–74 a Viking army camped at Repton and destroyed the monastery but fortunately the crypt survived. The tall and elegant spire of the parish church (212 ft) is a landmark for miles around – and a tale is told about it.

'There was a steeplejack in Repton in 1804, named Joseph Barton, who was called upon to repair the spire. This he did, watched by an admiring crowd. He received £10, and a goodly collection made among the villagers. He was also given a new suit of clothes. These he took with him when he returned, in a spirit of bravado, to the very apex of the spire. He climbed his ladders as far as possible, then threw up a rope and skilfully hitched it to one of the arms of the cross on top of the spire. He then climbed hand over hand until he reached the bend of the ball, when he crawled up and seated himself at the foot of the cross.

Two or three minutes elapsed during which he was donning the presentation clothes, but at length he stood erect and proceeded to throw into the air, one by one, the discarded garments – the crowd below meanwhile cheering loudly as each garment fell fluttering earthward. Suddenly there was a cry of fright, followed by a deathly hush. The steeplejack had dislodged the rope – his sole connecting link with the earth – and it now hung dangling from the top of his ladder, 30 ft below where he stood. Before anyone could move, his daughter, about 16 years old, went up the tower, then the ladders, rung by rung, until she looked no bigger than a doll. Hanging by her left hand, nearly 200 ft in the air, she threw the rope to her father, and both descended safely. No wonder

Repton Cross and Parish Church

the good people of Repton were proud of little Bessie. The rope hung on the steeple for many years until time and winter's storms finally carried away.'

The Norman building known as the Old Priory was the work of the Augustinian canons who came to Repton from Calke about 1172. They built a splendid monastery that survived for nearly 400 years.

In 1538 the Dissolution of the Monasteries ended the religious life of the Priory and it passed into the hands of the Thacker family. One of them achieved notoriety as the man responsible for destroying the Priory buildings. Alarmed at the prospect, under Mary Tudor, of a religious community being re-established at Repton, he assembled an army of workmen and – so it is said – had the greater part of the Priory demolished in a single day. He said later that it was necessary 'to destroy the nest for fear the birds should build therein again'.

One remaining part of the Priory – the guest house – was sold to the executors of Sir John Port of Etwall, whose will provided for the foundation of Repton School, which still flourishes today. In its time the school has produced three Archbishops of Canterbury: Dr William Temple, Dr Geoffrey Fisher and Dr Michael Ramsey.

Against this long historical background the life of the village has continued over the centuries. Until the end of the 19th century regular markets and fairs took place in the area between the cross and the priory arch. Indeed the cross was – and still is – the heart of Repton and reputedly where Christianity was first preached in the Midlands in AD653. And it was to the cross that in 1848 a man brought his wife, with a halter round her waist, and offered her for sale for a shilling!

Riddings

The earliest recorded reference to Riddings is in the 12th century when it was, as its ancient name 'Ryddynges' implied, 'a clearing in the grove'. This was the grove of Alfreton, part of woodland which swept down to the river Erewash, a mile away, and over the boundary into Nottinghamshire, where it eventually became part of the great forest of Sherwood. Apparently it remained a small agricultural hamlet on the south-east edge of Alfreton manor until the Industrial Revolution.

Within the first decade of the 19th century the ironworks had become the most efficient producer of pig iron in the country. It was towards the end of this period that the Oakes family acquired the local mineral rights and extended the industrialisation into coalmines, brickworks, clayworks and other allied industries including, and quite by chance, a short lived oil industry. Records tell that in 1847, following complaints of the 'canal setting fire', a strange oily liquid was discovered seeping from workings in a Riddings mine. Scientific investigations instigated by chemist Lyon Playfair, James Oakes' brother-in-law, pronounced it to be petroleum, and for a short while a small refinery operated in the corner of the ironworks. The oil was of poor quality and soon ran out, but it can be claimed that the British petroleum industry had its birth in Riddings in the year 1847.

James Oakes provided extensive housing for his workers, repairing old property, building new, and within two generations Riddings was transformed from a decaying medieval hamlet into a prosperous industrial village. Small businesses and shops sprang up, ranging from candlemaking, building, ironmongery, concrete works and milling to a bakery, butchery, grocery and druggist.

But from all accounts, in its early days, Riddings was a rough, tough spot, lacking spiritual guidance and leadership and with no place of worship since the dissolution of St Mary Magdalene chapel in 1650. A memorial cross in Riddings churchyard bears testament to William Shawcroft, died 16th June 1831, who first 'raised the standard of the Cross amongst the benighted inhabitants of the hamlet'. In 1833, as a result of public subscription, and on land given by James Oakes, the present fine church of St James was erected.

Oakes built himself Riddings House, a model farm close by, and surrounded it with an extensive park with recreational facilities, cricket and football pitches. The present infants school on West Street was also provided in 1883. In 1877, at the summit of Greenhill Lane, the highest point of the village, twin windmills were erected to mill flour for the Oakes family, their tenantry and feedstuffs for the livestock on the estate farms and the pit ponies in the mines. Named Sarah and James after members of the Oakes family, they stood as proud and well loved landmarks dominating the skyline for the next 86 years until their sad demolition in 1963.

Today the heavy industries – coalmining, iron, brick, clay and concrete have gone, so have the candle and flycatcher factories, but employment is now provided on a modern industrial estate by lighter industries such as Granwood Flooring, Derwent Upholstery, Standard Soap and Charnos. There are adequate shopping facilities and modern housing developments have extended on all sides of the village. Happily there have been no great changes to the village itself – here the Guinness Housing Trust has modernised the old cottages and built new ones in keeping with their original character. The Moulders' Arms (the Thack) retains its thatched roof and across the road the Seven Stars, built in 1702 on the site of the old St Mary Magdalene chapel, has changed very little. Riddings House is now a residential home for the elderly, the Model Farm has been tastefully converted into charming mews cottages and the green and pleasant park is in regular use.

Ridgeway 🦋

The name of the village is derived from its means of approach, along the ridge where the old road south from Sheffield passed via Gleadless to Mosborough and Eckington, and eventually to Nottingham. Its location and early agricultural activities in Eckington parish gave rise to a traditional gathering known as rent suppers, when tithes would be collected.

Not only was the land good for farming, there were deposits of iron ore and coal to be found. Evidence suggests that both Romans and Danes excavated here in search of the former. Towards the end of the 16th century, Flemings, who came to England to escape persecution, started the scythe and sickle industry for which Ridgeway continued to be known. They realised that the combination of iron, coal and local water power were ideal: a fact which did not escape the notice of the head of a well known local family, Joseph Hutton. He purchased a small scythe works at Birley Hay about 1750, one of several along the Moss valley, below the village. The growth of the Huttons' business made it necessary to move to larger premises and this works was in operation producing scythes and sickles until 1988, on the retirement of the existing directors.

Modernisation was slow in coming to Ridgeway in its secluded valley. Early owners of cars were known to garage them at the top of the hill and walk or horse-ride to collect them as they were unable to cope with the steep gradient on the outward journey. Electricity was a luxury and until the 1960s gas supplies were not available in the lower end of the village.

More recent 'industry' has again arrived, and the recently restored farmstead in the village houses the rural craft centre, where knitting, sewing, woodworking, glass cutting, chocolate making and natural cosmetics are some of the items produced and sold to visitors.

Other names with connections in Ridgeway would indicate that it was quite a closed community in the past; Rodgers, Nicholsons and Bolsovers being prevalent, whilst the name of Archer can be said to be associated with one of the minor scandals of the past. John and Sarah Archer were the first couple to be married in the newly completed church, only to find that, as the church was unlicensed for marriages, they had in fact been living in sin for several days and matters had to be speedily corrected by a visit to Eckington, where their union could be legalised.

More recently the name of Renwick upheld the law in the person of Sir John Renwick, knighted as President of the Law Society and his wife Lady Renwick, who was for many years a local Guide Commissioner. Each summer a Guide camp was held on their land. The house in which the Renwicks lived is named St Cross and was built in the shape of a cross by its owner, in the early part of the 20th century.

Modern day Ridgeway has a sports hall and thriving cricket club supported in part by an annual Carnival Week in July where all groups including the WI sponsor and run events to raise money. There are still four local hostelries and the former vicarage now houses a restaurant.

Ridgeway still retains some connections with its past, as it is set in an area of special scientific interest, where birds and wild flowers enjoy a sheltered habitat. Whilst farm buildings and old workshops have been renovated to provide modern country dwellings for escaping city folk, the ghost once thought to inhabit the churchyard can still take the form of a barn owl perching on the Hutton Memorial, living in peace in a quiet corner of the valley.

Risley ✤

Risley, spelt Rislie and Riseleie in the Domesday Book, means 'rush meadow' but whatever it was in the 11th century it is now a village with some 648 inhabitants, steeped in history but with no village store or post office. However, one farmer has a saddlery and a pick-your-own fruit and vegetable business and another a greengrocery shop. There is also a petrol station and garage repair and recovery service for the nearby M1 and bypass. The single pub, once called the Ffych Arms after a past owner of the Hall, later changed to the Blue Ball, was demolished and rebuilt as a 'road house' before the Second World War.

The majority of adults commute to work in the towns. The village lies on the old A52 road halfway between the towns of Long Eaton and Ilkeston and the cities of Derby and Nottingham. It is mainly a ribbon development of modern houses with some farm tracks and two avenues leading off. The avenues are imaginatively called First and Second Avenue! In Second Avenue are eight bungalows for retired people.

The old windmill which stood at the brow of Rushy Lane and the old toll house and cottages at the east end of the village have disappeared long ago, but towards the west end where Risley brook passes under the road there is a conservation area, within which is the small Elizabethan church of All Saints. The present church is a rarity, in that it belongs to a period when churches were being pulled down rather than built. Inside over the west arch hangs a replica of the Royal Coat of Arms which survived when many of its contemporaries were destroyed.

The church was built by Michael Willoughby and his wife Katherine, who also founded a free school. The Willoughbys lived at Risley Hall opposite the church. A descendant of theirs, Elizabeth Grey, built or endowed four other buildings of interest in the area, the Latin and English school houses and the Latin school and English school. The latter is a Church of England school and caters for up to 90 pupils. The Latin school is now used by the pupils as a music room and an extra classroom.

Behind the church, along the brookside, is the old post office, now a private dwelling, as is the forge which once operated near the pub. Of the other two cottages along the brook, one was replaced by a modern house before the conservation order was passed, the other has been renovated and is now a very pleasant cottage. Beyond here the path continues to

Windmill Hill, where it is believed a second windmill was situated.

In June 1729 a Roman silver plate was found in Risley Park. Unfortunately, it was broken and the finder, not realising its value, broke off even more pieces. It passed into the hands of Lady Aston of Cheshire who owned the Park.

There is a march for piano by Niccola Zeppili called *Risley* and dedicated to Madame Hooley. No history of this is known but Ernest Terah Hooley bought Risley Hall in 1889 and owned it until 1942. He was a well-known financier who made and lost several fortunes. Although a bit of a rogue in his business speculations he was reputed to be generous to people in need. The local church received many gifts, including a chalice and paten.

Risley Hall was rebuilt in the early 18th century. The balustrade and gateway on the terrace are all that is left of the original great house. After the Hooleys, the Hall was bought by Nottingham Corporation and used as an approved school for boys. It is now a private nursing home for the elderly, with a complex of small homes for the more independent. The village cricket team play their home matches in the grounds and for several years the church have held a garden party there.

Rosliston 🌿

The name Redlauseton found in the Domesday survey probably derived from Rodlaueston, an Anglo-Saxon name meaning the farm of Hrolf, a Norseman.

Rosliston was a pleasant agricultural settlement and in 1801 it had a population of 257, which rose to 360 by 1831. In 1849 a school was built by public subscription. The present school opened in 1876 with 44 pupils. Fees ranged from tuppence halfpenny to sixpence depending on age and social class.

In 1802 Rosliston and other neighbouring parishes were united for poor law purposes under an Act of 1782. A workhouse, or 'House of Industry' as it was described on a plaque above the door, was built at Rosliston. In 1838 the combined salary of the master and matron of the workhouse, Mr John Campion and his daughter Elizabeth, was over £36 per annum. The workhouse was sold in 1840 to Joshua Hardy for £200 and converted into tenements. These have long since been demolished and part of the Yew Tree estate now occupies the site.

A crime was committed in 1859 that upset the tranquillity of the village. A reward of £2 was offered for the apprehension and conviction of the 'evilly disposed person who did on Friday night or early Saturday morning, wantonly and maliciously pull up a quantity of onions and seriously damage a quantity of beans growing on a plot of ground occupied by William Whittingham.' The culprit was never discovered.

The church was largely rebuilt and extended in 1819, and today the church of St Mary the Virgin consists of a small apsidal chancel, nave and south porch, and at the west end a tower surmounted by an octagonal spire. This, the oldest part of the church, dates back to the first half of the 14th century.

In addition to its church, Rosliston had a Methodist chapel for over a hundred years. There is reference to a chapel in the village in Circuit documents dating back to 1851 but the chapel still remembered today celebrated its centenary in 1973, a year before it closed. The chapel, now alas demolished, was built on to the side of the Plough inn, although, as far as is known, there was no inside means of access from one to the other!

In 1955 the Milligan family of Caldwell Hall donated a packet of land to the inhabitants of Rosliston and Caldwell for the purpose of providing a village hall. The actual building was based on a prisoner of war hut transferred from the camp situated off Linton Road.

Historically the main occupation of Rosliston's inhabitants has been farming, but in more recent times many people have been employed in coal-mining and at nearby Drakelow power station. Since the mid 1960s, with new housing developments, there has been an influx of newcomers to the village but Rosliston has maintained its essentially agricultural character.

Rowsley 🌿

Great Rowsley, sitting astride the A6 leading to Bakewell, is one of the gateways to the Peak National Park, as also is Little Rowsley, on the Chatsworth Road.

Great Rowsley has long had strong links with Haddon and with Bakewell. In 1636 Grace, Lady Manners founded a school 'for the better instructing of the male children of the inhabitants of Bakewell and Great Rowsley, in good learning and Christian religion', today's Lady Manners School. The people went to the churches at Bakewell and Beeley, and earlier still the chapel at Nether Haddon. Today the village is still in the main part of the Haddon estate, only small portions having been sold for private households.

The village with its turnpike gates (two toll-bar cottages still stand) was on a main stage coach route, then in 1849 the railway arrived. The life of the small farming community must have been rudely disturbed by this intrusion into its midst. A lot of building took place in those years, giving much of the shape of the village today. Not only the railway, with its bridges, viaduct and new station (now gone), but also the school 1840, Wye bridge 1844, the church and vicarage 1855, and a new corn mill. Some of the roads were realigned. In the 1890s came the railway houses, the Midland Cottages, with the Methodist chapel in 1910. The earlier years of this century saw the widening of the old narrow bridge over the Derwent to its present state, the village hall built and the Express Dairy by the station.

The railway, with its extensive marshalling yard – Rowsley sidings – and locomotive shed, went under the 'Beeching Plan' in 1967, and shortly afterwards the dairy (although some of the buildings are used today for small industry). Caudwell's Mill has become a popular water-powered working museum with craft workshops including glass blowing, wood turning and ceramics. But the days when Rowsley had found employment for a wide area around have gone.

Probably the best-known building is the Peacock Hotel, with the inscription above the front door of 'John Stevenson 1652'. It was a one time dower or manor house and farmhouse. In the 19th century Rowsley, 'embosomed in hills', with its thatched houses and two rivers, was the haunt of artists and anglers, who stayed at the Peacock. Mrs Gaskell stayed on a visit to Chatsworth House in September 1857, as did the Emperor Maximilian of Mexico.

Equally popular as a roadside hostelry is the Grouse and Claret (formerly the Station Hotel), built around the time of the coming of the railway, and in recent years extensively developed and modernised. East Lodge nearby is now a country house hotel.

Mention must be made of the recreation ground, given to the village by the Duke of Rutland in 1926. The tennis and bowls are no more, leaving football and cricket, the latter celebrating its centenary in 1990 with a new pavilion. There is also a children's play area.

Of the numerous small farms of 50 or 100 years ago, four larger ones remain. Today there is a village shop and post office. At the sawmill (once a fulling mill with a dyeworks nearby in 'Blue Street') pine furniture is made. The blacksmith's shop has long gone. It was part of one of the two coaching inns, the Nag's Head and the Red Lion, which are said to have stood in the village square. There are two shops in Little Rowsley.

The village fete takes place during the last weekend in June, with a Well Dressing and Flower Festival in the church, at which time opportunity should be taken to view the tomb, in Siena marble, of Lady John (Catherine) Manners, described by one writer in 1893 as 'the most exquisite monument I ever saw'.

Sawley 🦢

The village of Sawley lies in the extreme south-east corner of the county and on the north bank of the river Trent. It centres around its ancient church dedicated to All Saints. Constituted a town in 1258, it is still regarded as a village. The original name of Salloe referred to the willows which grew on the river banks and a tablet in the priest's vestry of the church bears this name. The willows were used in basket making.

Sawley has had a parish church since approximately AD800 and parts of the present church date back to Saxon times. In its early years it was quite famous and around 1345 hundreds of priests and deacons were

Bridge over the River Trent at Sawley Village

ordained there. A tomb dated c1320 in memory of the first vicar of Sawley has unfortunately been destroyed but the carved 'Sawley Angels' which adorned it have survived and are now in the Victoria and Albert Museum as fine examples of sculpture. The church has a ring of eight bells, the oldest dated 1591, and a dedicated group ring them for all services.

During the hey-day of river transport so many inhabitants worked the barges that the nickname 'Sawley Nose-Baggers' originated due to them leaving their donkeys feeding from their nose-bags outside the inns while they imbibed inside. One of the three inns, visible from the church, the Harrington Arms, is an old coaching house.

To the east of the church, excavation has revealed the presence of a Roman fort dated about AD47 which was a guard post for the river crossing but never inhabited.

The lace trade originated in Sawley, from where it later spread to Long Eaton and Nottingham. It was a thriving industry and the art of 'flossing', which was a type of silk embroidery on lace, was native to the village. The wedding dress of a Princess Royal was made here using this material. Many villagers were engaged in knitting hosiery, which they did in their own homes. Cheeses, mainly of Stilton type, were made and sold at the annual Wakes or Fair which took place every November.

Situated as it is on the banks of the Trent, Sawley is closely associated with water. The rivers Derwent and Soar join the Trent nearby and the Trent-Mersey canal runs beside it. The marina, which has recently been extended on land freed by gravel extraction, is one of the largest in

Europe. Boat building is still one of the local trades. A Severn-Trent water treatment works lies in the village and purifies vast quantities of water to supply many surrounding counties.

The present village is a mixture of old and new, rural and urban. Approaching over the river the fields still stretch on either side of the road and the farmer can be seen collecting his cows in for milking. The church spire still dominates the scene and the inns stand where they did in coaching days. Gone are the manor house, the smithy, the cottages housing the lace frames and knitting machines, the stocks and the pinfold where stray cattle were housed. Modern housing estates extend the village far beyond its original boundaries.

Although formerly much more important than its neighbour Long Eaton, in recent years the position has been reversed and the village fights a constant battle against being absorbed into the town and deprived of its identity. The WI were responsible for Sawley identification signs being placed on all approaches.

Most residents now commute to the near-by towns for employment although Carters, the famous soft drinks firm, have a large factory close to the church. Its enormous lorries come and go all day long carrying their products far and wide and some local people work there.

Scarcliffe

Scarcliffe is eight miles south-east of Chesterfield and three miles from the M1 motorway.

The earliest documents date from the Restoration period. Scarcliffe Manor was the residence of the de Frechville family, but the Manor was demolished in 1964 before restoration became the vogue. Many other old dwellings were also demolished including a thatched cottage with farm buildings lying between the church and Vale House, now replaced by two cottages and the post office. The gable end of this farmhouse can still be seen in the yard of Vale House (which was once a butcher's shop). Other old relics are the water pumps still in existence, one on Fox Hill and one at Jasmine Cottage on Station Road.

The old buildings which remain are lovingly cared for, and the village still retains its rural character, having been awarded 'Best Kept Village' several times. In recognition of this trees have been planted in front of the church and along Fox Hill. There is very little room for expansion, so the population of around 600 is not likely to increase.

Most of the land in and around Scarcliffe is owned by the Duke of Devonshire, a group of houses having been built for the Chatsworth estate on the site of the Old Manor.

There are two well-known farming families in the village today, the Wigleys of Manor Farm and the Wildgooses of Hall Farm. In addition, Mr Field farms Station Farm on Station Road. There is no railway station today, having been closed in 1951, but Scarcliffe was once a station on

191

the Chesterfield-Lincoln line of the London North Eastern Railway. This line ran through a tunnel under Scarcliffe and there is a story that during a bombing raid the King and Queen, travelling along this route, were halted for a time in this tunnel. Today, the old stationmaster's house now belongs to the gamekeeper.

The only 'industry' was an agricultural engineering business supplying the farming community, but this was closed in 1983.

The focal point of the village is the church dedicated to St Leonard. It dates from the 12th century, having Norman pillars and a priest's door. Until 1842 the church had a spire, but this was removed and a tower now replaces it. The most well-known part of the church is the tomb of Lady Constantia, an alabaster tomb of mother and child. It is believed that Lady Constantia was one of the de Frechvilles. She and her child were lost in the woods around Scarcliffe when she heard the ringing of a church bell – the curfew bell of Scarcliffe, and made her way towards the sound. In gratitude she bequeathed to the church four acres of land with the proviso that the bells be rung three weeks before and three weeks after Christmas in perpetuity.

Scarcliffe is still fortunate enough to have a post office and general store. There are two inns in the village, the Horse and Groom and the Elm Tree inn. The Elm Tree inn is bordered on two sides with new buildings which have taken the place of Shaw's Row, demolished in 1964.

There are two well-known sporting families in the village, the Elliots and the Heaths, and there was once a good cricket ground and bowling club.

Shardlow 🦑

Shardlow is a village of contrasts. One is between the speed of the traffic on the A6 and the gentle four mph pace of those travelling on the Trent and Mersey Canal. Another is between the quiet, misty calm of the winter, when the village visitors are mainly anglers and walkers, and the bustle of midsummer, when boats travel through the lock in a steady stream and moor along the canal banks, while the pubs and restaurants are full of cheerful holiday makers.

Shardlow is known to all who love the inland waterways, but there was a settlement here, between the Derwent and the Trent, long before the 18th century canal engineers set to work. Known in the Domesday Book as Serdelav, the open fields of the village belonged to the Abbey of Chester. The settlement clustered round the crossroads where the track from Aston to Wilne crossed the route from Derby to the Trent.

At the crossing on the Trent was Wilden Ferry, a rope-hauled ferry which was replaced in 1760 by Cavendish Bridge. Tolls had to be paid by travellers on the road, which from 1738 was a turnpike and the stone giving the toll charges is still displayed on the roadside, approaching the present modern Cavendish Bridge. This bridge was built in 1956; the old one had collapsed spectacularly one day in the bad winter of 1947.

Then came the canal. Warehouses were built to store the goods, and wharves to moor the boats. Ropeworks, saddlers, blacksmiths, ostlers and boat builders and repairers were needed to service the horse-drawn boats. Brewers, innkeepers, shopkeepers, clerks and managers organised the traffic and supplied the wants of the boatmen. Small wonder that from 1788 to 1841 the village population quadrupled, and a whole new group of buildings rose along the canal banks.

But once the railways began to spread, the canals were too slow for all but the most bulky cargoes, and in 1846 the Shardlow section of the Trent and Mersey canal was bought by the North Staffordshire Railway. The canal warehouses became grain stores, and other small industries developed such as woodworking and a wireworks. Malting continued, as did farming, and Dickinson nursery became nationally known. Other places of employment for Shardlow people were the cotton mills at Wilne and factories in Kegworth and Castle Donington.

What can be seen today of Shardlow's past? Many of the old cottages were replaced by modern developments in the 1960s; others were saved by the designation of much of the canal side as a conservation area in 1978. Shardlow Hall, dating from 1684, is an imposing mansion, now used as offices. It is opposite St James's church, dating from 1839. Before this the village was in the parish of All Saints, Aston. When the canal opened, villagers were able to go to Aston church by boat, instead of on foot.

The wealthy canal merchants built themselves fine houses, some of which can still be seen, such as Broughton House on the A6, The Lady in Grey in Wilne Lane, the houses on the Canal Bank and The Wharf. Attractive cottages still stand in Long Row and on the green. There are interesting new developments, including the conversion of old warehouses for modern housing, and these have increased the village population and the range of its activities.

One of the most striking developments of the last 20 years is the growth in leisure use of the canal. With this has come increased prosperity for the inns and restaurants, of which the village has a wide selection, and the development of businesses providing services for holidaymakers.

Shipley

The village of Shipley, situated in the Erewash valley midway between Ilkeston and Heanor on the A6007 is somewhat different from the rural picture of a village clustering around the ancient church. The village has no church or chapel, no state school, no policeman, no shop or post office, no traffic lights or pedestrian crossing.

The estate of Shipley from which the village takes its name, is very old, there being evidence of two manors here before the time of William the Conqueror. In 1729 the heiress of Shipley, Hester Miller, married Edward Mundy of Allestree, making their home at Shipley Hall and taking the name of Miller Mundy. For almost 200 years this family held the lordship of the manor of Shipley.

During the Victorian and Edwardian eras many famous people enjoyed the lavish hospitality of the Squire and his Lady, notably the visits of King Edward VII and Lillie Langtry. Flourishing today is a blue cedar planted by Edward VII in 1907 and also several beech trees well over 250 years old – reputedly some of the oldest in the country. With the death of Alfred Edward Miller Mundy in 1920 the dynasty came to an end. His heir sold the estate to the Shipley Colliery Company and some of the farms to the sitting tenants.

The next 25 years saw intensive colliery workings with also a brick-yard, woodyard and gasworks, the houses in the village being mainly occupied by colliery and estate officials and workers, but with the beginning of ribbon development by private householders along the main through road. The Hall was demolished in 1942 following extensive subsidence damage due to the extraction of coal from underneath.

The character of the village started to change with nationalisation of the coal mines in 1947, the subsequent working out and closure of the pits, transfer of labour and closure of the mineral railway, culminating in 1976 with the transfer to Derbyshire County Council of some 900 acres of farm and woodlands, together with about 25 houses and farms remaining from the Miller Mundy estate.

Today the village bears little resemblance to its past; the Hall has gone but its redelineated foundations form a focal point of interest to the Shipley Country Park established in 600 acres of the land now owned by Derbyshire County Council. The two lodges designed by Sir Edwin Lutyens still survive, along with the water tower, gardens, a dower house and the Home Farm with its dovecote and unique octagonal-shaped dairy, which have been tastefully restored and now house 'Farmcraft', a business and educational venture specialising in the preservation of rare breeds of domestic animals and birds. The remaining 300 acres belonging to Derbyshire County Council has been developed as a theme park.

The eastern part of the parish retains its rural character so loved by D. H. Lawrence, following the successful campaign to prevent the open-casting of a large area of the Erewash valley.

Shottlegate 🦢

Well before the hamlet of Shottlegate was so named, the Romans discovered that the area was suitable for starting up kilns to make pottery. It is said that specimens of this pottery have been found at Hadrian's Wall.

Today, activities at Shottlegate centre on Shottlegate Farm, an imposing stone-built edifice built by Strutt in 1855, and on the Women's Institute hut where monthly meetings bring together women from a wide area.

The busy A517 Belper to Ashbourne road through the hamlet was licensed as a turnpike in 1764. The Gate inn and toll house built in that year still stands, but is now a private house called Bye-Ways. The Hanging Gate now stands further down the hill, an attractive place but much altered since the Second World War.

The next village is Blackbrook, where in Longwalls Lane one passes the ruins of Holly House Farm, once the home of Samuel Slater. After completing his apprenticeship with Jedediah Strutt, Samuel went to America where he introduced the cotton industry and became known as the 'Father of American Manufacture'. Now, close to the ruins, stands imposing Holly House, said to have been erected by the Slater family of America. Longwalls Lane is believed to be a prehistoric road leading to the north.

Also in Blackbrook, in Plains Lane, stands Shottle Wesleyan Methodist chapel, erected by Thomas Slater of Chapel Farm, who was so fervent a preacher that he was called 'Parson Slater'. Wesley, it is said, visited Chapel Farm during his preaching tours. Now the chapel is derelict, no more singing children or fervent preaching.

Further along Plains Lane stands Holly Seat Farm, nestling close to Handley Wood. Here a friendly ghost has been felt and seen on several occasions.

On the edge of the area stands Cross Roads Farm. A coaching inn known as the Owl from 1850 to 1880, it is said that Dick Turpin once slept there!

The land around Shottlegate abounds in springs, and wells stand in several gardens. A local saying is 'Go to Shottle on a bottle and come back on the cork'. A walk down quiet Lambhouse Lane from Shottlegate brings you to Shottle, an ancient manor which, together with the adjoining manor of Duffield, was given to Henry de Ferrars by William the Conqueror. Now Shottle and the surrounding stonebuilt farmhouses belong to the Chatsworth estate. St Lawrence's church, a daughter of Hazelwood church, is still used, but the school is closed, and the Baptist chapel is now used by a potter.

Two landmarks are Alport Stone and Firestone Hill, both beacon sites and giving excellent views of the rolling farmlands and the villages in the area.

Simmondley

Simmondley was once one of the seven hamlets that became the township of Glossop. The first written mention of the village is in the Domesday Book, as Symond's Ley, Symond being a Saxon chief whose land was seized by William I.

Simmondley Hall was built in the reign of James I and one wonders to what use its Priest Hole was put during the Civil War. The oldest house, Dingle Cottage, nestles in the lee of Whiteley Nab, and between these two old dwellings are a cluster of stone houses and cottages which form the old village.

Now the centre of Simmondley has moved from the old village and its pub and Sunday school, to the small supermarket, county school, few shops and amenities and a new pub on one of the estates. The surrounding farmland is rapidly disappearing and the barns and outbuildings are being converted. Simmondley Hall is now divided into two, Dingle Cottage has been restored and extended, and the Sunday school now houses a thriving play group. One Cow Lane has disappeared to make room for the commuters to Manchester and Stockport who daily clamour for a ring road.

Its a far cry from the 16th century when the wool trade brought prosperity to the area, or the time when the whereabouts of illicit stills eluded the law officers because so many were involved in their use. Eventually the stills disappeared as the climate became too hot for the miscreants, and alehouses took their place, spring water which makes the best ale being so readily available. The Hare and Hounds was one of these, and it didn't get a licence for spirits until around 1960. Few can now recall the existence of a mineral water factory (the 'Pop Shop') near Ailsa Craig, and the Simmondley Society which once planted and tended shrubs in the old village is now defunct.

Memories have receded of the 1920s murder in the ventilator shaft of the drift mine for Simmondley Pit, the Simmondley seam of coal whose workings finished in the 1940s. Even tales of the exploits of Billy the Donkey and his stablemate and partner in crime, the goat, are now becoming legendary.

However the magnificent views remain and the old and new are blending with the old village, now a quiet cul-de-sac through which walkers stroll on their way up the Dingle and onto the Nab, or down the Roman road which led from Melandra to Brough. But Fickle Spring is still living up to its name.

Smalley ✍

Smalley, situated on the Derby – Heanor road, six miles north-east of Derby, has come a long way from its early beginnings. At the time of the Norman conquest Smael Leah or Smaellage meant narrow clearing – a tranquil spot, surrounded by forest. Smalei is recorded in the Domesday Book in 1086 as having 'a church, a priest and a mill. . . .' Now with a population of more than 2,000 it is desirable commuter territory, with a strong sense of community.

A family who helped to shape the history of Smalley was that of the Richardsons. In 1610 they bought the Smalley Farm estate, with coal workings under the local clay. Their descendants prospered as the need for coal grew and the coal was transported to Derby and Leicester. In the early 18th century the brothers John and Samuel Richardson founded a Colliers' Charity, which benefited the village miners, and also endowed a free school for 'twelve poor boys' built in 1721. The endowment continues to this day, though the school is now administered by the local authority.

Pre-war Smalley was a linear village, with houses strung out along Main Road and Heanor Road. Now it has taken on a new shape with two large housing estates extending deep into the countryside. With the growing population many new organisations have arrived. But the organisation that draws the widest cross-section of people is the Smalley Community Project.

The Smalley Dam was created at the end of the 18th century by John Radford of nearby Smalley Hall, the High Sheriff of Derbyshire. During this century, after years of neglect, it became silted up. The Community Project workers took on the task of its restoration, including cutting back encroaching trees and undergrowth and removing tons of silt. Gradually the area, presented by its owner to the village in 1990, is becoming an amenity to be enjoyed by all who appreciate the peace of the countryside.

Smalley is not one of Derbyshire's most picturesque villages. Only a few houses are more than 100 years old, but it has lovely gardens and is well-cared for. Sadly its most distinctive building – the Round House –an old-fashioned toll house was pulled down in 1956. Its other claim to fame is the chime of five bells in the parish church. They were given by the Rev Charles Kerry, who was born in Smalley, and whose tomb is in the shade of the ancient yew in the churchyard. A bell-tower was built to house this gift in 1912. They were brought to the church from the Loughborough bell-founders, garlanded with flowers on a large dray in a procession headed by a band for their consecration. It was only recently discovered that the chime of five bells is the heaviest in England, the largest bell – the tenor – weighing over 40 cwts. The church of St John the Baptist was built in the 18th century on a much earlier site. In the wall of the porch is inserted a 7th century Saxon cross.

It was through the Squire, then Robert Sacheverell Wilmot-Sitwell, that cricket was introduced to the village in 1863. His son continued the tradition of a strong cricket team, and it was no coincidence that, as patron of the living, he appointed two parsons who were cricketers of distinction.

Smalley now has two general shops and a butcher's. Traditionally village life centres on its public houses and Smalley is well-endowed with three – the Bell inn, the Nag's Head and on the southern boundary with Morley, the Rose and Crown. All offer a warm welcome, good food and companionship. But, to get a complete picture of a village, the visitor must explore it on foot. Turn from the busy main road and a network of paths connects Smalley with the surrounding villages. Walking along them is like putting back the clock and it is possible to imagine one is back in the Smalei of long ago.

Smisby ❦

Smisby is a small village on the southern edge of Derbyshire. The Derbyshire/Leicestershire boundary forms part of the parish boundary, and because of its close proximity to Ashby-de-la-Zouch many attempts have been made to transfer the village to Leicestershire. However, it is determined to be 'Derbyshire born and Derbyshire bred'.

Smisby can trace its roots back to the Norman Conquest, for in 1068 the monks of nearby Repton built a chapel of ease here. The memorials in the church show the influence of the lords of the manor. The manor house is close to the church of St James. It is the third house to be built on the site and dates from the 1500s.

Ann Comyn, whose alabaster figure is the first in the church, was the widow of the 14th century lord and she had the present church built incorporating the chapel of ease as the south aisle. Her descendants raised the roof of the main aisle – and added clerestory windows, but Ann Comyn's church is still there. Her descendants were the Kendalls who in 1660 sold the manor and the village to the Crewes of Calke Abbey and, although much property had to be sold, a considerable part of the village still belongs to the Harpur-Crewe estate.

Smisby was originally Smithesby – the village of the smiths – and as the tournament field for Ashby Castle lies between the village and the castle, it is possible that the smiths made and repaired the armour for Ashby's knights as well as for the Kendalls. The proximity of the Tournament Field made an impression on Sir Walter Scott. When his host took him on to the top of the church tower, the scene before him gave him the setting for *Ivanhoe*. Many houses in the area have used this title in their name. The original posting inn – the Three Tuns – became Ivanhoe House when the present public house, the Nelson inn, was built.

There are many signs of the medieval village still to be seen. Photographs taken from the air show the three field system of farming to have been centred on the manor house. The village itself is still arranged in the medieval block system as the streets have followed the old tracks.

Sixty years ago the village consisted of six farms and 20 cottages. The farmhouses were within the confines of the village. Each farm had tied cottages for its labourers and the other cottages were occupied by miners and clay workers. There was a working flour mill with a bakehouse attached (what memories that invokes – waiting for a loaf to be peeled from the oven – the smell of real hot cross buns – was it only 60 years ago?)

It is in the last 20 years that the greatest change has taken place. The small farms have gone and in their place are two rival racing stables and a stud farm. The land has been sold from the others and the farm house and buildings turned into small residential complexes. Cottages have been removed or enlarged until very little space is left in the village. The young population has dwindled, resulting in the closing of the school.

Smisby is still an extremely pleasant village and its position in the proposed new forest will hopefully surround it with trees in place of those that elm disease removed.

The village receives many visitors through its connections with Ivanhoe and the Kendalls of the manor house, whose descendants are mostly American. Another dedicated group of visitors are the descendants of a Smisby farmer's daughter, Hannah Bailey, who married Charles Baker from Packington. In 1828, the day after their wedding, they sailed for New Zealand as two of the first party of missionaries to work there. They were instrumental in bringing the Maoris to agreement with the settlers and are so revered by their many descendants that any visit to Europe must include England and in particular Hannah's birthplace.

Snelston

Snelston is a small village situated three miles south-west of Ashbourne, between Clifton and Norbury. It nestles in a valley bounded on its eastern side by Darley Moor through which the A515 passes, and on its western side by the river Dove, beside which the railway used to run. A small brook, which joins the river Dove, flows through the centre of the village and due to torrential rain, houses along Brook-side were badly flooded in 1957 and again in 1970.

In 1828, Cottingham was commissioned to build an immense Gothic revival-style Hall – a mini version of the largest house in Europe, the Earl of Shrewsbury's Alton Towers. The mansion had a baronial-type entrance hall lighted by a large imposing window with stained glass heraldic devices. The whole place was richly furnished and hung with many pictures and had much fine internal panelling. Thirty acres of pleasure grounds which included terraces and sunken gardens surrounded the hall. From gate lodges, coach roads passed through 300 acres of parkland planted with a variety of trees. A unique feature was a plantation of

80 monkey puzzle trees – the first to grow successfully in Europe. This beautiful hall was occupied until around 1945, and it was demolished in 1951.

Well satisfied with the Hall, the Squire John Harrison commissioned Cottingham to design and remodel his village, which is the one we see today. Many houses feature Flemish brickwork with Tudor chimney stacks, and lacy-style Gothic windows set in deep stone mullions. There are some timber-framed houses, the best examples being the former inn – Stanton Arms – and the old post office which closed in 1989. The school, built in 1847 to educate 40 pupils, was erected and maintained entirely at the expense of John Harrison.

The tavern close by the brook bridge, was called the Three Horse Shoes, probably named because of the blacksmith's forge nearby. The bracket for the inn sign many still be seen on the wall and here stood the ancient stocks which disappeared about a century ago, when the tavern was disused. By the side of the smithy the old village pound, made of stone, was standing until some 70 years ago.

The Stanton Arms, which bears the Stanton coat of arms, had only a six day licence, as ordered by Mrs A. F. Stanton – to prevent Sunday brawling. Snelston's only inn now is the Queen Adelaide, whose landlady was born at Snelston.

It stands in a small field on the B5003 – Snelston Common/Cockshead Lane, formerly known as The Turnpike. Close to the inn is Mine Farm, which takes its name from the old lead mine about 500 yards along the road. There was a warning sign which told all to 'Keep Out', and understandably so, as just over a five ft wall was a sheer drop of 83 ft, with other deep holes from where lead had been mined. Just opposite the old lead mine was Birchwood stone quarry. Here around 20 men were employed until its closure in 1957.

In just over 150 years John Harrison's extensive estate is almost non-existent; only four large farms and a few cottages remaining. Farms have been sold, mostly to occupiers, and vacated houses put on the open market.

Visitors to the village enthuse over it, much to the joy and satisfaction of the residents who are happy that Snelston remains totally unspoilt by modern additions.

South Wingfield 🦢

According to old records, the village was known as Winfeld, the 'winne' being the Old English name for gorse and ling. On Church Lane is the cornmill, dated from the mid 17th century, but there had been a mill of some kind on the site long before this date. A medieval document says there were two mills at Winfeld, one under the very walls of the manor house.

In the churchyard, near the chancel, is a tombstone cover of a Crusader knight lying cross-legged. This almost certainly belongs to the ancient Norman family of de Heriz, who were lords of the manor of Oakerthorpe. Opposite the churchyard, three brick cottages have now been renovated into one large dwelling. Before the brick cottages came into being, it is thought the priest's house was on this site and was known as Bakewell Hall. The meadow near to this site is still called Bakewell Meadow.

Wingfield Pit yard was known formerly as Foundry Yard. A foundry was working in addition to the pit and was owned by Bess of Hardwick. It has been said there were once 14 mine shafts in Oakerthorpe, and seven inns. Of course, the Peacock Hotel is in a class of its own; before the hotel came into being, the grange of the Abbot of Darley occupied this site, and before that the ancient Manor of Oakerthorpe, which was occupied by the Norman family of de Heriz.

There is a 'Holy Well' (now filled in) to the rear of the council houses on High Road. This well is believed to have had special healing powers, with steps leading down to the water for people to walk in.

Field End Cottages, across the road from the Yew Tree inn, were built by the stonemason family of Turners. Their name is carved in the stone lintel over the front door. One member of this family was hanged at Derby, for his part in the doomed 'Pentrich Revolution'. It has been said there is a concealed well in the floor of one room in Field End Cottage; and in despair, the frightened, misled rebels flung their muskets and what other arms they had down it, to conceal their identity when they had been betrayed and were hiding as fugitives.

The railway came to the village in 1835 and was built by George Stephenson. The lord of the manor at that time stipulated that the railway must be at least half a mile away from his Hall, hence the railway station was outside the village. The station buildings were built by Thompson and it was said that Queen Victoria stopped at Wingfield Station and had a cup of tea.

There still remains the Toll Bar House on the Nottingham to Ashover turnpike, now a private dwelling.

Wingfield manor house was built by Sir Ralph Cromwell and building was commenced in 1441. The manor was dismantled in 1646 by order of Parliament, although the ruin is still standing and shows a fine crypt and surviving tower.

Sparrowpit 🪶

Sparrowpit, a strange name for a village, but this has nothing to do with 'sparrows', it is taken from Spar Row, the row of cottages which cling to the hillside on the old coach road to Chapel-en-le-Frith, open to sun and wind but never actually seeing the setting sun. It is said locally that one could throw water out at the back door and it would drain into the Humber, but throw water out at the front door, it would drain into the Mersey. The old stone cross just above the village is 1,300 ft above sea level.

During the 18th century when miners found spar or lead in the pits around the area, the village sprang up, with the huddle of cottages we see today, close together yet no two alike, each with a character of its own. The people were self sufficient, with a blacksmith, three inns and a Methodist chapel. Each cottage would have a smallholding with cows, sheep, pigs and hens. Fresh water was abundant with a well and a village pump, and some of the cottage cellars had their own wells and pumps until the advent of a piped water supply.

There is just one inn in the village now, the Wanted Inn, as the Pig and Whistle and Brown Cow closed long ago, with the opening of the New Road to Chesterfield. The Wanted Inn at the bottom of the village, facing Barmoor Clough was originally the Devonshire Arms, being on part of the estate belonging to the Duke of Devonshire until the 1950s, when the lands were sold off because of rising death duties. The inn was not sold privately for almost two years, then at last a buyer was found who really 'Wanted the Inn'.

The Memorial Hall was originally an army hut and was brought from Oswestry in 1919. Its journey nearly ended in disaster when the old lorry and trailer went over in a ditch near Sparrowpit having taken the wrong turning! It was hauled out safely and put onto a solid base on a piece of land later to be given to the village in the will of George and Sarah Beresford of Macclesfield. The hall has been well preserved and in later years bricked around and modernised inside in every way.

The village is quite small, with a population of about 80. There are just one or two holiday cottages, and some newcomers to the village, but there is still a good community spirit and warmth up there in the hills, where the weather in winter can be rough and snow can block the roads.

Spondon ❧

By the time the Domesday Book was written in 1086, Spondon was already a well established agricultural village and so it remained for several centuries. The village was almost completely destroyed by fire in 1340 but the determination and hard work of the residents meant that Spondon was soon rebuilt and in 50 years also had a huge new stone-built church. Remaining essentially an agricultural village, Spondon grew very gradually until the late 18th century.

The advent of the Industrial Revolution changed the character of the village – cottage industries, the canal and railway and finally heavy industry all brought new residents to Spondon. They in turn brought new money, skills and ideas, particularly religious and educational, with them. The new money meant that the new houses were built, especially many larger 'gentleman's residences' for the new professional middle classes.

In the 19th century the population trebled; by 1900 it was approximately 2,500 but from then on it just mushroomed. Houses were needed in ever increasing numbers and estates were built by industry, the local authority and private builders. Spondon maintained its popularity as a residential area and that brought about another change to the landscape as several of the larger houses were demolished and replaced by small houses for commuters. In 1968 came the biggest change of all when Spondon was absorbed by the then Borough and became a suburb in the north-east of the now City of Derby.

Now a little puzzle! What is the connection between Spondon, the painter Joseph Wright, the Minack Theatre in Cornwall and the industrial giants, Courtaulds? The answer is the Homestead, the magnificent red brick Georgian house which stands at the top of Willowcroft Road.

A Grade I listed building, the Homestead was built in 1745 for John Antill, a member of an old Spondon family, who made his money as a tanner. John never lived at the Homestead but his brother William lived there until his death in 1787 when the property passed to their great-nephew, Dr James Cade. He was a surgeon in Derby who mixed in society with such eminent people as Dr Erasmus Darwin, father of Charles Darwin, and Joseph Wright the painter and in 1795 he married Wright's only daughter, Anna Romana.

In 1893 Rowena Cade was born. The Cade family left the Homestead in 1912 and Rowena and her parents moved to Cheltenham. It was Rowena Cade who built the open air Minack Theatre on a cliff edge near Porthcurno. The Greek style amphitheatre was first opened in 1932 and is now a well known tourist attraction. The next resident at the Homestead brought a link with industry. Sir Henry Fowler, who was later to become the Chief Mechanical Engineer with the LMS Railway, lived there until he purchased Spondon Hall. That link with industry continued and the present owner is Courtaulds, which uses the Homestead as a guest-house for important visitors, particularly overseas visitors.

The 19th century gentlemen's residences of Spondon all seem to have been surrounded by high walls. A walk through the 'jitty' from Potters Street will give you a feel of the old Spondon; following the path between the grounds of the Homestead and Ingle Nook you are hemmed in by walls, just as you would have been a century ago. Although the walls are all that is left of the other houses, the most elegant, the Homestead, remains to bridge the centuries which changed Spondon from a small agricultural village into a busy suburb.

Stanley ❧

Stanley is a small village that has escaped the seemingly inevitable housing explosion of many of the neighbouring villages. It lies about halfway between the towns of Derby and Ilkeston, sharing a parish with Stanley Common which is about a mile away by winding country lanes.

In the centre of the village stands St Andrew's church, of 12th century origin, but restored and enlarged in 1876. Though small it has an attractive light interior with an interesting carved Jacobean pulpit and screen. There is also a Methodist church in Morley Lane built in 1882, a post office and newsagent on Station Road, and two public houses, the White Hart and the Bridge inn, both on Derby Road and converted from old cottages. Near the church is the small Church of England primary school and opposite, magnificent beeches almost hide Stanley Hall. Between the church and the old vicarage lies the picturesque and last remaining thatched cottage in the village.

Off Station Road and bordering Dale Abbey parish is Stanley Grange Farm, one of the oldest and most historically important of the local residences. Parts of the present buildings originate from the 17th century when neighbouring West Hallam was a Roman Catholic stronghold and the Grange operated as a Jesuit headquarters and boys school. During this period it was the subject of a debate in Parliament and was raided twice by government forces.

Although the village is now pleasantly rural, during the last 200 years coalmining was the main industry, as can be seen by the remains of several pits on the outskirts. Drift mining operated at the Footrills and evidence can be seen of the longest 'continuous rope' haulage railway which ran from there to Cemetery Hill, Derby. In the 1960s much of the farmland in that area was opencast for coal and the old Manor Farm was demolished. This is now the site of a very large modern farm. Stanley Colliery closed in 1959 and the large spoil heap was taken away during the 1970s and used partially to refill the disused railway cutting.

Now, farming is the main industry, but another local longstanding business is the Felix Bus Company which was started in the early 1920s. The first proprietor, Norman Frost, began by transporting local people to football matches and workers to the pits. The name derived from the famous cartoon of the day 'Felix kept on walking' and true to its namesake is still running a regular service between Ilkeston and Derby today, remaining a family business despite considerable expansion.

Evidence of past industry can also been seen on either side of Derby Road as it starts to climb the hill out of the village. The sandstone quarry which used to be 100 ft deep is still apparent although now filled in. Originally the stone was quarried for use as a very fine quality polishing stone exported as far away as India. In 1929 however, the enterprising owner, Mr Anthony of Chaddesden, discovered another use for the considerable amount of waste produced and started to manufacture concrete building blocks – the Stanley Building Block. Several houses in the village are constructed of these blocks, including those higher up the hill and the Felix bus garage at the other end of the village, but many more may be seen in the Derby suburbs especially Chaddesden and Allenton.

Opposite the shops and behind Station Road lies the recreation ground and at the back of this the very recently built village and sports hall, the culmination of years of fundraising by the whole community.

To the rear of the recreation ground is the line of the old railway cutting, much of which has been left untouched providing a pleasant quiet walk up to the 'Klondyke'. Klondyke was the nickname locally for a group of houses built for workers of a colliery company after the opening of a new mine, and from here the glimmering lights of glow-worms may be seen by walkers along the railway cutting on summer evenings.

Stanley Common &

Before the 1792 Act of Enclosure, Stanley Common was almost comple-tely undeveloped, being purely common land attached to the village of Stanley. Now, with its council estate and more recent housing develop-ments, it has become by far the larger of the two villages. It also incorporates the adjacent hamlet of Smalley Common, officially designa-ted part of Stanley parish in 1938.

In the days of common grazing land, gates were placed at parish boundaries to stop cattle straying and the gate between Stanley and Smalley was originally sited at a spot near the public house previously called the Gate inn and now known as the White Post. The other pub in the village, the Bateman Arms, also on Belper Road, is named after the squire of Stanley residing at Stanley Manor when the common land was enclosed. As with Stanley, coalmining soon became a vital industry, but other trades were also prominent as shown by surviving place names such as Rope Walk and Brickyard. For the traveller passing through, a feature along the roadside is a long line of terraced houses, mostly renovated, and forming a distinctive frontage. Further renovation can be seen at Smalley Common where complete refurbishment of old terraces combined with harmonising new development has revived the commun-ity there.

Stanley Common church dedicated to All Saints was not built until 1913 and was the result of a building fund to which many notable people with local connections contributed. Two Methodist chapels closed down in the 1960s but the one situated at Smalley Common is still active. The small Church of England primary school, now bursting at the seams due to the population explosion of recent years, is hopefully to be replaced in future on land reserved at The Crescent.

Of the local personalities, Mr George Stafford, butcher, must rate as the most widely known, having won medals internationally for the excellence of his black puddings. Indeed, in 1965, the White Post was the scene of a sausage-eating contest at which a local man, Mr Brian Julian, was declared world champion after eating 82 inches of Mr Stafford's own cooked sausage.

Many people will remember the carnival band of previous years 'The Western Echoes', and the musical tradition is carried on at present with the Stanley Common Silver Band which provides entertainment at many events around the district.

Stanton-by-Dale 🪶

High above the Erewash valley lies the quiet little village of Stanton-by-Dale. This area, said to have been known by Bronze Age men, derived its name from stone quarries in the area, several of which exist in and around the village.

Of the old customs, few remain, but local folk recall the village Wakes which took place on the weekend nearest to Michaelmas. On the Saturday there was bowling for a pig, swing boats and stalls, and the first Christmas puddings and mince pies were eaten. The festivities concluded with the special Anniversary Service held in the 12th century village church of St Michael and All Angels. The Wakes were discontinued in the late 1920s.

All the local land was owned by the Earl of Stanhope until 1912, when it was purchased by the Stanton Ironworks Company Limited – later to become world famous for its cast-iron products. Mr Charles Crompton, a former banker, was Chairman of the ironworks and resided at Stanton – now a nursing home for the elderly. A generous benefactor in his lifetime, he was responsible for forming the Erewash Golf Club, the Village Men's Institute for indoor games and providing cash to convert this institute to a hospital during the First World War.

Only Stanton workers were allowed to live in village houses. These were let and maintained by the Stanton estate department. On payment of rent, a beer ticket was issued to be spent in the works pubs. Villagers remember the days when water was drawn from wells, no gas or electricity was available and a 'flush' lavatory was a privilege of the rich. Tales have been told of outside 'loos' by candlelight and banging on boards to scare away rats.

In the parish there were six farms, owned by Stanton, now there are none in the village and only two in the parish. Most have been sold to developers for conversion into country homes – thus showing the trend towards dormitory accommodation. The village boasted numerous characters. Frank Riley, who until 1930 functioned as smallholder, coal merchant and night soil man, was said to have a horse which would not pass the Chequers inn without a pint! Harry Thornley, for many years landlord of the Chequers, not only drew a good pint from the wood, but also extracted a painful molar, cut hair or provided veterinary care for sick animals. Dick Scattergood, owner of the Stanhope Arms, was additionally local undertaker, who laid out the corpses, made the coffins, took them to church and did the burial.

Latterly the village fought to retain the post office, but in years past there were two general stores, a post office, a cobbler's and a shoe shop, as well as a horse and cart service in greengrocery, fish and game, paraffin, hardware and butchery. The forge, used until 15 years ago but now sold to provide a modern dwelling, has a wheelwright's hearth listed for conservation and said to be the only one of its kind in Southern Derbyshire.

Parts of Stanton-by-Dale were designated a conservation area on 4th July 1978. It is deemed a village with a well-preserved character – due in some part to the influence of the Stanhope estate and Stanton Ironworks.

Stanton in Peak

Stanton in Peak is a hillside village, of houses mainly built of gritstone from the Stanton Moor quarries. Also in the parish are Stanton Lees, Pilhough and Congreave, the last two being very small hamlets. The name Congreave means 'rabbit hole', and this is where rabbits used to be kept for the Haddon Hall tables.

Many of the houses date from the 17th and 18th centuries. Holly House, opposite the inn, was probably built 50 or so years before the window tax of 1697. Eight of the 14 windows at the front of the house remain blocked up to this day.

William Pole Thornhill built a good many of the estate houses in the first part of the 19th century; these have the initials WPT in stonework above the door. Now, nearly all are privately owned. Around the time that this building was going on, the stone quarrying industry thrived. The population increased from 512 in 1851 to 717 in 1881, and the number of quarry workers from 21 to 103. Now there are only a couple of quarrymen in spite of there being three local quarry firms operating, a reflection of the change of methods over the years from manual to highly mechanized.

Holy Trinity church has a very unusual feature in that the nave lies from south to North. One of the artefacts is a bronze Italian water stoup from the workshop of Bellini.

In its heyday Stanton had at least three public houses, a general store, post office, butcher's shop and a smithy. Now there is just one inn and a combined post office and store. The public house is named after a racehorse owned by the fourth Duke of Devonshire – the Flying Childers.

The church, the school and the reading room were all built by members of the Thornhill family, as was an unusual feature at the side of

Coach Lane just beyond Beighton House, and known originally as 'The Belvedere'. This is a viewing platform with a stone seat overlooking the Wye valley, and now referred to as 'The Stand'. Before the church was built parishioners used to walk to Rowsley church, and the Belvedere was a convenient resting place with a magnificent view of Haddon Hall and surrounding countryside.

Immediately south of Stanton village, and rising to a height of over 1,000 ft, is Stanton Moor. This is a great attraction to visitors on account of the Nine Ladies, a Bronze Age stone circle. There are numerous Bronze Age burial chambers on Stanton Moor, some of which have been excavated and the finds exhibited in local museums.

The steep hillside on which the village has grown up is a very attractive feature, enhancing the appearance of the buildings and providing a beautiful view as far as Longstone Edge and beyond if weather conditions permit. The gradient can cause problems, especially in times of snow and ice. There are usually several days each winter when cars and lorries cannot reach beyond the lower part of the village.

Having a sloping cricket pitch might be considered a disadvantage, but it does not seem to have hindered generations of boys and young men from developing their cricket skill. Stanton Cricket Club was a hundred years old in 1985, and the teams have many successes to their credit.

The observant walker through the village will notice a number of sturdy stone posts at the side of the streets. These were used to prevent horse-drawn carts from rolling backwards when being unloaded.

The village of Stanton-in-the-Peak

Stapenhill ❧

Geographically, Stapenhill is in Staffordshire, but the majority of its residents look to Derbyshire as their 'home county'.

Stapenhill in the 19th century was a farming village and self-sufficient; it had many shops to cater for the needs of the community ie bakers, tailors, boot and shoe maker, doctor, butcher, post office, four alehouses, a lawyer, wheelwright, plumber, shopkeepers and undertaker. St Peter's church was and is an outstanding edifice in Stapenhill Road. The clock has four faces on the church tower and dates back to 1890. The church was offered the gift of church bells by a wealthy Stapenhill parishioner, but this was rejected by the Rev Warbreck on the grounds the church tower was not safe enough to take them. The old bier and charity boards are still in the ringing chamber.

A number of coopers lived in the village. It was considered one of the top paid jobs in the brewing industry and required an apprenticeship of four to five years. Sons followed fathers and nephews followed uncles. It was very much a 'closed shop'.

The North Pole was the name of the alehouse in St Peter's Street. It has deeds 126 years old but is thought to be much older. It was originally two houses, the pub and the butcher's, and Mr Harvey was the butcher, his shop being the front room and his slaughterhouse the back room; the remaining half of the building being the pub with the maltings in the back yard. Rumour has it, the Rev Warbreck objected to the alehouse being open on Sundays and he was responsible for the licence being taken away. The property is still standing, the two houses are now one private house, but the name 'North Pole' has been retained.

The post office in Woods Lane shows deeds for 1898 but as this building was empty for 40 years it is thought to be much older. A Mr Shotton acquired the property and had a mock Tudor balcony placed halfway up the front of the building. He had three sons, one was a plumber, one a painter and decorator and the other a taxi driver; all business was done from the post office and a display of hardware, toilets, sinks etc was always on show from the Tudor balcony.

Stapenhill village now has beautiful gardens alongside the river Trent. This was made possible by the Goodger family, who gave the land to Burton-on-Trent Council in early 1930.

Starkholmes ❧

The buildings in Old Matlock date back to the 17th and 18th century and at that time some were inns for the benefit of the passengers travelling on the coach road, which is what Starkholmes Road used to be. A little further down the road is the hamlet of Starkholmes looking quite sleepy and respectable now, but it must have been quite a lively area in those days.

There has been a church on the site of St Giles since medieval times, although today only the tower is really ancient. Immediately next to the church, there is a very impressive building which, over the years, has been a public house, a farm and a family residence. This building, the Wheatsheaf, date stone 1681, is said to be haunted. In front of the Wheatsheaf there is a small green and in days gone by this was a site for the stocks, which must have been quite entertaining for some.

The days of the two very happy village schools in the Starkholmes area are numbered. After many changes of Government policy, at last a new school is being built on a site in the vicinity of both schools.

Like most villages, Starkholmes boasts a village pub, the White Lion. Once there was a thriving lead mining industry in the locality and in fact the pub used to be called the Buddles. The term 'buddle' means an inclined hutch for washing ore. As is the case with most village pubs, what you didn't know when you went in you know when you come out! The village is very fortunate in having a small post office and general shop, which is a boon for the elderly in the village.

Starkholmes village is situated on the side of the hill, so even the most humble of dwellings has magnificent views over Matlock Bath and up the valley towards Wirksworth.

Staunton Harold

Staunton Harold is on the border of South Derbyshire and Leicestershire. Staunton (the farm on stony ground) was with many other manors in this area, an appendage of Tongue at the time of the Domesday survey in 1086.

The parish consists of farms and cottages situated in this very rural area. Nestled in the centre of a valley of grass and woodland is the Palladian-style Staunton Hall with the beautiful lake in its foreground, which is overlooked by the church.

The present Hall was built in the 18th century in brick with stone dressings. On the south front on the parapet a massive lion can be found. The leaden figures of Minerva, Apollo and Ceres are to be seen on the eastern front.

The church is a superb example of Gothic architecture. The tower and the body of the church has changed very little, still having box pews and Jacobean furniture and fittings. The nave has a painted wooden ceiling representing the Creation. The church is now owned by the National Trust but there are still some services held in it and also the occasional wedding.

The first family to live at the Hall were the Ferrers, later followed by the Shirleys who in the 1700s reverted back to the family name when the title of Earl Ferrers was created.

Staunton Harold Parish Church

In 1760 a murder took place, when Laurence, the 4th Earl Ferrers, who was separated from his wife, shot his steward, a man called Johnson, after accusing him of administering the estate in favour of the Countess. After a notable trial he was sentenced to be hanged. Dressed in his wedding suit which was embroidered with silver, the Earl was driven to the place of execution in his own landau. He was escorted by a body of constables, horse grenadiers and foot soldiers accompanied by the Sheriff and Chaplain.

Another notable character on the Staunton estate was Samuel Great-bach, who was the head gamekeeper at the turn of the century. He was awarded a pension but still carried on his duties. At that time the park was a sanctuary for many different birds; owls, kestrels, jackdaws, stockdoves and nuthatches were found in the trees. Kingfishers and grey wagtails nested in the stream and swans, coots, moorhens and wild ducks were found by the lake.

In 1955 the estate was dispersed and Group Captain Leonard Cheshire VC, DSO, DFC purchased the Hall and it became one of the famous Cheshire Homes. At the same time, a scheme was approved to build a large dam near Melbourne, and so a large area of countryside between Staunton Park and Melbourne became Staunton Harold Reservoir, which covers 209 acres. The Hall was later purchased by the Sue Ryder Foundation.

The people living in this area are mostly farmers, but during latter years the stableyard at the Hall has been opened into a craft centre and there is also a nursery close by. There are two public houses on the estate, both of which are named after the famous Ferrers coat of arms and crest. They are the Ferrers Arms at Lount and the Saracen's Head at Heath End.

211

Stoney Middleton

Our village of 600 inhabitants nestles among the limestone cliffs and rocks in the beautiful Peak District. Why 'Stoney Middleton'? Well, it is built of stone, many early inhabitants were miners and the village is surrounded by stone. Situated on an ancient highway between Chesterfield and Brough, it is mentioned in the Domesday Book as 'Middletune'. Here Roman coins and a 3rd century bracelet were found and there were cupolas for smelting lead and lime.

Middleton Dale has always been an awesome place. It is particularly beautiful with its high limestone cliffs and caves attracting climbers and potholers from all over the world. These high limestone rocks are the homes for jackdaws and gilly flowers and each spring the sandmartins return and the cowslips bloom. Also in the Dale is the Lover's Leap Cafe so called after a beautiful young local girl named Hannah Baddaley, who in 1760, heartbroken after a lovers tiff, jumped off one of these cliffs. Luckily her dress and petticoats billowed out acting like a parachute, thus saving her life.

Candle, besom and boot manufacturing, lime burning, quarrying and light engineering have all been occupations of the past, with quarrying still employing the largest proportion of workers today. Still in business, and family-owned for over a century, are Mason's Joiners and Lennon's Boot Factory. The village can boast two butchers – both Hancocks, a general store and post office, hairdressers and bakery.

There were several dame schools before the present school was built on High Street in 1835 by public subscription. It consisted of one room with a gallery and later enlarged in 1893 to enable 120 children to be educated there. Since the reading room was sold, the school is the meeting place for the Parish Council, PTA, WI, Horticultural Society, Tennis Club and other activities of the village.

The Toll House, now our chip shop, was built at a cost of over £87 and features 14″ thick walls.

Our village is full of history; Lord Denman, Lord chief-justice of England lived here, lord squire of the Hall. He was a great Victorian reformer, a man with high morals who advocated the abolition of slavery. Lady Denman was the first National chairman of the WI formed in 1917. For many years our WI were privileged to use the Denman Room in the Hall for its meeting place. Denman College now proudly bears her name. The local WI formed in 1951 is still going strong.

July is well dressing time when the village comes alive, with the young and the old mixing together, sharing the work and pleasure, with three wells to be dressed in the Nook. The whole village takes part in the many varied activities. After a service of 'Blessing the Wells', and the opening of the festival, the local school children dance round the maypole to a local band. The flower service in church performed by the school children on the Sunday is a delightful custom still carried on, the flowers going to the elderly and sick of the village. Yes, well dressing time brings the village alive as the wakes did in the old days when families were re-united and dancing bears and donkey races were the attractions.

The cross at the bottom of High Street is a reminder of the repeal of the old corn laws. Quite rare and exceptionally charming, the tower is all there is left of the 15th century church of St Martin built by Joan Eyre in thanksgiving for the safe delivery of her husband from Agincourt in 1415. This octagonal church, where the congregation sit in the round, was mainly completed in 1759. The nearby spring water is reputed to have healing qualities. The Wesleyan Reform church is on the Bank and recently held its Anniversary service.

The old Roman Baths in the Nook is where the Middleton lads used to swim and dive and have great fun just as in the past the Roman soldiers did. The constant 63°F of the water is its main attraction. These baths are now in the process of restoration with help from the Parish Council and the Peak Park Planning Board.

Sudbury ✒

Sudbury – meaning South Fortification – has a population of a little under 500, a similar figure to that of 100 years ago. It is situated in the lower valley of the river Dove, within ten miles of the gateway to the Peak District, and is one of the few remaining feudal villages in Derbyshire.

Once mainly an estate village and farming community, many of the cottages are now tenanted by people of varying trades and occupations. The predominant building is the Sudbury Hall, former seat of the Vernon family, now owned by the National Trust. This beautiful house, built during the reign of Charles II, was, for three years, the home of Queen Adelaide, the widow of William IV.

Beyond the Hall, but hidden from view, stands the church of All Saints, which was recorded in the Domesday Book but has been extensively restored in later years. The east window was given by Queen Victoria and Prince Albert in memory of George Edward Anson, brother of the then rector of Sudbury. The six bells in the tower are rung regularly, and the 1870 organ leads a very strong choir every Sunday.

A modern bypass, constructed in 1972, has brought a measure of peace and tranquillity to the largely 17th century village. To the north stands an imposing 18th century deer cote, where herds of deer once roamed in the surrounding parkland. Here the Second World War brought changes with the building of an American army hospital. In 1946 this became a rehabilitation centre for returning British troops and in 1948 its role changed yet again to become HM Open Prison, with accompanying staff accommodation.

The kennels of the Meynell Hunt are situated on the outskirts of the village, meets taking place three days a week during the season.

The sweeping curve of the road through the village is lined on the south side by terraced cottages, little changed since the 19th century. As tenants have come and gone, the interiors have seen many alterations, but their facade of mellow brick remains. The lane to the south takes one past the Victorian butcher's shop to the school, built in 1831 by the 4th Lord Vernon. In the days when pupils were kept at their desks for hours on end, the nature walk to the bottom of this leafy lane was a wonderful treat. Here there is a modern telephone exchange, and farm buildings have now become blacksmith's and joiner's workshops, whilst opposite, still in use, is the local butcher's slaughterhouse.

On the north side of the main road stands the Vernon Arms, an old coaching inn, and the village shop, now incorporating the post office. At the rear of the shop, where bread was once baked, the warehouses have recently been converted into an up-to-date medical centre. At one time Sudbury boasted its own brickworks and gas-house, the latter now a farrier's shop.

A 19th century dairy, the first in the country to be subjected to tuberculin tests, sent milk to London twice daily from the adjoining railway station, sadly closed in the late 1950s. The dairy is now a residential home for the elderly.

For the wayward the village provided its own lock-up and stocks; the latter can still be seen and sometimes 'used' by school children visiting the Museum of Childhood at Sudbury Hall.

The 17th century estate yard and office, bearing the Vernon coat of arms, is still in use today. At one time part of this building comprised a reading room and games room solely for the use of the male inhabitants of the village. In his recollections of 1844, William Warren Vernon recalls going, as a child, with his grandfather to the estate office on Christmas Eve to watch the distribution of joints of beef, together with red cloaks, blankets, flannel petticoats and other warm clothing to all the cottagers. He also tells of how, in 1804, Elizabeth Lane, the beautiful sister of the village shoemaker, was seen by the second Earl of Massarene whilst changing horses at the Vernon Arms; he fell in love with her and they eventually married.

A strong community spirit still exists. Thriving clubs, including cricket, football and archery, compete in the idyllic setting of the sports field opposite the Hall. In equally attractive surroundings is the bowling green and clubhouse.

Sutton on the Hill

For a village only eight miles to the west of Derby, Sutton retains a rural appearance, since there has been comparatively little new building. As its name suggests, the part of the village round the church is slightly elevated and there are excellent views, particularly of the Peak District. Generally the village is scattered round a number of narrow lanes.

Farming, particularly dairy farming, provides a way of life for some, and its importance in the past is reflected in the construction of a cheese factory in 1875, used also for dances and converted into two houses about 50 years ago. This is a good grassland area, with many of its hedges still intact and we have a hedgecutter who is a national champion. It is in the middle of good fox-hunting country, with various coverts in the parish ringing to the cry of the Meynell foxhounds. Parts of the Longford brook, which runs through the village, are fished privately for trout and coarse fish: one stretch is fished by a Derby angling club.

The Domesday survey describing Sutton mentions 'a church and a priest; one mill'. Sutton has the successors to these buildings nine centuries later. The mill, standing near the brook, ceased to function as a water mill before the Second World War and has more recently been converted into a private house. The dried up mill pond and former watercourses are still clearly visible. The church of St Michael, standing on a hill, was very largely rebuilt in 1863, on its old foundations. The earliest parts of the church are the 14th century arches between the nave and the north aisle and the south wall of the chancel.

The 19th century vicarage, built by the Rev Rowland Ward, was a 'castellated mansion' and must have been quite grand even in the times when vicarages were spacious. This has become the Hall, with its turrets and Gothic appearance, a contrast to the more mundane village architecture. Across a sunken road, lie several fields which are ablaze with daffodils in springtime. The Buckstons have remained at the Hall and there are inhabitants who remember life behind the green baize door, donning best cap and apron in readiness for serving afternoon tea. In a retired position behind the Hall, on part of its land, lies the cricket club.

The 19th century village school, with its one large partitioned room, was closed in the early 1970s through lack of pupils and, although this was a loss to the village, the building provides a venue for daytime activities.

Sutton is not a closely knit village since it has now no school of its own, no shop nor post office, no public house and no regular bus service. Nevertheless it has a thriving church community. Certainly one of the occasions when most of the villagers meet is the Church Garden Fete, held near the Hall. Sutton was not always the quiet place that it now seems to be. George Ashmore, a counterfeiter of guineas, was executed and buried in the churchyard in the 18th century. His corpse was removed the following week.

Taddington 🌿

Taddington is one of the highest villages in England, being 1,000 ft above sea level. Approached by way of the A6 from Buxton via Topley Pike, there is a 1 in 6 hill to climb and by way of Bakewell through the picturesque Taddington Dale a similar climb along the A6.

Taddington and Priestcliffe are separated by the A6 bypass, with a combined population of 466. The removal of heavy traffic from the main road through the village on to the bypass, together with a now regular bus service operating daily through the village to Manchester and Nottingham, is a great improvement to village life, but there is always a reminder of bygone days with the old iron London milepost standing at the side of the road.

Many of the newcomers to Taddington are employed in nearby towns, with easy access to work via the A6. Taddington is surrounded by pasture land, mainly used for cattle and sheep farming and tended by local farmers. In the past the two main industries were lead mining and farming. Of recent years the passing of milking cattle through the village has ceased, compared to times when milk was transported from Millers Dale station as far away as Liverpool.

The village is sectioned off by lanes leading to High Well, where many years ago the only water obtainable had to be carried down. Houses are mostly built of stone and limestone abounds everywhere, which on a sunless day can present a sombre look, giving the village a rather cold and bleak appearance.

Taddington in summertime, with its 17 miles of splendid footpaths, becomes a popular place for ramblers. One of the finest views over the fields and houses, giving a marvellous view of the church, can be seen dropping down from The Jarnett near Humphrey Gate Quarry (disused) on one side and the children's play area on the other. Many tourists use this point to take photographs of the lovely view. The thriving primary school for Taddington and Priestcliffe children was rebuilt in 1845, to accommodate around 50 children.

Much of the social life centres on the Queen's Arms public house at one end of the village and the Waterloo Hotel, which caters for passing trade and is popular for local functions, at the opposite end.

Taddington, like most villages, has a chapel and church. The chapel, situated at the lower end of the village, was built in 1903 with the help of local people – services are held monthly.

St Michael's church, part of which was built in the 12th century and rebuilt in the 14th century, has a stone lectern said to be rare beyond Derbyshire, and a 13th century stone font. Sadly the church roof has been badly damaged, presumably in an attempt to remove the lead, and recently two antique chairs were stolen from inside the church. Events are frequently held to raise money to repair the damage to the fabric of the church, and there is also a grant from English Heritage. Considering the small population the money raised is a great credit to the inhabitants.

Tansley

The village is situated on the edge of Tansley Moor, about one and a half miles east of Matlock. In a hollow surrounded mainly by gritstone hills, its westerly aspect is an open valley to Matlock.

The population today is about 1,300. Tansley has two churches, Methodist and Anglican, three public houses, a primary school with about 100 pupils, the village hall, situated alongside the village green, the youth club building, and the last remaining village shop, the post office general store. There are approximately 350 houses. There is a variety of industrial development, mainly on the periphery of the village.

Industry came to Tansley in the latter part of the 18th century in the form of a variety of mills and associated works, making use of the copious supply of water, flowing down small valleys from the gritstone moors. The streams were dammed to provide water storage and power for the mills. A map of the 'Township of Tansley' in 1840 shows ten dams. Several of them remain today and provide the ideal habitat for water birds and a sporting ground for anglers.

Two of Tansley's largest mills, down the old Coach Road, were built in 1783 for the manufacture of cotton tapes and shawls. Both buildings still stand, one being used for storage and the other has recently been divided into several factory units. Older residents of the village recall working in Mr Scholes' tape mills, and of making khaki tape for 'the soldiers' puttees' in the First World War.

Perhaps the largest mill complex was that built in 1799, by Edward Radford for bleaching, dyeing and mercerising, in the lower reaches of Lumsdale. This is the only one of the textile mills which is still worked today. Edward Radford was, in 1840, one of Tansley's chief landowners.

Nineteenth century Tansley was a self-sufficient village. Several grocers, butchers, greengrocer, market gardener, blacksmiths, boot and shoemakers, a tallow chandler, builder, joiner, plumber, cab proprietor, a yeast dealer and several farmers, must have catered for most people's needs.

The parish church was built in 1839/40 on a site which commands such an extensive view that one could imagine that it had been purposely left for just such an important building. Prior to 1840, Tansley people walked the five miles to Crich to attend church. It is interesting to note that the church was extended only 30 years after completion, to accommodate visitors staying at the hydropathy establishments on Matlock Bank. There were 300 seats, when the village population was little over 500!

The first place of worship for the Methodists in Tansley was the octagonal building, now a house, next to the post office. It was reputedly the village cockpit, before being converted to a chapel in 1811.

Tansley House was owned and managed by William Mycock, who had learned the system of hydropathic treatment during his eleven years working at Smedley's famous hydro in Matlock. On coming to Tansley he ran The Grove as Tansley's first hydro, but by 1893 Tansley House was established and being advertised in the most glowing terms. After the 'hydros' faded from popularity, Tansley House was a private residence for many years, but it has recently opened as a residential home for the elderly.

Tansley is perhaps best known, to people outside the village, for its garden centres and nurseries. James Smith & Son (Scotland) Nurseries at their hill-top location off the A615, are the oldest established and proudly hold the Royal Warrant. Down the hill towards the village, Matlock Garden and Waterlife Centre is reached. Increased indoor shopping and restaurant facilities have promoted an all-weather interest in both centres. Several other smaller outlets, Lorna Cross Landscapes, Whitelea Nursery and Stan Smith's, all add to the provision for any gardening enthusiast to enjoy 'a day out in Tansley'.

Tibshelf ✒

The village of Tibshelf began as a tiny settlement of nine peasant families around the year AD800. In the Domesday Book of 1086 it is called Tibecel which is thought to mean 'a place of worship on top of a hill'. Various other spellings have been recorded but the present one has been in use for the past 400 years.

The village had notoriety as a place of one long street, beginning at Overmoor in the east and ending at Nethermoor in the west. Farms and cottages were dotted along this main thoroughfare, widely spaced in the early days, with the gaps being filled in over the years but never much depth of building, and this to a large extent still applies. The church stands centrally on the highest point of this long street and was begun around 1200.

For hundreds of years the economy depended on agriculture, the people growing corn and using the land for pasture and hay to feed their cattle and sheep, but in 1500 Bess of Hardwick (Hardwick Hall is only two miles away) started a coal mine and this was followed over the years by many others. The two longest surviving, Top Pit and Bottom Pit, remained until the 1930s. During this period the growth of population was swift and in 1891 over 2,000 men were employed in the village mines. During the early part of the 19th century many small pits were sunk; these were 20 to 30 yards deep and coal was raised using chains and horses. There were many accidents, the worst being at the Drum and Monkey mine on 2nd March 1833. Three boys aged nine, four aged eleven to 17, and two older men were all killed. This was a tremendous disaster for a small village.

Agriculture remained important, however, and also during the 18th and 19th centuries many were employed in framework knitting of cotton hose in their houses, and the noise of the frames could be heard through the village. By 1939 the coal had run out and miners had to take employment at other local pits, of which there were many, but in more recent years with the run down of the mining industry as a whole, small factories have sprung up varying from the manufacture of textiles to aluminium extrusions.

Throughout the centuries local farms and land belonged to only a handful of families. In 1553 the Tibshelf estate was given to the Crown as a source of revenue for the newly built St Thomas's Hospital in London, and this unusual landlord continued until the arrival of the National Health Service in 1946 when the revenue was no longer required. All the properties were sold off, mostly to sitting tenants, but the association has continued in the St Thomas's Close complex of bungalows for the elderly and council houses in the village.

In recent years British Coal and the local council have co-operated in reclaiming the old colliery spoil heaps and unused railway land, creating a network of footpaths and country parks between Tibshelf and surrounding villages. These provide access for the public to enjoy the heritage of natural beauty all around. Due to its considerable height about 500 ft above sea level) the village has wonderful views – Hardwick Hall and Park to one side and the Pennines and Peak National Park to another. At one time it was said that eleven churches could be seen from the vantage point of Marlpits Farm.

Due largely to the proximity of the M1 motorway which runs along part of the village boundary, considerable new housing schemes have been generated, mainly bought by commuters from the nearby cities of Nottingham, Derby, Sheffield and even further afield. However, the friendly village atmosphere has been maintained. Children to the age of 16 are educated within the village and facilities are provided for scouts, guides and other youth activities. At the other end of the age scale there is a thriving old people's club and two old people's homes in the village main street. Also centrally placed are a modern health centre, pharmacy, post office and a number of shops, with two Methodist chapels, one at each end of the village.

Ticknall 🦋

Ticknall is a picture postcard village on the southernmost tip of the county, and close enough to neighbouring Leicestershire and Staffordshire to warrant two spare telephone directories. It is best seen by a leisurely amble on foot. Three aspects strike a visitor – the beauty of the front gardens with their ancient pines; the wayside water taps, some still functioning; and the random arrangement of attractive dwellings set at curious angles to the road. It is a village of irregular ribbon development where handsome farmhouses, rosy brick houses, rough hewn stone cottages and substantial public houses happily combine. Several modern developments, where former farmhouse buildings have been updated, are settling harmoniously.

Formerly Ticknall was a remote village at a fold on the map. Two events changed all that; the arrival of Edward Moult at Scaddows Farm, and in 1981 the sudden death of the local squire, Charles Harpur Crewe. This was to cast a huge pebble into the local waters. The Harpur Crewes, owners of the misnamed 'Abbey', exerted a strong feudal influence on the village, employing a large staff. Most families had at least one member in their employ. Pay was basic and conditions grim, balanced by the security of a cottage in the village at a peppercorn rent. Things had begun to change by the middle of the 20th century, when the Harpur Crewe family had shrunk to just one in the great house. After Charles' death nothing was the same. Calke Abbey in its beautifully wooded park finally passed to the National Trust, and since 1989 has attracted thousands of visitors. Villagers lost much in privacy and peace but gained access to a hitherto closely guarded estate.

To return to 'Ted' Moult. He soon became a popular figure who made it his concern to know and greet by their first names all who lived in the village. At strawberry picking time (he was a pick-your-own pioneer) he would gather up all the retired men and leave them on rickety chairs at the field gates in front of a pair of old-fashioned scales to dispense the gleaming fruit. Their age dropped off; panamas were pushed back from sunburnt brows, and for one glorious fortnight they lived again. With his tragic death that bonanza came to an end, and many of us will forever eat strawberries with a sigh.

Visitors' steps will eventually lead towards the church, which, though not particularly elevated, is visible from the several attractive approach roads to the village. A word of explanation of the ruins alongside a comparatively modern building in so old a place is necessary. When the population was at its height (1,281 in 1831, about 750 now) it was decided that the existing church of Thomas a Becket was too small. It was demolished and a new larger building erected nearby. The old structure proved very substantial and two fragments, the west wall and altar window, defied contractor's gunpowder and stand now, a silent reproach to an unfortunate decision. The present church has clean lines, mellow stones and a graceful spire, but none of the romantic history which would have accrued to its ancient predecessor. The churchyard is best explored in early spring when snowdrops bloom thickly under the walls, and before summer vegetation has rampaged over the more interesting monuments.

Few fail to notice a conical building on the main road although almost obscured by ivy, and set back into the wall of an adjoining garden. It is the village lock-up, in use until about 1917. Here the local inebriate, or disturber of the peace, was incarcerated for the night with nowhere to lay his throbbing head. Rumour has it that one Mrs Soar kept a secret key, and for a consideration – unspecified – could be persuaded to release the miscreant. With seven alehouses and beer at 8d per gallon, the lock-up was probably in frequent use.

Tideswell

Tideswell, with a population of approximately 2,000, stands 1,000 ft above sea level on the limestone plateau of the Peak District.

The 14th century parish church of St John the Baptist – 'Cathedral of the Peak' – stands on the site of a 11th century chapelry recorded in the Domesday Book. The patronal festival is celebrated with well dressings, and a week of festivities culminating in a torchlight procession and the Morris Dance, the form and tune of which is unique to Tideswell. The church contains many fine wood carvings, worked by three generations of the Hunstone family. There are also some interesting brasses, including one of Bishop Pursglove, founder of the grammar school in 1560 and of an educational foundation bearing his name. The document still ensures educational assistance for students. The grammar school closed in 1927 and a secondary modern school funded by this trust opened in 1936.

The main occupations in times past have been lead mining, quarrying and agriculture. The village accommodated two velvet cutting mills, while cotton and silk weaving were a cottage industry. Today, quarrying and agriculture survive and a small, light industrial estate has been established providing local employment.

Tideswell has a long established musical tradition. William Newton, 1750 – 1830, was a poet and known as the 'Minstrel of the Peak'. Samuel Slack, 1737 – 1822, was reputed to have sung before George III. It was said that his voice could be heard a mile away. The musical tradition is upheld with a renowned male voice choir, a silver prize band, and several smaller choirs.

Tideswell was a prosperous market town, with a charter granted in 1250. There were five markets a year for cattle and local produce. This tradition has been revived and is held twice a year, selling local crafts and produce, although sadly no longer cattle. However a Cow Club, founded in 1838, is still active. It originally acted as a form of insurance against veterinary bills and death of cows. It is understood that this club is the only surviving one of its kind.

Oatcakes can still be bought in Tideswell and a few areas in Northern Derbyshire. They were the staple diet for farm labourers. Many houses had their own 'bakestone'. This was a type of griddle with a fire below to heat the stone. Many housewives baked these fresh in time for breakfast, and they would sell them to eke out their meagre income.

At some unknown date, stone crosses were erected on all roads leading into Tideswell. These were probably resting places for bearers and friends of the departed, as they carried the dead to the parish church.

Water collects in the bases, and local people maintain a tradition of placing two pieces of grass, or straw, to form a cross, at the same time making a wish. Butterton Cross base now forms part of the wall on the old road leading to Millersdale, and on the road to Wormhill another base is part of a gate post. This is dated 1761, probably the date it was placed there. Another cross, Poynton, cannot be traced. This was on the road from Tideswell to Windmill. Approaching the hamlet of Wheston, a base of an unnamed cross can be found in the grass verge, whilst perhaps 'the most elegant cross in Derbyshire' can be found in Wheston, just beyond the hall. This is 14th century, the upper part older than the base, and it has the figures of the Virgin and Child on one side, with the Crucifixion on the other.

The hamlet of Wheston, with a population of approximately 50, is chiefly a farming community and lies two miles to the west of Tideswell. The present Hall was erected in the late 17th century. Close to the Hall is the 14th century cross which is a scheduled Ancient Monument.

Tintwistle

Dating from Saxon times and referred to in the Domesday survey of 1086, Tintwistle (or 'Tinsel' as it is called) is situated towards the west end of the Longdendale valley on the main Manchester to Sheffield road. It is on the boundaries of Cheshire, Yorkshire, Lancashire and Derbyshire. It has a population of 1,420 inhabitants, with 580 dwellings, with panoramic views of glorious countryside. There are many old buildings at the 'Top End', most of which have now been renovated and made into most desirable residences, whilst at the 'Bottom End' newer houses were built from approximately 1936 onwards.

At the turn of the century there were twelve shops in the centre of the village. Unfortunately, due to the advent of cars and supermarkets, most of these have closed and are now dwelling houses.

There is still a good community spirit existing, centred around Christ church and the United Reformed church. There was also another place of worship in the village – the Ebenezer chapel, – 'Little Ebbey', which was a Wesleyan Methodist chapel situated on the old Roman road, towards the east of the village.

There is also a church of St James at Woodhead, where monthly services are still held. It is over 500 years since the original church was built, funded by Sir Edward Shaa (Lord Mayor of London) who did not forget his early years in the area.

There is a legend that Dick Turpin, when pursued by the King's officers after one of his hold-ups, made the village smith, at pistol point, put his horse's shoes on the wrong way about, to give the impression that he was travelling in the opposite direction. This story is not confirmed by any concrete evidence.

Another story related for decades is that of an old travelling sweep, who was found dead on the roadside. He was given a common burial in the churchyard and his clogs were buried with him. It has been said that the trees now growing in that corner of the churchyard sprouted from the wooden soles of his clogs.

Tintwistle prize band is still flourishing and other prized assets are the cricket club and the football club. There are five reservoirs to the east of the village, where in recent years a water park has been created, with sailing and surfing facilities, and a Youth Hostel at Crowden (opened 1965) caters for walkers of the Pennine Way etc. The southern boundary of Tintwistle is marked by the river Etherow, a tributary of the Mersey.

Tissington 🌿

Tissington is a small Derbyshire village which, together with the surrounding land, forms the Tissington estate. This has been the home of the FitzHerbert family since the 17th century. The family home is the Hall, which dates from Jacobean times.

The village is known for the well dressings, which is a Christian ceremony to give thanks for pure water, dating back to the time of the Black Death. In years past Ascension Day was looked forward to with great excitement as a large fair arrived each year. The well boards were erected at daybreak on Ascension morning and at one time a young man used to fire a gun at the top of the village to let everyone know it was time to be out of bed.

There was a butcher's just across from the village store with its own slaughterhouse, this still stands but is no longer used. The villagers purchased produce from the kitchen gardens run by the estate. Everyone had their own vegetable garden and a few kept a pig, there are still a few old sties around. Quite a few were employed on the estate; farming, grooms, gardeners, with a large house staff. There was a joiner's shop where all repair work on the estate was carried out, an undertaker's business was also run from here.

The railway was another source of employment, opened in 1899 with three trains running daily to Buxton and Ashbourne. All the milk, coal and farmer's grains in those days went by train. Passenger services ended in 1954, freight continued until the railway was closed in 1963. Tissington station, once spotlessly kept, became derelict until the Peak Park demolished the old station to make way for the car park for the Tissington Trail.

No building has taken place in the village since 1900 when the baronet had some cottages built for work people, and about this time the railway cottages were built.

There is no inn, the nearest being the Blue Bell over the parish boundary in Fenny Bentley and the men used to go there drinking. Sometimes they had too much and had a job to reach home. One old Irish man spent a Saturday night on the funeral bier where the vicar found him next morning, fast asleep – it was cold weather too. Another one could not make it home and was found shouting for his wife, he was fast in a sheep trough. There was a resident policeman in the village at Church House, but it was rarely his services were needed.

The most important building in the village must be the Norman church of St Mary, with many interesting and historic features including the FitzHerbert wall monument. An old clarinet, used to lead the singing, before the organ, was stolen a few years ago but despite this the church is only locked at night.

The village is still thriving today but things have changed. Very few people work on the estate now and only a few of the family farms remain. Many of the villagers work in nearby Ashbourne or at one of the nearby quarries. The school was closed, it's now a tea-room and the children go to Fenny Bentley school. The beautiful avenue of lime trees was cut back in 1970 and a second avenue planted. It looked terrible at the time but now the young trees are established and growing well.

Tupton ❧

Tupton lies on the old Roman Rykneld Way and was recorded in the Domesday Book of 1086. The original settlement was probably founded AD550 to AD878 near the now Tupton Hall School, where some ancient trees are reckoned to be a thousand years old.

Tupton has a population of 3,230. New Tupton rapidly grew in size around 1830 to accommodate the mining families brought into the area to work the local mines. Rows of houses were built leading off Queen Victoria Road and on the site now occupied by the present village hall. These rows were pulled down as the need for them disappeared and the mines became worked out and closed down.

George Stephenson began to drive the Clay Cross Tunnel in 1834 and the London Midland Railway line was built. This created more work for the population of Tupton and more coal and ironstone was struck.

Old Tupton has developed to its present size as a mainly residential area although its origins were mainly farming with some small scale ironstone 'Bell-mining'.

There are several fine old manor houses in the area. Woodthorpe Hall and Egstow Hall built about 1600 are still in fine state of preservation. Egstow Hall stands in the grounds adjacent to those in which Tupton Hall School is now situated.

Near the west drive to Tupton Hall School stands a large stone house. This building served for a long period of time as a meeting place for the Quakers and their burial ground was nearby. A wheelwright's shop and a smithy stood on Derby Road. These have long since disappeared but two new houses on the site bear the names.

St John's church on Queen Victoria Road celebrated its centenary in 1991. Until recently Tupton was part of the North Wingfield parish but is now a separate parish within the team ministry of North Wingfield. There are two stained glass windows in the church. One depicting St George and the Dragon is behind the altar and is in memory of the late Col H. H. Jackson of the Clay Cross Iron and Foundries Company.

The infant and junior school nearby was built in 1875 for the Clay Lane Board School. A Methodist chapel is nearby. A second Methodist chapel near the Chesterfield to Derby Road was converted from the workshops of the worked out Tupton Green colliery. Red Tile Row, now demolished, just below the chapel was originally stables used for the pit ponies. A railway ran from the colliery to the London Midland line and the Clay Cross Tunnel.

Tupton did not escape enemy action during the Second World War. Three bombs fell on the village killing eleven of the villagers. Their names are recorded on the war memorial in North Wingfield church.

Turnditch

Turnditch is a small village on the A517 between Belper and Ashbourne. In the Middle Ages this was the ancient forest road linking the two towns. Turnditch is in the valley of the river Ecclesbourne with splendid views towards Wirksworth and Hazelwood.

The church of All Saints was an early chapel of ease, started, it is thought, about 1250, with many later additions. It only had church status in 1847. The date 1630 is clearly written over the south door. The stained glass windows on the south side of the nave came from the redundant church of St Werburgh, Derby.

Opposite the church is the village school, a charming listed building. Its original date, 1846, is displayed at the front but the clock tower which gives so much character to the facade was only added in 1910. The school was built on orchard land belonging to a Turnditch farmer, one George Milne. At first there was no room for a playground and the children used the road! Unfortunately several were attacked by a cow passing through the village, causing slight injury.

A vicarage was built in 1863 on a site given by Lord Scarsdale and still houses a clergyman today.

By 1800 there were two pubs – the Cross Keys and the Tiger, still flourishing today. Hill Cliff (now Lane) was a hamlet in the parish. 'Cross-o-th'-Hands' was the scene, in 1851, of a prize fight watched by 1,000 people. Such bouts were illegal and this resulted in a prosecution, 86 rounds were fought in 95 minutes between the contestants who came from Redditch and Nottingham.

Tutbury 🦢

There are two outstanding features in the village, which is just over the border in Staffordshire. At the top of the hill overlooking the valley is the castle and its ruins, and just below is St Mary's Priory church. Many visitors come to see the church with its beautiful Norman doorway, pillars and arches.

The castellan of the castle was Henry de Ferrers but the castle was given to the monarchy, with whom it has since remained. Mary Queen of Scots was imprisoned here in one of the dungeons, and her son James I stayed at the castle when he came for the hunting season. Queen Elizabeth II comes to Tutbury to meet her tenants. She and Prince Phillip planted trees in the castle grounds in 1957; they now stand proud and strong alongside the excavations which have been carried out.

In the last century a lady by the name of Ann Moore deceived the villagers with the claim that she lived without food or any nourishment. This went on from 1807 until 1813. Her fame spread around the whole country and people came from miles around to see her. In 1811 a committee of investigators watched her for 16 days, but with help from her accomplices she fooled them. Finally the Rev Richmond and Sir Oswald Mosley of Rolleston put a strict watch on her from 21st April 1813 and after nine days she was forced to admit that she did eat, but only small amounts. In fury at being made fools of, the people who had gained from her claims drove her from the village, and her house in Ludgate Street was later demolished and formed part of the site for the Tutbury Glassworks.

Tutbury glass is known all over the country and also in some parts of the world, and even in the 1880s glass was being made by craftsmen here at Tutbury. This craft was passed down by father to son and still exists today.

Also at Tutbury, on the outskirts, is the gypsum mine, known as Fauld mine. Here alabaster has been mined from as early as 1303. A monument of a knight in chainmail is in Hanbury church, and in Westminster Abbey on top of the marble tomb of Queen Philippa, who died in 1369, is a life-size figure of the Queen in Fauld alabaster. Today the mine is still being worked but the gypsum is used in the building trade.

The village has altered over the years; now it is a tourists' haven, with two glassworks who have conducted tours and a factory shop. Gone are a lot of the old terraced houses which were also little shops and small pubs. This was to make way for a large free car-park and a community and health centre. On the corner of the major High Street is a pottery shop where the owner makes and sells his own designs. The post office also has a shop selling toys and gifts. There is now a mews corner at the bottom of the High Street, with a selection of shops.

The 14th century Dog and Partridge Hotel is in the High Street – this is one of the Burton inns and is still kept in line with its historical background. There is a museum in the village too, where you can browse away your time, looking at photographs of people and places that have long since gone, also read about the explosion at RAF Fauld where so many men lost their lives. In the summer there are guided tours of the village which are very popular. It's quieter now in the main street due to the new Tutbury A50 bypass, once again the street is safe for children and the elderly can cross at leisure.

Two Dales

Two Dales, now a commuter village, was once a thriving community on the main Chesterfield to Bakewell route. The route ran down Flash Lane past the ghost haunted Quiet Woman, now Darley Forest Hotel, straight down the notoriously steep Sydnope Hill, along Oddford Lane, through Bakewell Old Road, passing the toll house standing in what is now the Dales and Peaks car park.

The village was served by four public houses, of which the Plough is still serving. Two Dales brook goes merrily through the middle of the square on its way to the river; this has now been piped underground until it appears again on the opposite side of the road and runs sparkling clear through the gardens of several cottages. A lazy trout lies under the stones of one of the cottages waiting for the owner to feed it – it is now becoming a very large, fat fish!

The main industry of Two Dales, established at the Ladybrook Mill by the Dakeyne family, first produced flax. Later it became a lace factory and now produces animal feed. The mill was powered by water contained in three reservoirs lying in the valley and now provides a pleasant walk through quiet woods abundant in wildlife and woodland flowers. The Dakeyne family, now transcribed to Dakin, has been responsible for much of the prosperity of Two Dales, or Toadhole as it was known until 1850.

The area has also been renowned for its nurseries owned by the Smith family. Forest Nursery in Oddford Lane is still run by descendants of the original family. Another member of the Smith family bought the Red House in 1939 and presented land now known as the Promenade to the village. This property became a riding school in 1946 and is well known all over the world as a carriage driving school. There is an interesting museum next to the stables. The magnificent carriages and horses are a common sight in the area.

The original Darley Hall built by the Columbell family in 1400, backing onto Hall Moor Road, was pulled down by Richard Arkwright, son of the Richard Arkwright of Spinning Jenny fame. The present Darley Hall is now a nursing home for the elderly. A field owned by the Darley Hall estate known as Underhall Field was eventually purchased by the local council, who in conjunction with a Leicestershire builder built an estate of starter homes and bungalows for senior citizens. A large complex of sheltered flats, day centre and short term care accommodation was opened by Her Majesty Queen Elizabeth II in 1985 and has been much acclaimed as a forward looking project for the care of the elderly.

Unstone 🪶

Unstone and Unstone Green nestle in the top corner of north-east Derbyshire on the former A61 (now B6057) between Chesterfield and Sheffield. To the north and the top of the hill a mile away sit the hamlets of Apperknowle, Summerley, Hundall and West Handley.

Visitors passing through the area today would never guess its history. In 1870 the Midland Railway came through Unstone, for which a very impressive seven-arched viaduct was built. The station was very busy as goods trains carried coal from the local pits and with the prospect of regular work people flowed into Unstone from as far away as Wiltshire and Suffolk. Unstone became a mining village with ugly spoil heaps dominating the view. However, the last pit closed in the 1930s and after the Second World War miners' dwellings were pulled down or altered beyond recognition. All that was left were coke ovens almost hidden in the surrounding woods and an enormous tip 369 ft high and covering some nine acres. This was finally removed and used as hardcore under the M1 motorway. A football pitch and community centre now stand on the site. The Miners Welfare Institute has outlived the miners and it is still a very popular meeting place. In the past whole families went 'at'stute' at the weekends.

In the 1820s Unstone Green was known as 'a rough place' and this was confirmed in 1822 when William Twelves set up a Methodist prayer meeting in a thatched cottage in Crow Lane. His first meeting was held behind locked doors while an angry mob tried to break in with an axe. Nevertheless a Methodist church was built in 1847 and thrived for many years until the membership started to decline in the 1960s. In 1977 it finally closed its doors to worship and is now a private house. All was not lost for the small congregation as they were invited by the rector of Dronfield to worship at St Mary's church across the road and so began one of the first ecumenical churches in the country with a very happy relationship between the two congregations. St Mary's church was started on 8th July 1915.

Between the wars Apperknowle became famous for its 'Tea Gardens'. Many people from Sheffield and surrounding districts came at the weekends and enjoyed walking around the gardens and partaking of afternoon tea provided by the Marsons and the Massinghams.

Although only eight miles from Sheffield, which was bombed extensively during the Second World War, the area was relatively unharmed. However in April 1961 Mr Orton, a local farmer, had been ploughing and unbeknown to him had disturbed a bomb, which exploded about 7.30 am a few days later.

Today Unstone is a very different area to that of the mining era, although its attractions are not immediately obvious. Turn off the B6057 towards Apperknowle or down Mill Lane past the old Mill House and you are in a truly rural setting.

Waingroves ✎

In the 12th century Waingroves was known as Wayngrif meaning waggon-hole or valley. The hamlet belonged to the Knights Hospitallers to whom it was given to found a house of that Order. No preceptory was built and the land was tenanted. An early landowner was a Robert Strelley who resided at Waingroves Hall, which is situated apart from the village. It is still a residence.

Waingroves is marked on very few road maps, being situated west of Codnor off the A610. It was mainly a one-street village, but now has small off-shoots of new developments. The road narrows in parts and rises steeply to join Peasehill Road on the outskirts of Ripley. It is flanked on one side by small fields, mainly grazed by horses, on the other by farmland and spinneys and at the top by what was once common land.

Originally it was a mining village, until the great strike of 1921 when the pit filled with water and could never be reopened. Local author, Mr Walter Brierley, wrote about the poverty of the area following this period in his novel *Means Test Man*, published in 1935 and republished in 1983.

On the outskirts of the village is situated a brickworks. This was started in 1913 by the Butterley Company, and in recent years has expanded and is now a flourishing concern.

A spirit of friendliness and village pride prevails throughout Waingroves, centring around the chapel, the two public houses, the village shop, the post office and the old school, which is now the community centre and is mainly run by public support. There are a variety of groups of children and adults using the centre. The two pubs, the Jolly Colliers and the Thorn Tree, help to support the groups and the centre by cash raising events.

The main highlight of the year is the show weekend held in September. This brings a gala-like atmosphere throughout the village. It consists of a horticultural, handicraft and baking competitive show, staged in the community centre.

Walton 🌿

The present day Walton lies about four miles to the west of Chesterfield. Reference to Walton in the Domesday Book is as Waltune. Without doubt the most important building in the ecclesiastical parish of Chesterfield in the 16th and 17th centuries was Walton Hall, belonging to the Foljambe family. It was here that Mary Queen of Scots spent two nights in 1569. Nothing remains of the old Hall but on its site is the 18th century farmhouse known as Walton Hall Farm in Foljambe Avenue.

Opportunity for worship was available as far back as 1224 in Walton chapel, but then solely for the lords of the manor. It is known that in the late 19th century there was a mission church converted from two cottages on a site opposite the present church of St John.

Walton as a village came about with the development of the mission church, the fact that there were two hostelries – the White Hart and the Blue Stoops – on the old Matlock to Chesterfield turnpike road, and in the vicinity of this some cottages, farms, a few larger houses like Park Hall, Walton Lodge and Walton House, a post office and a school house.

Private schools played a significant part in educational life in early Victorian times. Normally these were very small and conducted in the homes of the proprietors. This was the case in Walton. The old schoolhouse stands almost opposite the White Hart and in the front part of the upstairs room the Walton children were set schoolwork to do whilst the schoolmistress got on with her household chores downstairs. Consequently the academic standards were low and enquiries were made concerning the backwardness of the pupils. This resulted in the school being closed. In 1895 the foundations of the Walton infants board school were laid. It ceased to be a viable proposition, closing its doors in 1952.

The Walton Wakes were held in July and lasted five days. The Wakes commenced with a cricket match played on the parkland of Walton Lodge opposite the White Hart, followed by skittles and dancing in the club room at the inn. During the Wakes considerable drink was consumed at the White Hart and Blue Stoops, causing a sergeant and two constables to be on duty.

During the last two decades the development of the Park Hall and Walton Hall estates with some 6,000 inhabitants has changed the face of Walton. Reminders of the past have been incorporated into the naming of this housing development, which is now part of Chesterfield Borough. With this urban encroachment has come a change in the lifestyles of the majority of the residents as increased mobility enables them to seek their pleasures and recreations further afield. Similarly one notes a change in occupations from farmers to pharmacists, labourers to lawyers and artisans to accountants and architects. However despite the changes which time has wrought on Walton one still senses and catches glimpses of its rural past.

Walton on Trent 🦢

If you are driving from Staffordshire into the south-west corner of Derbyshire then be careful. You have to cross the Trent at Walton and this is by means of a Bailey bridge which bounces gently even if you walk across it. Anything wider than a big car can be scraped or stuck – as many drivers discover to their cost.

From the Staffordshire bank the village has a traditional look about it. A church amidst scattered houses, with a cricket field alongside. On a gloomy night through mists over the water you might even imagine the ghosts of Celts, Saxons, Danes and medieval figures who all passed here and influenced the place. It is steeped in antiquity.

No bridge seems to have existed before 1836. Before then there was a ferry, the traditional privilege of ferryman belonging to the landlord of the Black Swan, an inn on the river bank, now replaced by modern houses whose gardens stretch down to the river.

To the south of the present village stands the earthwork known as Borough Hill. This commands an imposing view over the river and is probably the site of an Iron Age fort and the first Walton settlement. Today, the village is anchored firmly near the church and bridge.

The Domesday survey indicates a village of some 200 people with a priest and church. The present church of St Laurence (at one time called after John the Baptist) has some remnants of early Norman building but, like many churches, has been restored or added to over the centuries. The first definite record is of the construction of a chantry in 1334 by the rector, Richard Waleys. His tomb and mutilated effigy are to be seen there. The church is well-known for its proliferation of wood-carving. This was carried out by two former rectors from 1860–1940. Each was called Frederick Fisher, father and son.

Walton has a fine new C of E voluntary controlled primary school. Its origins may be traced to a charitable foundation of 1760 set up to teach the poor children of the village. The first specific building of a school seems to have taken place because the barn then in use caused so much absence through winter colds.

The present Walton Hall is a minor stately home built in Georgian style in 1723. For centuries Walton must have been a closed agricultural community having little contact with the outside world. In 1801 there were 343 inhabitants – 427 by 1871. The trades represented in a directory of 1874 are only those of butcher, dressmaker, innkeeper, joiner and wheelwright, shopkeeper and farmers. Another directory of 1936 shows little change.

Streets, fields and houses have old-fashioned names and one at least illustrates the conditions that existed. This is a dwelling known as Dripping Pan Cottage. It is situated near the Hall and apparently after the squirearchy had dined well the dripping that remained from their feast was taken in a pan and donated as a charity to those impoverished labourers living in cottages at the foot of their drive.

After the Second World War a large power station was constructed at nearby Drakelow. This led to considerable employment opportunities and the village doubled in size, with further building taking place. Fortunately, the old character of the village was not greatly affected.

Once the young son of a rector broke the peace of the village by landing his aeroplane in a field by the river. Today its peace is broken by low-flying jet fighters almost brushing the church tower, commuter traffic rattling over the bridge and the occasional juggernaut going to and from the power station. Yet farm tractors still trundle through and horses and even a pony and trap are to be seen and heard.

Wardlow ❧

Wardlow, a small village with limestone walls and buildings, lies approximately five miles from Bakewell and three miles from Tideswell, and is in walking distance of the spectacular Cressbrook and Monsal Dales. The name Wardlow means 'watch hill and slope', with the hill known as Wardlow Hay Cop, now a nature reserve, rising to over 1,100 ft. The farms and houses are strung out adjacent to the sloping B6465 road.

It was formerly an agricultural and lead mining community, and part of the Chatsworth estate. Twenty five years ago many of the farms were producing milk, but today there is only one, and former barns and farmhouses are now residences for commuters or providing holiday accommodation, which is a sign of the times. The village has a population of 82 excluding the 30 or so children who are transported daily to various schools outside the village.

The Gothic-style church of the Good Shepherd was built in 1872, and before this in 1835 the attached schoolroom had been built, which was then used as a day school and a small chapel. The day school closed in 1947 owing to insufficient children, but today the building is used for social events.

St Peter's Stone, or Gibbet Rock as locals call it, is a circular mass of limestone with a grass dome, which stands near the village. It marks the spot where the body of Albert Lingard was hanged in 1815 after he had been found guilty of the murder of Hannah Oliver, who kept the toll bar cottage (now gone). This was Derbyshire's last gibbetting.

Before mains water was brought to the village, people had to collect their water from the village pumps. Although disused now, the remains of the pumps can still be seen. Another treasure in the village is the VR postbox, which is mounted in the wall near Manor Farm.

Wessington ❧

Wessington, with a population of approximately 600, is situated on the A615 between Alfreton and Matlock. The heart of the village is clustered around a fairly large green. Most of the outlying properties are farms or smallholdings.

Members of the Wessington and Brackenfield Women's Institute (formed in 1947) remember carrying water from wells on the green to their homes in the days before mains water was taken for granted. Rumour suggests that some young persons when sent for water for making tea would not make the effort needed to go to the furthest and special Tea Well but would call either at Jubilee Well or Moses Well, whichever happened to be closest to home, and hope that mother wouldn't notice! Jubilee and Moses Well water was used mainly for washing. A young bride really had some hard work ahead of her on washday. First she needed to make numerous visits to the well for water, enough both for washing and rinsing. Then came the ponching of the clothes and boiling nappies over the open fire, always a very dangerous procedure should there be any small children around. After all that effort the dirty water had to be carried out to the nearest drain. The wells are no longer a feature on the green; when every house in the village had mains water they were no longer needed and were filled in for safety.

At about the same time the green was often used for grazing, particularly horses and goats, but in recent years this custom has lapsed and the main users are the Wessington and Ivanhoe football clubs and a group of villagers interested in wildlife conservation who have planted a number of trees.

Many changes have taken place. In the lower part of the village there was a complex of 16 houses built in horseshoe formation and known as Friday Yard, reputed to be the site of an old friary. These no longer exist, though the private home built on the site retains the name. In those days the village could boast many shops, a hardware store, cobbler, butcher's, a grocer's, a post office and a smithy. No need for a journey into town to keep the family fed. Pork pies, sausages and all other pork delicacies were delivered to other villages by our pork butcher driving his pony and trap. The pies and sausages were made on the premises by his hard working wife.

The two pubs are still here but, sadly, the village has lost many of the shops. There is still a post office, a fish and chip shop, a furniture store, a garage and a garden centre.

Wessington county primary school was built in 1839 in order to educate children of the village and an influx of miners' children when a pit was sunk in nearby Oakerthorpe. The school developed a good reputation locally for pottery and weaving and was visited in 1935 by the Duke of Kent.

The main occupations in the village were mining and farming but with the closing of local pits and the arrival of the motor car this has changed. Even some of the farmers are having to look at other ways of making a living. Being close to the Peak District National Park, some find income from summer visitors. Bed and breakfast and summer cottages (converted barns) are now a feature of the village. However one or two of the larger farms still give it a country look and, now and again, a real country smell!

West Hallam 🌿

The first record of West Hallam is in the Domesday Book, when it was called Halum. The Cromwell family were lords of the manor for 300 years and it is possible that the second Ralph de Cromwell built the church in 1275, named St Wilfrid's. It is thought that the local wakes day fell around the 12th October, this being the saint's day. The church still stands today at the top of an avenue of lime trees which becomes alive with flowers in the spring. At the bottom of the drive stands a fine war memorial, carved from Sicilian marble, commemorating the fallen of two World Wars.

West Hallam had three schools which still stand today. The oldest, situated in School Square, was a boys school known as Scargill Boys School and now converted to a private house. The second to be built was an infants and girls school, now used as the village hall. A new school was built on Beech Lane in 1935.

There are also three public houses in the village, the Newdigate Arms, the White Hart and the Punch Bowl, which stands opposite the church and was the centre from which the West Hallam and District Ploughing Match first started and is still going strong today.

On Station Road stands the 'Cinder House' erected in 1833 to commemorate the birth of the squire's son, Francis Newdigate. As the name suggests it is built of cinders, which were made by burning local clay. The walls are very thick and the windows a special feature, making it unique in many ways. Another local landmark is the Bottle Kiln, now featuring a buttery cafe and gallery. This stands on the site of the old brickyard which later became a pottery, hence the bottle kiln chimney which is still preserved.

Mining in the area is now a thing of the past, but two mines to the north of High Lane Central and High Lane East were known as West Hallam Collieries, besides numerous small pits dotted about the area. Bordering on the village was 'Nibby' Pit at Stanley and 'Simon' Pit at Mapperley. Much damage was caused to local property and roads by subsidence prior to the closures in the 1960s.

West Hallam has supported a cricket club, the White Rose, since 1880 which plays on the recreation ground on Beech Lane. An athlete West Hallam is proud of is Mr Jack Winfield, who represented England in the

Olympic Games of 1936. He could regularly be seen running round the district long before the days of 'joggers'.

West Hallam has changed dramatically in the last 20 years with the development of a large housing estate covering land which was once farmland. The residents of this estate commute mainly to Derby or Nottingham, as the only industrial centre which has connections with the village is the old ordnance depot that lies on Cat and Fiddle Lane and now houses mostly storage sheds for various companies. This all seems a far cry from the days when the centre of the old village supported a smithy, cobbler's shop, Bosworth's the butcher's, the post office and a builder. Today in the same area there is a mini-market, takeaway food and a video hire shop!

Westhouses

Westhouses is comparatively new. There was a Westhouse Farm there possibly in the 16th century, but it was classed as in Blackwell.

The LMS railway passed through Westhouses from Nottingham to Sheffield in the 1850s and a station was built there, but due to lack of use was closed in 1865. It reopened in 1881, when the collieries were opened at Blackwell and B'Winning, also Huthwaite. The LMS railway decided to build sheds to house 24 locomotives and service 40 at Westhouses. This occasioned dramatic changes.

The railway company built about 100 houses known as 'The Terraces' in Tibshelf Road, an hotel, church, chapel and school, the railway institute and stationmaster's house. Development later took place on the Main Road, all of which properties were occupied by persons connected with the railway.

In February 1928 during a long period of severe frosty weather, at a point near to the bridge which takes the bridlepath over the railway on the Doe Hill side, during the early hours of the morning, a train of goods wagons travelling towards Westhouses was accidentally running on the passenger 'up' line towards Doe Hill. A passenger train travelling in the opposite direction collided head on, causing a tremendous crash in which the engines were overturned and coaches impacted and overturned. Fortunately, as the driver and fireman of the goods train had earlier sensed the error they had stopped their train and gone down the line to attempt to give warning. It was also fortunate only the driver and fireman of the passenger train were the fatalities.

During the summer season, Westhouses station was a hive of activity with excursions going to most popular holiday resorts. The railwaymen were noted for their keen interest in gardening and a site of six acres was at one time used as allotments.

Weston-on-Trent 🍂

Weston-on-Trent is a small village of about 500 people which lies seven miles south-east of Derby.

Once a farming village, Weston now has only two working farms, one predominantly a sheep farm and the other producing food crops for sale in supermarkets and other retail food outlets. Most working residents now commute to nearby towns to work, thus following the pattern of life in many villages these days.

Surprisingly for an old village (Weston is mentioned in the Domesday Book) the parish church of St Mary the Virgin is situated away from the village near to where the canal now passes, on an elevated site known locally as The Cliff. The stone for the church and some of the old outbuildings was excavated from here in earlier times. The church dates from the 13th century.

Buried in the churchyard are two soldiers who were killed in a skirmish at Kings Mills during the Civil War in 1642. The church may also have been used as a look-out post during the Jacobite Rebellion in 1745. The story is that a man was supplied with a musket and instructed to stand on the church tower to defend the people from the army of Bonnie Prince Charlie, which is reputed to have turned back at nearby Swarkestone Bridge. All this for one shilling a day. Inside the church is an interesting monument to a 17th century rector, Sir Richard Sale, his wife and ten children, all of whom are represented in a stone carving.

On the outskirts of the village and close to the church is a Ukrainian Youth Centre used as a campsite by visiting Ukrainians. Also in the grounds, housed in the old rectory, is a Ukrainian old people's home.

Although many cottages have been demolished there are still some old buildings in the village, the most notable being Weston Hall, a five storey brick building which, had it been completed, would have rivalled Hardwick Hall for size. Local gossip records that part of the Hall was used as stabling for horses during the Civil War and from about that time onwards no further building work was undertaken on the house due to the bankruptcy of the owner. It is one of the few private houses in the country that was moated.

The river Trent which forms the southern parish boundary has been navigable from the Humber to Nottingham from earliest times and boats could continue upstream as far as Kings Mill at Weston when there was a sufficient depth of water to enable them to be hauled over the shallows.

Until the 1940s there was a ferry across the river but it is not known if it was situated in the same place as the one mentioned in the Domesday Book.

Following the opening of the canal in the 1770s most waterborne traffic went along the Trent and Mersey canal, which passes through

Weston, taking plaster and alabaster from nearby workings to wider markets. Nowadays the canal is a venue for holidaymakers and fishermen rather than workers.

Whaley Bridge 🌿

Weylech or Weyley, the Anglo-Saxon name for Whaley Bridge, meaning 'the clearing by the road', speaks to us of a time when Macclesfield Forest covered the whole area. Long before this, though the Romans had established a crossing over the river Goyt at the spot, on the road they built from Manchester to Buxton. A curious feature of Whaley Bridge known as the Roosdyche, a shallow valley about three-quarters of a mile long and with banks on each side, was believed at one time to have been a racecourse for Roman chariots. Later research proved it to be, less romantically but just as interestingly, a geological fault caused perhaps by the passage of a monstrous iceberg in prehistoric times.

In 1670 'a great pillar of smoke, high as a steeple' swept through Whaley Bridge devastating houses and trees. It was possibly a freak whirlwind. At this time, as for several centuries, Whaley was no more than a few scattered hamlets, usually clustered around the family seats of the local landowners. Hockerley Hall, for several centuries the home of the Nixon family, was built in the early 17th century and is still standing today, as does Yeardsley Hall, once the home of the Jodrell family. The parish church of Taxal, St James's, was known to be in existence as long ago as 1287 although the church was mostly rebuilt in 1825. It contains an unusual memorial tablet:

'Underneath lyeth the body of Michael Heathcote Esq., Gentleman of the Pantry and Yeoman of the Mouth to His Late Majesty King George the Second, who died June 22nd 1768, aged 75 years.'

Michael Heathcote was born in Taxal but went to live in London on his appointment as the King's 'food taster' to guard His Majesty against possible poisoning. On his death, his remains were returned to Taxal for burial.

The coming of the Industrial Revolution transformed Whaley Bridge and by the mid 19th century the population had trebled. Coal mining had always been carried on in the district, but now textile mills sprang up on the banks of the Goyt, a cornmill was established near the old bridge, and an arm of the Peak Forest Canal was extended as far as Whaley, later to be linked to the Cromford Canal by a railway. A steeply inclined plane led down the canal wharf, trucks full of lime and coal being hauled up and down by a capstan worked by horses. In 1831 the Toddbrook Reservoir was constructed as a feeder for the canal, but the coming of the main steam railway to Whaley in the 1850s meant the gradual diminution in use of the canal.

At Stoneheads, on the road to Disley, in 1823 a luckless traveller was set upon by three youths and beaten to death for the £100 he was carrying. His body was later found beside the road covered by stones from the wall. This dramatic event was commemorated by a stone erected by local people, still known as 'the murder stone'. At one time, the spot was said to be haunted and nothing would grow there. In a field not far from this place, is another stone known as the Dipping Stone or the Plague Stone. There are two sockets in it which may once have held the shafts of two Saxon crosses which were found lying near the stone but have now disappeared. During the Plague, the Stone was said to have been used to leave money for goods as at Eyam.

Whaley Bridge is distinguished in English literature, both Carr Cottage (now Carr Lodge) and the then posting inn, the White Hart (which still stands besides the new bridge in Market Street), being mentioned in Mrs Linnaeus Banks' classic novel *The Manchester Man*.

Today the tide of the industrial revolution has ebbed away from Whaley Bridge. Coal mining is now non-existent, remembered only in the name of Bings Road and Bings Wood, 'bings' being the old name for pit spoil heaps. Only one mill, Edward Hall's bleachworks, is still in operation: the cornmill disappeared although the mill race can still be seen running beside the Railway Hotel in Market Street; and the inclined plane is now a pleasant Linear Park. Nevertheless, modern Whaley Bridge is a large and thriving village with a growing population. If the older industries have gone, other, lighter ones have been established and the village has much to offer to one of the newer ones – leisure. The canal is once more busy with narrowboats – seeking pleasure instead of trade. The reservoir with its wooded slopes so reminiscent of Switzerland, is the venue for a host of anglers, yachtsmen and windsurfers, and the network of ancient footpaths and bridleways reaching into the magnificent scenery of the Peak National Park are ever popular with ramblers and riders. Indeed, Whaley Bridge today is well-named 'The Gateway to the Goyt'.

Whatstandwell ❧

The village lies on the steep hillside above the Derwent valley some seven miles south of Matlock. Strictly speaking, Whatstandwell consists only of the bridge over the river, the Derwent Hotel and the cottage and old smithy buildings adjoining it. The rest of the village was known as Crich Carr. But over the years the distinction has become blurred and today, although the school is still officially Crich Carr C of E primary, the whole area, including Longway Bank and some farms on the opposite bank of the river, is covered by the name Whatstandwell.

The origin on this curious name is that the land on which the bridge was built belonged to, or was rented by one Walter (Wat) Stonewall back in the 14th century. It was on the site of an even earlier ford, used by the monks of Darley Abbey to gain access to their grange at Wigwell. The crossing is clearly visible today when the river level is low. Before the A6 was built along the valley in the 19th century, the turnpike road from Alfreton to Ashbourne crossed the Derwent at this point; the Derwent Hotel, known in those days as the Bull's Head, was an important coaching inn. Stage coaches, mail coaches and horse drawn waggons must have laboured up and down the steep hill through the village to Crich, South Wingfield, Oakerthorpe and so to Alfreton. The numerous stone troughs along the route bear witness to this traffic. There is a house halfway up the hill (now known as 'Bramble Tor') where the mail coach would stop on the way back from Crich and the driver would have a meal while the horses rested.

Florence Nightingale knew Whatstandwell, as she used to alight at the station (then located at the northern end of the tunnel, behind the Derwent Hotel) when travelling to her home in the next village of Holloway. She visited the school, and gave books to the reading room in the cottage next to the canal, where there was also a cafe and where billiards could be played.

Most of the older houses in the village are built of local stone from the quarries off the Holloway road. The quarries, once owned by the Sims family, had been closed for many years but one has recently been re-opened despite local protests and another has just been designated a nature reserve, where 78 species of plants have been listed.

It is said that the four main lines of communication – road, rail, canal and river – run closer together at Whatstandwell than anywhere else in the country. Once, there was much industrial activity in and around the village, not only quarrying, but stocking manufacture and the making of 'wisket' baskets for the lead mines. There were two red-lead mills; a small broom factory; brick and pipe works, and a rag mill, at Longway Bank; a joinery by the canal where doors were made; a smithy; and during the Second World War there was a small factory making barrage balloons. Now, the only industry left is a small foundry by the river behind the Derwent Hotel.

There were once three inns; now only one – the Derwent Hotel – remains. There is still a combined post office and stores, but in days gone by there were two groceries, a little sweet shop, and a butcher whose shop was a wooden hut on the corner of the Holloway road and who wore a top hat to serve his customers. Salesmen from neighbouring towns, travelling by bicycle or pony trap, called regularly, selling such necessities as paraffin and haberdashery.

There has never been a church here; Whatstandwell lies in the parish of Crich. The Methodist chapel, built in 1877, unfortunately closed in 1988. At one time the village had two schools – a dame school and the one still in use today, built in 1885 on land given by the Duke of Devonshire. It has recently become a community school which has given it a new lease of life. Its existence is important as it is the only place where all the village organisations can meet.

Whitfield 🐝

Men of the Middle Stone Age hunted in the woodlands which must have covered the surrounding hills at this time. At the end of the 6th century it appears that the valleys were filled everywhere between 600 or 700 ft above sea level with dense forests, and the hilltops covered with peat as today. Here in Whitfield residents still have the right to cut peat. Grouse shooting takes place on the thousands of acres of high moorland containing whimberry and heather; the home of the grouse. These moors, adjacent to Whitfield, are essential to the population as water-gathering grounds.

Farmhouses, cottages and mills which were built in the 17th century must have brought a new life into the gritstone quarries at Whitfield and Chunal. Chunal quarry must have been very busy selling large amounts of cut stone for field walls and other buildings in Whitfield.

In top Whitfield there are many very old houses that have been built of stone. The mortar is made of stone dust, cow dung and straw. Lime would have been too expensive as only the very rich people could have had it hauled by horse and cart over the rough mountain track from Buxton. The oldest cottage in Whitfield is dated 1638 and it is said that a forest warden once lived here. The surrounding land would have been King's land at this time, but later the Howards, especially Bernard Edward, who later became the 12th Duke of Norfolk in 1816, owned land for miles around and were ready to lease land for mills and cottages.

Looking across the fields to Chunal one is reminded of Joseph Hague, who was born there in poverty in 1695. In spite of his humble beginnings he managed to make a little money as a pedlar and at 21 he went to London and entered the cotton business. From the import of raw cotton he made his fortune but he never forgot his birth place and returned to live at Park Hall in Hayfield.

In the year 1779 Joseph Hague built the school which stands in Whitfield. Over the entrance door of the school there is a bee-hive carved in stone. This is a symbolic reminder to everyone that the school should promote a 'hive of industry' of course a perpetual reminder of Hague's own story of hard work. Joseph Hague left money in trust to help educate poor children, and also for his grave to be kept in good order.

A little way past Hague's school is Cross Cliffe. It was here that 20 years after the school was built, John Newton of Whitfield built a mill. A few years after this Whitfield's John Wesley chapel was built. In 1902 George Ollerenshaw presented Whitfield library and recreation ground to the corporation. The school remains, but not as a school. The school house is occupied but the school itself has been made into two flats. The mill is no more, and sadly Whitfield library was demolished about 14 years ago. John Wesley chapel still stands but is now used by a Masonic lodge.

In the late 1800s Ebenezer Street Methodist chapel was built. It continues today as a youth club and community centre.

Over 100 years ago Whitfield had its own well dressing custom and Whitfield well was the only one in Derbyshire that was decorated solely by heather.

Whitfield church, which is situated in lower Whitfield, was built about 1849. Hill Woods was the main benefactor of this church. Today, St James's is noted for its Christingle Services which are held every alternate year on the first Sunday in December.

During 1811 to 1861 there was a population movement towards the rapidly growing industrial centre of New Glossop (as it was then called). It is strange to think that at this time Whitfield had a bigger population than Glossop.

Whittington 🌿

Whittington, two and a half miles from Chesterfield on the old Sheffield Road and a few miles inside Derbyshire's north-eastern boundary, is reputed to be much older than the Domesday Book's recording of it as Whitintune, though no previous records have been found. A church and rectory are said to have existed since 1140 but known records are dated 1302. The original Norman church was small and much altered until replaced by a larger structure in 1865; this was destroyed by fire in 1895, the tower and bells only survived and these were incorporated in the new St Bartholomew's which opened the following year.

The Cock and Pynot inn stands at the junction of the old Sheffield and Rotherham road. It was here that in 1688 the plan was devised to bring 'William of Orange and his English wife' to the throne and so depose James II. For his part in the proceedings the Earl of Devonshire was made the first Duke of Devonshire; he later re-built Chatsworth House, one of the country's most beautiful ancestral homes. The Cock and Pynot inn, now known as the Revolution House, is a museum of its time. A new Cock and Magpie inn was built nearby and is still trading well.

In 1788 the population of the parish was 870 persons, now it is at least ten times that number. The northern end of the parish became New Whittington, a parish in its own right, in 1927.

Richard Dixon commenced making glass in 1710 at Glass House Common. It was to continue for 140 years, 'making a variety of Jacobean drinking glasses both plain and coloured also sturdy dark bottles for storage of wine, sack and ale'. They were the only makers in the area and traded by road routes and the Stockwith Canal.

This family were responsible for building Whittington Hall, living there until the business ceased in 1850. After the Dixons, the residence passed through several hands until in 1902 it was leased to Rev Burden for a period of 21 years for use as an Institute for Inebriate Reform, certified to house 50 persons under Home Office licence. By 1912 the character of inmates had changed under the Board of Control to that of 'care of the feeble minded'. Few institutions were better managed and controlled, an industry school was provided to teach crafts of all kinds to the inmates.

The railway coming in the mid 1800s was a boon to the up and coming industries, some of which still trade here. The station opened in 1840. It was quite a walk from the village but enabled residents to get to Derby or Sheffield. The passenger line ceased in 1952, but there is still an industrial branch line to several factories and marshalling yards. One hears trains, but rarely sees them as they work mainly at night. The station area made way for the sewerage complex. The 50 or so cottages in Bamford Street and the Square were demolished some 30 years ago to make way for modern council dwellings; thus ending the era of the market and the annual fair. For village occasions there is a church hall, Swanwick Memorial Hall and Mary Swanwick school. The 'New' end has two churches, a chapel and three schools, one with a class for deaf children. There are post office and shops enough for everyday use in both, and a good transport service. Both still have much of the 'village' though they are now incorporated into the Borough of Chesterfield.

Whitwell ぷ

Part of the Creswell Crags are within the Whitwell boundary; the caves are world famous as a home of early man. These hunters followed the great herds, and their bone carvings are in the British Museum. There are rich remains of animals such as the mammoth, sabre-toothed tiger, and a prehistoric hyena much larger than the present species. Thousands of years later a settlement was mentioned in the Anglo-Saxon Chronicle as Hwitan Wylles Geat; 'the shining stream in the valley'.

Welbeck Abbey, founded by the French Premonstratensian canons, flourished for about 400 years, until the Dissolution of the Monasteries. In 1593 the Abbey came into the Cavendish family, and the future Dukes of Portland greatly influenced the area. Their large estate provides employment to the present day.

The Old Hall became a residence and a school, and in 1853 a son was born to the headmaster. Charles Edward Wilson grew up to be a notable artist, and 40 of his paintings were exhibited at the Royal Academy. Several of his studies of Victorian village life are still popular as greetings cards.

The village church of St Lawrence, with its Saxon font and grey stone tower, is central to the village. Two miles away in the hamlet of Steetley the perfect little Norman church featured in Sir Walter Scott's *Ivanhoe* stands in a truly rural setting.

High over the village, on a craggy hill, is Bakestone Moor, apart, and yet part of the village. Hodthorpe, also separate, has St Martin's church. The Methodist church is in Portland Street, Whitwell. There were several earlier religious meeting places.

The well in the Square, with its pump, and another on the green, supplied the best drinking water. It used to be taken round the village by horse-drawn water tank, and sold for a halfpenny a bucket. Although many properties had their cistern the water from the wells was preferred, and some people carried it all the way up to the moor.

Several farms were situated within the village, and people remember the cows being herded along the roads for milking time. Peartree cottage stood in the centre of the Square; the site of the present war memorial. A turnpike road ran from the Half Moon inn to the George inn, where the old mounting steps remain. This road lost its importance when the new road was made in 1890, linking the Half Moon inn and the Dale inn, on Whitwell Common.

An old mill sank into dereliction. The grindstone is now an ornamental feature in the Mill Lane housing estate. The old brewery provided winter quarters for travelling folk. The farriery is modern, but notable for holding the 'All England' Championship in farriery, and many other awards.

Whitwell has many activities, including the Women's Institute, the History Group, and the Natural History Group. The Natural History Group is particularly involved with Whitwell Wood, which was laid out as a replica of the forest of Versailles. Before the era of chlorinated pools, generations of Whitwell youngsters learned to swim in the 'Dosh', the stream in the wood. Shutters, kept at a nearby farm, were used to dam the stream. It was also used as a sheep dip. The Ginny Spring provided pure clear water; locals provided the gin. Surface streams are not common in the area, and one wonders if the Saxon Hwitan Wylles Geat was the shining stream in Whitwell Wood, long before the trees were planted.

Immediately after the closure of the pit the superstructure was dismantled, and the winding wheel embedded in what was once the school playground, now the parking area of the community centre. The tall chimney of the processing plant of the dolomite quarry represents continuing industry. The dolomite material is crushed and burned, to provide the fireproof lining for blast furnaces.

Despite the changes the village has retained its character, absorbing generations of change and newcomers. The old stone houses, farmhouses and more humble abodes, are now desirable residences. Their occupants do not go now to the well for water, but help at the annual Well Dressing.

Willington 🌿

Willington is situated on the wide, flat fertile gravel plain of the north bank of the river Trent. Its history has been traced back for at least 4,000 years. In 1970 archaeologists discovered the graves of the Beaker People, dated at 2,000 BC. Other artefacts from this dig, now on display in Derby museum, include Bronze Age and Roman pottery.

Willington has always been a convenient crossroads for many forms of transport. Despite the ferry crossing from Meadow Lane across to Tanners Lane in Repton, it is listed in the 1600s as the highest navigable point on the Trent. The port here was used for transporting china clay, flints and local cheeses. The old cheese factory is now Trent Alloys site. 1770 saw the building of the Trent and Mersey canal, with its horse-drawn barges. 1840 brought the Derby to Birmingham railway line, cutting off part of the village green and providing off-loading for the canal barges where the marina now lies. The far side of the village also has the Derby to Crewe line creating two level crossings, with a shunt line for the coal trucks travelling to the generating station which was built on the outskirts of the village in the 1950s.

The old Roman way to Chester Green, Rykneld Road, which runs parallel to the river, has become the A38. The development of the new Toyota factory at the side of this is leading to further changes, a motorway link road will cross the fields a quarter of a mile from the village. In 1835 a toll bridge was built over the Trent, the toll gates remaining until late 1898. The faint remains of the toll cottage and garden can just be detected at the foot of the bridge.

Egginton brook, known locally as the Molly, runs under the canal, down Repton Road, round Trent Alloys and joins the river. It has provided safe 'jam-jar' fishing for many generations and is home to a pair of ducks, who manage to rear a small family every year despite their habit of halting traffic by wandering across to nearby gardens. In winter when the mile-wide flood plain surrounding the raised road to Repton is like a lake, the Molly occasionally backs up and overflows.

There are very few of the old cottages left. Potlocks Farm, mentioned in the Domesday Book, has a cedar tree. Bargate Lane has a timbered cottage still standing. Perhaps this is where the young man lived who was to marry his sweetheart at a distant church. Having no transport and needing to arise early for his long walk, he made sure of an early alarm call by tying a cockerel to the banister. The Baptist chapel is fairly new, but in the old wooden-floored building two elderly gentlemen used to punctuate the Hallelujahs by banging their long walking sticks on the floor, to the great delight of the children. St Michael's church still thrives; the main building is relatively new but parts of the nave are thought to be Norman. The Methodist chapel has been converted to a dwelling house, its main structure beautifully preserved.

The centre of the village has been altered to accommodate the increasing road traffic. The old building now occupied by 'Computer Lines' lost its right of access for a coach and horses when the post office built an extension. The old cottage next door used to house Sammy, who panicked strangers by driving his father's Rolls Royce around. Unfortunately Sammy never grew very tall and was totally invisible behind the wheel. The large, old beech tree at the junction with Oaks Road is still intact, complete with Ron Gaskin's initials, despite the building of a block of shops. The Green Man still has its 'mounting step' outside. The thatched cottage remains opposite Woodisses farm on Repton Road and the Canal Cottages have been renovated.

No one mentions ghosts, despite Frizzams Lane being named after a gipsy buried there, or three men hanged for sheep stealing buried beneath the current village hall. Rather, village memories are of the community spirit in the village, the outings, the dances, the many bicycles fished out of the canal after the war where they had been dumped by servicemen on short-leave passes in a hurry to get home. There are still green fields and small farms, with a pretty marina providing recreation for canal boats and cars alike.

Windley 🌿

Windley is a rural hamlet, set in the Ecclesbourne valley. The name means 'pasture clearing'. Originally Windley was part of the Duffield Frith and at one time was owned by Lord Scarsdale, as part of the Kedleston estate.

The soil is light and sandy, the subsoil being sand and gravel. It is very much an agricultural area, with many of the farms having belonged to the same family for generations.

It has a Baptist chapel which was built in 1846 and the Sunday school was started in 1855 and still flourishes today.

The village also contains two large Grade II listed buildings. The largest is 'Flower Lilies', which was built of brick and stone in 1819 by John Crompton, who was five times Mayor of Derby. The house sits on a small hill, set in gardens and surrounded by fields, with a drive nearly one mile in length. It is now divided into flats. In 1928 Lord Baden-Powell was staying at 'Flower Lilies' when a fire broke out in the garage. The fire engines were sent for from the nearby town of Belper, but the firemen had trouble catching the horses needed to pull the fire engines, and the garage was gutted. Lord Baden-Powell's car, a yellow Standard, was destroyed. At the Jamboree at Wirrall that year, all the scouts donated one shilling each and bought Lord Baden-Powell a Rolls-Royce car.

The other large house is Windley Hall, which was built in the 18th century and replaced a previous house on the site. There has been a Windley Hall on this site since 1577. The brewhouse and malt kiln were converted into a cheese factory around 1869 and was the first farmer co-operative in England. The building is still called the Cheese Factory and is now a listed building.

Windley has one pub, called the Puss in Boots, which is situated a mile away from the main cluster of houses that make up the village. The Puss in Boots dates from 1686 and was originally the dwelling house of the local miller who worked the old mill. In 1824 it was remodelled and the mill, which had fallen into decay, was rebuilt and considerably enlarged. The estate was sold to the Crompton-Inglefield family by the Kedleston estate and on the death of Lady Inglefield in 1951, the estate was divided up and sold.

Wingerworth ❧

Wingerworth is situated three miles south of Chesterfield, mainly to the west of the A61 road to Derby. Although there was probably a settlement in Anglo-Saxon times, the first documentary record of its existence appeared in the Domesday Book of 1086, when it was called Wingreurde meaning Winegar's enclosure.

The original village was in the area south of the church, but at various times off-shoots appeared at Hockley, Nethermoor, Hillhouses, Swathwick, Stubbing and Harper Hill, all of which are now part of Wingerworth.

The manor of Wingerworth was given to the Brailsford family by the king in about 1100, and then it passed by marriage to the Curzons of Kedleston. In 1545 Nicholas Hunloke obtained leases on the ironworks, the manor and other property, but about 1590 his son Henry purchased the manor outright and built Wingerworth Old Hall.

Public worship was first permitted in the Roman Catholic chapel at the Hall in 1791 and when French prisoners from the Napoleonic War were interned in Chesterfield, they were invited by Sir Henry to attend Mass. As the prisoners were not allowed on parole past the first mile-post out of Chesterfield, the story goes that they carried it with them to Wingerworth.

The baronetcy died out in 1856 and in the summer of 1920, the estate was offered for sale by auction. Besides the Hall, advertised as 'a handsome early Georgian mansion standing 500 ft above sea-level', was 'a grandly timbered deer park containing three lakes; 38 stock-rearing and dairy farms; three fully licensed public houses; several attractive smallholdings and a large number of cottages'.

No buyer could be found for the Hall and it was eventually demolished in 1924, leaving only the north and south wings. The estate was sold piecemeal to sitting tenants and others. Haphazard housebuilding began on individual plots which were available on Longedge Lane, Derby Road and Central Drive.

Wingerworth lies on the western outcrop of the coal measures and this accounts for many of the industries which arose at various times in the past – coalmining, iron smelting, red-lead making and sandstone quarrying. Few traces remain apart from names such as Furnace Hill and Redleadmill Brook.

The carbonisation plant, opened in 1956, was built on the site of the old Avenue Colliery and produces smokeless fuel for domestic and industrial purposes. The huge cloud of steam which arises from the plant can be seen for miles around! Also in the same area, to the east of the A61 road, are the offices of Coal Products Ltd, whose canteen supplies dinners for the Meals on Wheels service.

The parish church of All Saints, first recorded about 1130, still shows evidence of its Norman origin. Over the Norman chancel arch is a rare rood loft dating from around 1500, said to be the only one surviving in Derbyshire. The tower, with its curious gargoyles, was added about the same time. In 1783, the Roman Catholic Sir Henry Hunloke added a mausoleum to the church for members of his family. A large extension of modern design was built out from the north aisle and dedicated in 1964. The former chancel is now the Lady chapel and the former nave has become the entrance porch.

Salem Methodist chapel was founded in 1849 by Joseph Fletcher, a colliery official and evangelist. Because of opposition from the Hunlokes and the local curate, it was built near the Great Pond at Stubbing Court on land outside the Hunloke estate. One John Norman was asked to give up playing his fiddle to accompany hymn singing because he used the same instrument to play for dances in the village schoolroom. As a result he transferred his worship to All Saints and was eventually churchwarden there for 25 years.

Most people go to work outside Wingerworth, although there are still several farms on the outskirts. The Finney family, of Stubbing Court Home Farm, breeds prize-winning Shire horses; Mrs Allen of Longedge Lane breeds and shows Shetland and miniature Shetland ponies, and another resident, Mr Crosby, shows donkeys.

Despite having no real centre, Wingerworth is a thriving community within easy reach of undulating wooded countryside, with many public footpaths.

Woodthorpe ✄

The 'thorpe' has lost its wood, the remains being a tiny copse in a derelict quarry. The adjoining village, separated from us by the black river Doe Lea, is Netherthorpe, which, of course, is the 'lower village'. This land houses the former grammar school, built in 1572.

The bridle path leads through fields from the grammar school over the bridge of the Doe Lea, where sixth formers traditionally threw their caps into the slurry black waters when finishing schooldays, and where one headmaster sadly finished his days. The clear, fish-laden waters became polluted by emissions from Coalite Products and mining industries. The slag tips of Ireland Colliery fringe these fields which were once the home of skylarks, cornbuntings, peewits, owls, rabbits and glow worms. They retreated and in marched the massive pylon giants which supply modern day electricity needs. Thankfully the cuckoo still calls every spring from the old copse.

Entering Woodthorpe on the hill, the end of the bridle road is now lined with private houses and compact gardens. Once this road housed Butcher Milner's shop – he also had a farm. It was tithed land owned by St John's College, Oxford. There was also a bakery owned by Miss Ivy Watkins' family, which later ended as the school tuck-shop where children savoured their bulls eyes and liquorice. A village 'beer-off' was kept by dumpy, lovable Mrs Windle, who served beer from the wood and vinegar and candles in her dark, dark corner shop lit by gas lantern. These were all unforgettable characters and life in the village was self contained.

The church school, over 100 years old, is down the lane to Seymour. Seymour was a mid 19th century mining community. Built in 1860, there were about 129 houses in four rows with four 'gaffers' houses. It had its own baker, cobbler, barber, shop and chapel. The mine was sunk in 1853 but it was all ended by 1955 by part closure and evacuation of the cottages. Today Seymour is only a screening and sidings site on the colliery branch line to Oxcroft Pit.

The Woodthorpe road extends from church to Woodthorpe Hall, before it turns to Bolsover. Woodthorpe Hall, reputedly haunted by the Grey Lady, was lived in by the De Rodes family until they built Barlborough Hall in the 17th century. Sir John Rodes, who died at Woodthorpe Hall, sold the estate to Bess of Hardwick in 1599, hence the connection with the Devonshires to whom the farms still pay rent. There were nine farms – the old farming community of Renshaws, Lees, Tomsons, Milners, Bennets, Tomlinsons, Stubbins and Lincolns. Today, there is one main farm run by Jackson Bros and the field patterns are large acres with yellow rape in flower.

Woodville 🌿

Woodville is a sprawling industrialised village sitting astride the busy A50 road on the Derbyshire-Leicestershire border. Five roads converge onto a traffic island which is referred to as Woodville Tollgate.

Until 1845 this area was known as 'Wooden Box' and consisted of a string of cottages and a tavern along the road to Ashby de la Zouch. The name was derived from an old port wine butt which was a shelter for the toll-keeper; this was located near to the present traffic Island. Many people still refer to this area as 'Wooden Box' or, more colloquially, 'Box'.

In 1845 the name Woodville was given to the village, and the consolidated chapelry of Woodville was formed by Queen Victoria.

From being a rural hamlet it took off into the industrial revolution; there was an abundance of clay in the area and that provided the raw material for the flourishing sanitary earthenware trade. These items were purely functional and it was a proud boast that you could go anywhere in the world and use examples bearing the trademarks of either Outrams or Nadin & Parker.

The potteries needed packaging for their wares so crate shops sprang up, adding other employment to the village.

Brunt, Bucknal & Co lost no time in opening up a brewery to satisfy the thirst of the workers. The only part of the brewery which remains is the old bottling store in High Street, which is now a discount warehouse.

The sanitary trade has declined but Bretby Art Pottery – established 1883 – still manufactures ornamental ware. A variety of their early pieces are much sought after by collectors.

Remnants of the past remain; a Victorian post box set in a wall adjoining Butt farm, and, although they are without their outer brick-work, two bottle kilns still stand. One is near the Tollgate, the other behind a furniture shop in High Street.

The area between Butt Lane and Sun Street was considered to be the oldest part of the village; it was named 'The City' and no doubt it was the hub of Woodville in the 19th century. Butt Lodge is reputed to be the oldest house, it stands back from its larger neighbour Butt House. The 'Butt' referred to has nothing to do with wine or water, but with the archery butts located down the lane.

St Stephen's church was built in 1846 along Moira Road. One of its benefactors was Queen Adelaide, widow of William IV. A Church of England school and church hall were built nearby. The school was moved to High Street some years ago, but the building is now used as a community centre.

Not one, but four Methodist churches have been erected since 1816. The present church, built in 1969, is an attractive modern building, which provides meeting facilities for a number of organisations.

Redevelopment has taken place along High Street, making way for sheltered housing and flats. New houses have been built over the last ten years which have brought fresh people into an otherwise static village. Shops are varied and most everyday needs are catered for. Along with the traditional 'chippy' there are now other fast food outlets of a more exotic kind, eg Indian and Chinese.

Finally, a mention should be made of the local dialect – 'Ay up, me duck' is the South Derbyshire way of saying 'Hello, nice to see you', and, if storm clouds are looming, 'It's black over Bill's mother's' – though who Bill is, no-one knows!

Woolley Moor 🦢

It is claimed by the original villagers that the name of the village came about from the tufts of lamb or sheep wool caught on the brambles and hedges on the moor. Historians, however, claim the name comes from the old English words 'Wul au leah' meaning 'wolves clearing'.

The village has existed since medieval times but little is known of its history. The earliest known buildings are Handley Fields Farm, which shows a date carved in stone of 1590, and Bottom Farm built about 1600.

The village was formed on the old packhorse route and takes in the hamlets of Handley – 24 dwellings, Woolley Moor – 98 dwellings, and Woolley – 16 dwellings. It is difficult to bring a scattered area together but Handley church and Stretton Handley school are both in Woolley Moor – that's integration! The new school is a church school and was opened in 1970, serving 28 pupils by day with play school facilities and offering classes for all in the evenings. The old school was in the church premises and records show that in 1908 there were 94 pupils on the register going through to the age of 13.

In the 1920s and 1930s there was a sweet and oddment shop, a post office selling groceries and hardware, and visiting lorries selling paraffin and greengrocery. Now there is nothing and villagers have to travel two miles to the nearest post office – this is progress.

Characters have included poachers, one exceptionally good who lived well and was never caught or appeared before a magistrate, the other apparently have invisible bells tied to his feet as he was always being caught and 'hauled up'. Another was a local farmer and milkman. He delivered the milk in a horse-drawn cart but, being rather partial to the 'local brew', his cart was often seen outside the pub. On occasions he rushed outside, a little the worse for wear, leapt upon his cart and cried 'gee up', encouraging the horse to go not realising the poor animal was still tied to the tree! After mechanisation came to the farm, he could be seen driving his tractor and yelling 'Whoa' when he wanted it to stop, completely forgetting his brakes! A great event came to the village in 1949/50 – Indoor Plumbing. Imagine, prior to this there were only earth toilets and an outdoor toilet is still the only form of sanitation for one farm today!

In 1960 the Ogston Reservoir scheme changed the village in as much as areas of beautiful countryside disappeared under water. In spite of the regret felt at the loss, however, there is a lovely view to be seen with the dinghies sailing on the reservoir on a beautiful summer evening, the reflections of the sun in the water and the arrival of various kinds of birds that birdwatchers from near and far come to watch.

Yeaveley 🌿

Yeaveley came into being in the year 1189, previously being called Gheveli. The village was the birthplace of one of the greatest architects of the Middle Ages, Henry Yevele, who travelled to London at the time of the Black Death and was responsible for the rebuilding of the great naves of Westminster Abbey and Canterbury Cathedral.

The original Hall of Yeaveley, Stydd Hall, is reputedly haunted and was once the hub of village life. Today it lies largely forgotten, somewhat off the beaten track, occupied by a farmer.

The church of Holy Trinity dates from 1840 and is one of the few brick churches in this part of the country.

The current population is approximately 280. It is in a very rural area, which has been intensely farmed, most of the families having lived there for generations. The school and post office having closed over the last five years, the only amenity remaining is the public house, the Horseshoe, at the rear of which there is a thriving clay pigeon shooting ground. There has been considerable development in the village over the past 20 years, mainly infill, the boundaries remaining the same, with most of the newer residents commuting to work to nearby towns.

In an effort to help the younger generation to remain in the village, the sale of the current development of nine houses is restricted to local people.

Yeldersley

Now only a hamlet, it was spelt Geldeslie in the Domesday Book and was held first by the de Ferrers. One of the holders was Thomas Pegge, whose daughter Katherine became mistress of Charles II. She bore him two children, one whom was created Earl of Plymouth.

Yeldersley still has two halls: the Old Hall, now converted into holiday homes, at the Bradley edge of the hamlet and a new Hall built in the 18th century at the Osmaston edge.

The estate was sold up in 1929 by Captain Fitzherbert Wright as a direct result of the Wall Street crash. He was great-grandfather of Sarah, Duchess of York. Other large houses are Lady Hole and Ians Oak, built for and named after Sir Ian Walker Okeover. It is said that in one of the barns at Lady Hole Farm are the ancient foundation remains of a convent. Lady Hole supposedly gets its name from the home of the holy ladies.

The hamlet has no centre, no school, no church and no longer a public house. Originally it did have one, the Running Horses, located where the bridle path from the Old Hall and Lady Hole emerged on Painters Lane, now part of the A52.

Youlgreave

Youlgreave on the church pulpit, 1778; Youlgrave on the Derbyshire County Council road sign, 1978; Iolograf, medieval, translated as 'Yellow Grove', and Pommie, well known and often used local nickname, origin unknown. Few other villages in Derbyshire can boast so many different names, or so many different village societies – 53 of them at the last count and this for a village with a population of just under 1,400.

Today, Youlgreave Well Dressing is regarded as one of the finest examples of the traditional Derbyshire art and takes place at Midsummer each year, this date being linked with St John the Baptist's day and a most suitable time to give thanks for water. Five wells are dressed, all with traditional biblical pictures, and the village plays host to many visitors from all over the country.

Youlgreave again benefited when Mrs Waterhouse and the Misses Melland provided the village with a village hall. Over the years this has become a centre for the whole village to meet and once a year, magic and laughter are in the air when the famous pantomime takes to the boards, filling the hall for twelve performances. Indeed, it was on one such occasion that the bear, grappling with Dame Golightly, mistook his way, and fell off the front of the stage with a resounding crash. A moment's stunned silence and then, picking up its head from under the front row of the stalls and jamming it back on, the bear, Tommy Tomlinson in real life, made his unsteady way to the side door and vanished into the night. Word went round the village that 'that bear from panto' was on the loose, and there were no children seen playing out on the streets after dark for many weeks!

Another meeting place in times gone by was the monumental mason's shop, a small stone shed near the church. The mason, Mr Henry Carson, would be working and the retired gentlemen of the village gathered there, sitting round on the unfinished headstones, chatting over the week's news.

Youlgreave has its own version of the Co-op – started originally to help families whose men were engaged in the quarrying industries. When the frost was in the ground, they couldn't work, sometimes for many weeks, and with no 'income support' scheme to help the co-op was born, letting its customers have goods on credit until the better weather came and wages were paid again. The building is now a Youth Hostel, but keeps the names of the departments on its dormitory doors, so in Youlgrave one can sleep in 'Ladies Underwear' or 'Gents Underwear'.

Index